HISTORICAL ONTOLOGY

Historical Ontology

Ian Hacking

HARVARD UNIVERSITY PRESS

Cambridge, Massachusetts

London, England 2002

In memory of my mother, "Peggy,"
née Margaret Elinor MacDougall
b. 12 October 1905 in Tauranga, New Zealand
d. 19 July 2001 in West Vancouver, Canada

Copyright © 2002 by the President and Fellows of Harvard College
All rights reserved
Printed in the United States of America

Cataloging-in-Publication Data is available from the Library of Congress

ISBN 0-674-00616-X

Preface

These chapters are occasional pieces written between 1973 and 1999. Almost all are literally occasional, written for an occasion: an invitation to give a special lecture; to contribute to a volume of essays; to participate in a conference; to fill, within 24 hours, a blank spot in a magazine; or to review a book. Two closely connected themes predominate: some novel ways in which a philosopher can make use of history, and my uses of the early "archaeological" work of Michel Foucault. People sometimes take me to advocate *the* right methodology for philosophy in our times. Nothing could be farther from the case. There are many more ways for a philosopher to use history than I can imagine, and Foucault is an almost endless source of inspiration for people whose interests and abilities are very different from mine.

The essays have been revised only to avoid repetition, to correct outright errors, to make the style more uniform, and to change the tense where the present has become the past. The opening chapter is new; the closing one was published in 2001. I hope in the future to develop two groups of ideas presented here: about making up people (chapter 6), and about styles of reasoning (chapters 11 and 12). I have to thank my editor, Lindsay Waters, for encouraging me to put this body of work together, and for his patience in waiting for the results.

Contents

1 Historical Ontology   *1*

2 Five Parables   *27*

3 Two Kinds of "New Historicism" for Philosophers   *51*

4 The Archaeology of Michel Foucault   *73*

5 Michel Foucault's Immature Science   *87*

6 Making Up People   *99*

7 Self-Improvement   *115*

8 How, Why, When, and Where Did Language Go Public?   *121*

9 Night Thoughts on Philology   *140*

10 Was There Ever a Radical Mistranslation?   *152*

11 Language, Truth, and Reason   *159*

12 "Style" for Historians and Philosophers   *178*

13 Leibniz and Descartes: Proof and Eternal Truths   *200*

14 Wittgenstein as Philosophical Psychologist   *214*

15 Dreams in Place   *227*

Works Cited   *255*

Sources   *271*

Index   *273*

1

Historical Ontology

This is a revised version of the Robert and Maurine Rothschild Lecture, 22 April 1999, given at the Department of the History of Science, Harvard University. I was asked to discuss interconnections between the history and philosophy of science. Instead, I used the occasion to tie together some more general themes about philosophy and history, already broached in a number of the chapters that follow.

Ontology

"Historical ontology" is not, at first sight, a happy phrase; it is too self-important by half. Moreover, I have always disliked the word "ontology." It was around, in Latin, in the seventeenth century, naming a branch of metaphysics, alongside cosmology and psychology. Christian Wolff (1730) put it to use. He thought of ontology as the study of being in general, as opposed to philosophical reflection on individual but ultimate entities such as the soul, the world, and God. If, like myself, you can understand the aims of psychology, cosmology, and theology, but are hard pressed to explain what a study of being in general would be, you can hardly welcome talk of ontology. In the twentieth century the word attracted significant philosophers such as W. V. Quine and Martin Heidegger, but their pronouncements on the subject were sometimes bizarre as well as profound. Think of Quine's ontological aphorism, "To be is to be the value of a variable." And yet, and yet: suppose we want to talk in a quite general way about all types of objects, and what makes it possible for them to come into being. It is convenient to group them together by talking about "what there is," or ontology.

Ontology has been characterized as the study of the most general kinds that exist in the universe. Usually the emphasis has been on demarcation: which candidates for existence really do exist. Aristotle and Plato disagreed in their answers, and philosophers have gone on disagreeing ever since. In the chapters that follow I express very little interest in those disputes. As I say in chapter 6, I think of myself as a "dynamic nominalist," interested in how our practices of naming interact with the things that we name—but I could equally be called a dialectical realist, preoccupied by the interactions between what there is (and what comes into being) and our conceptions of it.

Yet some of the old connotations of "ontology" serve me well, for I want to talk about objects in general. Not just things, but whatever we individuate and allow ourselves to talk about. That includes not only "material" objects but also classes, kinds of people, and, indeed, ideas. Finally, if we are concerned with the coming into being of the very possibility of some objects, what is that if not historical?

Ontology has been dry and dusty, but I lift my title from an author whom none consider arid, even if he has now fallen from grace—in some quarters, into a mire of unkind refutations. In his remarkable essay "What Is Enlightenment?" Michel Foucault (1984b) twice referred to "the historical ontology of ourselves." This could be the name of a study, he said, that was concerned with "truth through which we constitute ourselves as objects of knowledge," with "power through which we constitute ourselves as subjects acting on others," and with "ethics through which we constitute ourselves as moral agents." He calls these the axes of knowledge, power, and ethics.

The notion of "constituting ourselves" may seem very fancy and far from everyday thought, but it isn't. After the Columbine School slayings in Colorado the lead editorial in *The New York Times* said that "the cultural fragments out of which Mr. Harris and Mr. Klebold [the two adolescent murderers] invented themselves, and their deaths, are now ubiquitous in every community, urban, suburban, and rural." I emphasize those words, *invented themselves*. I do not aim at explicating Foucault, but perhaps I do not need to, because on days of exceptional stress, like that 22nd of April, 1999, his way of speaking seems both natural and close to the bone.

In thinking of constituting ourselves, we should think of constituting *as* so and so; we are concerned, in the end, with possible ways to be a person. Foucault spoke of three axes on which we constitute ourselves. Do not be misled by the second axis, named power. Many readers picked up on Foucault's *Power/Knowledge* (1980). The resulting discussions often seemed to focus on domination from outside, and in English often appeared to confuse power in the sense of political, social, or armed clout, on the one hand, and causal efficacy on the other. When Foucault wrote of power, he did not usually have in mind the power exerted upon us by a discernible agent or authority or system. It is rather we who participate in anonymous, unowned arrangements that he called power (a theme that is amplified in chapter 4 below). It is as much our own power as that of anyone else that preoccupied him: "power through which we constitute ourselves as subjects acting on others," not ourselves as passive victim.

In deciding about my title, I am comforted that "historical ontology" is not one of the terms on which Foucault seems to have laid much public emphasis. It is not like "discursive formation," "episteme," or "genealogy." Those expressions have been picked up by his admirers and worked to death. He himself did not like to hang on to his made-up labels for any length of time, and it is possible that he used "historical ontology" only during one particular visit to Berkeley in the early 1980s. He then gave the text of "What Is Enlightenment?" to Paul Rabinow for first publication in *The Foucault Reader* (Foucault 1984a). About the same time he gave an interview that also referred to historical ontology (Foucault 1983). It was printed in the second edition of Dreyfus and Rabinbow's book about Foucault (1983). Neither before nor after that time did he seem to attach much weight to the phrase.

Paul Rabinow later organized the three volumes of the *Essential Works of Foucault* (starting with Foucault 1997) along the three axes of ethics, power, and knowledge. It was a good old-fashioned way to sort philosophy. "How we constitute ourselves as moral agents"—that is the program of Kant's ethics. Foucault regularly historicized Kant. He did not think of the constitution of moral agents as something that is universalizable, apt for all rational beings. On the contrary, we constitute ourselves at a place and time, using materials that have a distinctive and historically formed organization. The genealogy to be unraveled is how we, as peoples in civilizations with histories, have become moral agents, through constituting ourselves as moral agents in quite specific, local, historical ways.

Likewise, the constitution of ourselves as subjects is at the core of social and political philosophy. The reference to power is pure Hobbes, but Hobbes is exactly inverted. Instead of constituting the sovereign and investing Leviathan with absolute power in order to stop us from killing each other, we are the ones who constitute ourselves as subjects by the mechanisms of power in which we participate. And finally, the connections between truth and knowledge, the first of Foucault's three axes, warp yet another traditional theme, for instead of knowledge being knowledge of what is true, the objects of knowledge become ourselves, because of the possibilities for truth and falsehood that are woven around us. Such possibilities also involve ways of finding out what is true or false. Think for a moment of this obscure idea being bastard kin to Moritz Schlick's (1936) verification principle, according to which the meaning of a statement is its method of verification. Except here we realize that the possibilities for truth, and hence of what can be found out, and of methods of verification, are themselves molded in time. Historical ontology has more in common with both logical positivism and Auguste Comte's original positivism than might at first be noticed.

Foucault was concerned with how "we" constitute ourselves. I shall generalize, and examine all manner of constitutings. To mention only some that I have looked into: how what we now call probability emerged (Hacking 1975a). How chance, once the ultimate other, the unknowable, was tamed and became the increasingly favored means for predicting and controlling the behavior of people and things (1990). How something as painful as the abuse of children was made and molded into a focus for action, a vehicle for judgment, a lament for a generation's lost innocence, a scapegoat for the end of the nuclear family, and a ground for repeated interventions, the policing of families (1995c, 1992b, 1991c). How transient mental illnesses lurch into our consciousness and fade away, creating new ways to express uncontrollable distress, ways to absent ourselves from intolerable responsibility, and legitimating exercises in both constraint and liberation (1995c, 1998). But above all, how these various concepts, practices, and corresponding institutions, which we can treat as objects of knowledge, at the same time disclose new possibilities for human choice and action, the topic I begin to discuss in chapter 6 below.

These are disparate topics, and there is no need to find a unity among them; you would hardly expect a quest for commonality from someone who has tried to enumerate a hodgepodge of disunities among the sciences (Hacking 1996). Despite the element of self-aware irony in my title, the catchphrase "historical ontology" helps us think of these diverse inquiries as forming part of a family. The comings, in comings into being, are historical. The beings that become—things, classifications, ideas, kinds of people, people, institutions—can they not be lumped under the generic heading of ontology? But notice how, in all my examples so far, there is a cogent implication of Foucault's knowledge, power, and ethics. Although I want to generalize his historical ontology, I will try to preserve what was central to his ambitions, namely his three cardinal axes. Yet I could have subtitled this chapter "extensions and contractions." The historical ontology presented here is indeed a generalization, but is in many respects vastly more limited than Foucault's vision. It lacks the political ambition and the engagement in struggle that he intended for his later genealogies. It is more reminiscent of his earlier archaeological enterprises.

"Historical"

The explicit use of the adjective "historical" with philosophical nouns goes beyond "ontology." I believe that Georges Canguilhem (1967), the great historian of medicine and of life who was one of Foucault's teachers, was the first to state that Michel Foucault's "archaeological" method dug up the "historical *a priori*" of a time and place. The historical *a priori* points at conditions on the possibilities of knowledge within a "discursive formation," conditions whose dominion is as inexorable, there and then, as Kant's synthetic *a priori*. Yet they are at the same time conditioned and formed in history, and can be uprooted by later, radical, historical transformations. T. S. Kuhn's paradigms have some of the character of a historical *a priori*. For the nonce, I think that philosophy in the twentieth century drank its fill at the Kantian source, and should now turn back to more empirical springs. I learned from Karl Popper (1994) that we should abjure what he called the myth of the framework, and be firm in our resolve to stay, for a time, away from ultimate frameworks that constrain our thought. There is plenty of room for history plus philosophy without reincarnating the synthetic *a priori* in historicist garb.

I have now made plain that Foucault looms in the background of my discussion. I do not want to examine *his* work, but to use it to combine history and philosophy in a way that may or may not owe a good deal to him. Certainly "historical X" is not just Foucault. I have recently noticed quite a few instances of "history," "philosophy," and "science" (or their cognates) mingling in unexpected ways. There is even the "historical anthropology of science." That was how the late A. C. Crombie (1994, I, 5), a founding figure in modern history of science, described his monumental three volumes on styles of scientific thinking—there is more on that topic in chapter 12 below. Then there is "philosophical history." Jonathan Rée's (1999) engaging and iconoclastic *I See a Voice* is subtitled *A Philosophical History*. In an afterword Rée enters a plea for this new endeavor. It is not the history of philosophy practiced in universities, committed to philosophical epochs and schools, and dedicated to a canonical list of philosophers whom it regards as pen pals across the centuries. Instead, Rée tells us, it is "a discipline that may not yet exist, (despite some prototypes by Foucault and Deleuze), but whose arrival is long overdue." It will devote itself to "metaphysical notions that have infiltrated common sense and become real forces in the world." It will not be chronological. Like cinema, it will cut between close shots and distant perspectives. It will use the methods of autobiography, fiction, historical research, and philosophical criticism. It will fall under the broad framework of phenomenology, and will have learned from the teachings of Husserl, Heidegger, Sartre, and Merleau-Ponty. I admire this ambition, but cannot agree with the last sentence of Rée's book: "With luck then, a philosophical history will allow us to catch hold of the idea of scientific objectivity before it has broken away from subjective experience, and observe it in its pristine state, at the moment when abstraction enters our lives, and sense begins to separate itself from sound" (Rée 1999, 386). There we have it. The pristine state.

There is no such state, most certainly not in the case of scientific objectivity. I do not wish to saddle Jonathan Rée with a naïve belief in the existence of pristine states of knowledge. He wrote to me, apropos of my review of his book (1999c), that his mention of a pristine state was an unguarded "echo of something in Merleau-Ponty, and the idea is not that there's a single pure state of absolute objectivity, but quite the reverse. I meant to suggest that objectivity is constantly being renewed." I am not entirely in accord with this phenomenological stance. Rée did want to warn against the "danger that as [objectivities] grow old we forget their origins and take them to be infinitely old and preternaturally wise." That is a danger, but I doubt that objectivity is *constantly* being renewed. My picture is more like that which I describe in the next section, of significant singularities during which the coordinates of "scientific objectivity" are rearranged. These rearrangements are matters of discourse and practice, which I have seldom found to be clarified by the idioms of phenomenology.

But this is not the place to debate schools of philosophy. Why has there been, in so many quarters, a longing for the pristine, the innocent? Ah (we hear a whisper from the wings), if only we could do a certain kind of history well enough, we could return to origins. There may even be a vision of an Eden that we have polluted. Foucault fell into this trap in his first studies of madness, for he suggested that before the sequence that led us from incarceration through Bedlam to the moral treatment of the insane by talk, and on to the babble of therapies and anti-therapies that swirl around us today, there was a purer, truer madness. Happily, he renounced this romantic fantasy early on.

There are many other myths of originating purity. There is the social contract, which has been so powerful a tool in liberal political theory. There is Jung: "The dream is a little hidden door in the innermost and most secret recesses of the soul, opening into that cosmic night which was psyche long before there was any ego-consciousness . . . in dreams we put on the likeness of that more universal, truer, more eternal man dwelling in the darkness of primordial light" (Jung 1970, 144–5).

With only slightly greater modesty, there was once the fantasy of finding the original human language, Adam's language, more universal and truer than ours, the root and source of all human language. Since it employed the first names for things, names given by God himself, that was a language worth discovering (Aarsleff, 1982). That project once motivated much first-rate philology. Perhaps it is less extinct than mutated—to Chomsky's project of finding the universal grammar that underlies all human language. True, that grammar was not decreed in Eden, but it evolved in the first era of the human race and is what makes us human.

When history and philosophy intersect, their students must put aside the romantic cravings that so often occlude the vision of philosophers, whether they lust after a moment of original purity or long for an *a priori* framework. Some mingling of history and philosophy can, however, exhibit how possibilities came into being, creating, as they did so, new conundrums, confusions, paradoxes, and opportunities for good and evil. We can even address exactly that topic mentioned by Jonathan Rée, namely "scientific objectivity." The best present and ongoing investigation of it is being conducted under another label in the "history plus" roster, namely "historical epistemology." I refer to the work of Lorraine Daston and her colleagues at the Max Planck Institute for the History of Science in Berlin.

Historical Epistemology

Scientific objectivity has a history all right, with ramifications different from those imagined by Rée. Daston has studied the effect of the camera on our notions of objectivity (the objective lens, no longer the subjective eye). Then there are the massive international projects in the nineteenth century of collecting data about gravity or meteorology. They deployed hundreds of observers all over the world, and "thus" were free of subjectivity (Daston 1991a, b; Daston and Galison 1992). We judged that we became objective as we increasingly placed our trust in numbers (Porter 1995), More practices like these molded our conception of objectivity (Megill 1994). As Rée said, objectivity was constantly being renewed—but there was never a pristine state.

The label for this kind of study, "historical epistemology," may be catching on. There is Mary Poovey's *A History of the Modern Fact,* which begins by praising Daston's leadership and the phrase "historical epistemology" (1998, 7, 22). Arnold Davidson (2001a) subtitles his new book *Historical Epistemology and the Formation of Concepts.*

When that expression, "historical epistemology," was coined, it was meant to convey a concern with very general or organizing concepts that have to do with knowledge, belief, opinion, objectivity, detachment, argument, reason, rationality, evidence, even facts and truth. All those words suggest epistemology. Proof, rationality, and the like sound so grand that we think of them as free-standing objects without history, Plato's friends. But we see how local they are when we mention their opposites: myth, imagination, ignorance, folly, dishonesty, lying, doubt, madness, prejudice, overconfidence, commitment. Most recently, Daston and Kathleen Parks (1998) have added another dimension with their beautifully produced book about wonder. The important point of all these works is that the epistemological concepts are not constants, free-standing ideas that are just there, timelessly.

The ideas examined by historical epistemology are the ones we use to organize the field of knowledge and inquiry. They are, often despite appearances, historical and "situated." Historical epistemology may even claim that present ideas have memories; that is, a correct analysis of an idea requires an account of its previous trajectory and uses. Right now these concepts are ours, and they are often essential to the very functioning of our society, our laws, our sciences, our argumentation, our reasoning. We are stuck with them, which is not to say that we cannot change them, or that they are not changing as you speak—occasionally, even because you speak. There is also the suggestion that those who do not understand the history of their own central organizing ideas, such as objectivity or even facts, are condemned not to understand how they use them. Thus feminist critics of objectivity who have not studied its meanings in time, but who hold objectivity to be a patriarchal value, may be trapped in the same frame as those who embrace the ideologies that they oppose.

Meta-epistemology

Is this a kind of epistemology at all? Certainly it is not epistemology in that tainted sense that Richard Rorty assigned to the word in *Philosophy and the Mirror of Nature* (1979), his wonderful challenge to the entire enterprise of American analytic philosophy. He took epistemology to be not theory of knowledge but a search for the foundations of knowledge. Daston and her colleagues are not looking for foundations. Indeed, the very notion that knowledge has foundations—or rather, successive groups of such notions—might be a topic for the historical epistemologist.

There is nevertheless a problem with the name. In the fall of 1993 I organized a week-long conference dedicated to "historical epistemology." The participants were graduate students and a few teachers from Chicago, Paris, and Toronto. My Montreal colleague, Yves Gingras, reminded me that the label would not do, because Gaston Bachelard pre-empted it long before the Second World War. I have explained elsewhere how his idea differs from Daston's (Hacking 1999b). But we are not concerned with questions of who owns a label. The fact is that Daston and her colleagues do not do epistemology. They do not propose, advocate, or refute theories of knowledge. They study epistemological concepts as objects that evolve and mutate. Their work would be more truly named were it called "historical meta-epistemology." Where Bachelard insisted that historical considerations are essential for the practice of epistemology, the historical meta-epistemologist examines the trajectories of the objects that play certain roles in thinking about knowledge and belief. (That could include reflection on Bachelard's own role in transforming epistemological thought.) Historical meta-epistemology, thus understood, falls under the generalized concept of historical ontology that I am now developing.

Let us use Daston on the camera and the international projects for data collection as the paradigms (in the strict Kuhnian sense of the word—an achievement and exemplar for future work) of historical meta-epistemology. Although those two examples are quite different from any examined by Foucault, his three axes are plain to see. Daston's work was directed at the truth/knowledge axis, but it also implicates the other two. The camera became the agent for identifying and controlling criminals and immigrants. Even the passport, a long-standing device for regulating travelers, was completely transformed with the advent of the photograph. The coordination of observers all over the globe is one small aspect of the exercise of imperial power, but there was also a profound ethical dimension. The observers were morally bound to report absolutely truthfully. There, rather than in individual laboratory work, we formed the ethos of keeping a notebook in which one scrupulously records the data. The book must never be altered. That is a categorical imperative if ever there was one. The camera, it was said, "keeps us honest," for it showed how things really were. It was a great ethical leveler. Despite ruses in the past, only now have we learned how to outwit it with digital processing of photographed images. The person who used the camera for scientific work, or for police work, or for the photograph on the identity card, was a newly possible type of moral agent, as was the scrupulous observer of meteorological or gravitational facts on Baffin Island or in Polynesia.

Lively scholars do not stay still. The historical epistemology (which I insist is meta-epistemology) encouraged by Daston's group has expanded. Very recently (long after the present essay was, for most intents and purposes, complete), I received the latest production of the Max Planck Institute in Berlin, with the telling title *Biographies of Scientific Objects* (Daston 2000a). "This is a book about applied metaphysics. [In fact it is a collection of 11 papers revised from a conference held in Berlin in the fall of 1995.] It is about how whole domains of phenomena—dreams, atoms, monsters, culture, mortality, centers of gravity, value, cytoplasmic particles, the self, tuberculosis—come into being and pass away as objects of scientific inquiry" (Daston 2000b, 1). Here we have essays, by divers hands, on the coming into being, or going out of existence, of the study of just these objects. Does this applied metaphysics differ from historical ontology? Well, there are differences in emphasis.

One difference is not decisive, because it is likely to prompt too much argument, not to mention some equivocation. Daston is cautious: "come into being and pass away *as objects of scientific inquiry.*" Nothing overtly radical here: of course some objects are studied at one time and not at another. But atoms have been here, in exactly their present form, longer than the solar system, even if they became objects of scientific study (as opposed to Democritean or Daltonian speculation) only at the start of the twentieth century, and only, perhaps, in consequence of a curious transmutation in the study of the cosmic ether (Buchwald 2000). Buchwald is not writing about the coming into being of atoms, the objects. (There could be a history of the creation by human beings of atoms of transuranic elements such as plutonium; that would be a history of coming into being all right, but it would not be applied metaphysics.)

Tuberculosis bacilli, ancestors of the ones that still infect us, did come into being late in the history of our planet, but long enough ago to inhabit the world of the pharaohs. That coming into being is a topic not for applied metaphysics but for evolutionary bacteriology and historical epidemiology. There are questions about the confidence with which those two historical sciences locate the bacilli in the daily life of ancient Egypt. Bruno Latour (2000) raises these questions in his characteristically iconoclastic way. But only the most irresponsibly playful of writers (plus some fools who ape the playful) would assert that TB bacilli, or their baleful effects on humans, came into existence in 1882 under the gaze of Wilhelm Koch.

My historical ontology is concerned with objects or their effects which do not exist in any recognizable form until they are objects of scientific study. Daston describes her applied metaphysics as about the coming into being of objects of study—and not the coming into being of objects, period. Ah, but that is complicated. "Object" itself is an idea with a history, to which Daston dedicates an introduction rich with historical meta-epistemology (Daston 2000b).

I have a more direct reason for segregating what I call historical ontology. I should like it to retain a close connection with Foucault's three axes of knowledge, power, and ethics. These concerns are present to some of Daston's authors, but by no means to all. Let us leave it there and see how future inquiries develop. Say, perhaps, that historical ontology is a species of applied metaphysics, just as traditional ontology was a species of traditional metaphysics. But before giving examples of historical ontology, let us round out our discussion of historical meta-epistemology.

Has historical meta-epistemology anything to do with philosophy, or is it just a species of history? Well, "the problem of induction" is commonly taken to be one of the central problems of philosophy. I might add here that this is not strictly the way Hume put it: the very notion of philosophy coming packaged in "problems" of free will, induction, and so fort, may itself be an invention of the early twentieth century. Since I like fraudulently precise dates, I have long been saying that "the problem" as definitive of a mode of philosophizing was canonized in English around 1910 with titles by G. E. Moore, William James, and Bertrand Russell—for a few more details, see chapter 2 below. It is nevertheless almost unanimously agreed that what we now call the problem of induction was set up by David Hume. Of course there were anticipations, but they tended to be visible as precursors only after Hume created the issues—one thinks of Joseph Glanvill's work (1661). Unlike Garber and Zabell (1979), I do not rate the alleged anticipation by Sextus Empiricus very highly (see my 1975a, 178–9).

Why no problem of induction before Hume? Let us return to Poovey's *History of the Modern Fact.* By modern fact Poovey means the tiny particle of information, the capsule, the nugget, and such metaphors as come to mind; something compact, robust, down to earth, neutral, bite-sized, byte-sized, the very opposite of theory, conjecture, hypothesis, generalization. Facts are ugly ducklings, ungainly, unordered, "brute facts." But then they are supposed to speak, if only we get enough of them. And there we have the germ of a problem. Facts are these ugly dry little items. Why should they be so valued? Simon Schaffer and Steven Shapin (1985) have shown how the particulate fact was essential to the new sciences of the seventeenth century: essential for creating a rhetoric of trust and belief, while at the same time creating an elite society of self-professed equals. Poovey moves to where trust matters even more, in the keeping of accounts, and argues for an essential facticity for the new modes of commerce. She sees in double entry bookkeeping the origin of the modern fact, curiously timeless and temporal. Timeless, because the entries in the ledger are checked both ways to be right, for all time; temporal, because those entries refer to dated events, the state of the counting house at the moment of a transaction.

Yet such facts were supposed to speak for general themes and right-minded conclusions. How could anything so particular, no matter how well marshaled, support anything of general interest? That is exactly, Poovey implies, how David Hume saw it around 1739, when he formulated his problem of induction. We experience only particular bits of information, all in the present or the past. Yet that is our sole basis for expectations about the future, or for general knowledge. How can that possibly be?

A striking thesis arises: the problem of induction requires for its formulation a particular conception of the world. It may have had any number of sources, but it seems to be derived principally from commercial transactions, for whose purposes the world, or at any rate its wealth, is so abstracted that it consists only of particulate facts. All data, all rock-bottom givens, are permanent momentary items of fact like those that appear in a ledger book. That is a conception within which the problem of induction seems almost inevitable. Hume thought that all our impressions are of particulate facts. If you want to undo the problem of induction, you have to observe that our impressions are not of particulate facts but of the proverbial billiard balls in motion, and a billiard ball is not something particulate, momentary. In short, one has to undo the starting point. Both modern probabilistic evasions of the problem of induction are quite effective, even if not decisive. Here I mean both the Bayesian evasion—the so-called "subjective" approach that analyzes degrees of belief—and the Peircian one—the so-called "objective" approach that analyzes frequencies and confidence intervals. (I explain both these matters in an elementary way at the end of my [2001c].) But neither evasion can get started in a vacuum: they begin to work only when we conceive of our beliefs at a time as not encoded solely in particulate facts.

My cautious enthusiasm for evasions of Hume's skeptical problem about induction does not imply that all skepticism can be evaded. I refer only to Hume's inductive skepticism, couched in his examples of the postman's step on the stairs, and of the bread and whether it will nourish me. Maybe that skepticism can be evaded. A total skepticism, which we did not learn from Hume, remains on the cards. "For all we know," ANYTHING could happen next. If so, there is no point in worrying with Hume whether my morning's toast will be healthful. The worry that NOTHING might happen from now on was familiar to the schoolmen, some of whom very sensibly invoked God as a necessary condition for there being something, rather than nothing, after now. Their worry was not in the least like Hume's.

I mention the philosophical and skeptical problem of induction because it is taken to be a central problem of philosophy. Occasionally, it is relegated to the philosophy of science (as if science were concerned with my morning toast, billiards, or the delivery of mail). Hume's closely related queries about causality roused Kant. An even more profound philosophical difficulty occurred to Hume when he had got to the end of the *Treatise*—he had given no account of himself, of the "I" that gets impressions and is a unity. In his scheme of things the only impressions are particulate, and if there is a getter of impressions, it too is particulate. Whence, then, my idea of a person, of me? Kant took this so seriously that he proposed one of those massive absurdities that are the preserve of the truly great figures who take philosophical reasoning seriously and plunge on: I mean the transcendental unity of apperception. Every one of my noticings of anything is accompanied by a noticing that I notice it. Thus the particulate fact, child of double-entry bookkeeping and the new commercial practices, engendered transcendental philosophy. And when we realize this, we may want to store transcendental philosophy in the attic (do not throw it out: it might be needed again).

This discussion is the merest indicator of how historical meta-epistemology might bear on philosophy. Poovey does not say such things outright, and quite probably would think I am grossly overstating things. It is the philosopher's privilege to stand on the extreme margin. But these thoughts are natural for me because I had the idea, in the course of writing *The Emergence of Probability,* that philosophical problems are created when the space of possibilities in which we organize our thoughts has mutated. In line with that speculation, I offered my own account of "how Hume became possible" (1975a, ch. 19; the sentence "Hume has become possible" comes from Foucault [1970, 60]). I hope the account given there is not superseded by Poovey's but complementary to it.

The Creation of Phenomena

All sorts of things come into being in the course of human history. Not all, not even those of great philosophical interest, fall under my conception of historical ontology. What about what I have called "the creation of phenomena"? (Hacking 1983a, ch. 13). In 1879, a graduate student at Johns Hopkins University was following up a mistaken idea suggested by Maxwellian theory, or rather suggested to him by his teacher, Rowland, Maxwell's leading exponent in the United States. What Edward Hall found, largely by serendipity, was that when he passed a current through a sheet of gold leaf, in a magnetic field perpendicular to the current, he produced a potential difference perpendicular to both field and current. I stated that this phenomenon had never existed anywhere in the universe until 1879, at least not in a pure form. I was willing to be inoffensive and say that Hall purified a naturally existing phenomenon, but I did not really mean anything as mealy-mouthed as that. Hall brought this phenomenon into being.

The example was a happy choice, because when I used it, it was ancient history, but subsequently it came alive again, with two successive Nobel prizes for Hall effects: one for the quantum Hall effect, and one for the fractional quantum Hall effect awarded in the fall of 1998. The Hall phenomenon is quantized; that is, the potential does not increase continuously but by quantum steps. More surprisingly: build an extremely thin niobium supercooled "leaf," a leaf so thin that electrons do not have a chance to vibrate sideways. Then the potential steps are a quarky 1/3 of the standard quantum steps. This was not a theoretical prediction; the Nobel prize was shared with the man who, deeming himself a mathematician, not a physicist, figured out why the fractional effect occurs. Like the original Hall effect, this is a nice example for discussing the question, which comes first, theory or experiment? Experiment often comes first.

Hall effects are new things in the world, brought into being in the course of human history. For a more familiar example, nothing lased anywhere in the universe until fifty years ago. Today lasers are everywhere on the industrialized world, and especially dense in the vicinity of compact discs. This remark deeply offends some physicists, who triumphantly proclaim that masing (not lasing) phenomena would explain some weird astrophysical events. But what they really mean is that the universe was made, from the very beginning, in such a way that the laser was there, *in potentia*. Such talk is a sure sign that we have passed from physics to metaphysics—and a very effective and natural metaphysics it is, too. I had expected my talk of the creation of phenomena to be greeted with such resistance that it would be silenced. So I was very pleased to see *The Creation of Scientific Effects*, the title of Jed Buchwald's (1994) book about Heinrich Hertz.

Schaffer and Shapin's *Leviathan and the Air Pump* is the classic study of one of the first groups of artificial phenomena. One part of their truly innovative book that fascinated me was their translation of a little anti-manifesto by Hobbes (1985; cf. Hacking 1991b). He was prescient. He was afraid of these phenomena that we would create all over the face of the earth and beyond, and so, in the end, destroy the metaphysics, epistemology, and the approach to science that he held so dear. Hobbes believed in the thesis that phenomena are created, and, for his own reasons, hated it: we have quite enough phenomena already, thank you very much, he wrote, and lost the match with Boyle, forever.

I am dead serious about the "creation" of phenomena, phenomena of cosmic significance that come into being in the course of human history. Why not include the creation of phenomena as a topic for historical ontology? Because they do not mesh with our three axes of knowledge, power, and ethics. Obviously, Hall produced his effect only because he was properly networked into a microsociology of power. One can cite some ethical concerns. Certainly, he added to our store of knowledge, both of knowledge that and knowledge how. But there was no constituting of anything, not ourselves, electromagnetism, or anything else within those three axes.

Microsociology

Mention of "microsociology" invites a relevant digression. Thomas Kuhn's Rothschild lecture is well remembered, with some hostility, by sociologists of scientific knowledge. "I am among those who have found the claims of the strong program absurd," he said, "an example of deconstruction gone mad . . . There's a continuous line (or continuous slippery slope) from the inescapable initial observations that underlie microsociological studies to their still entirely unacceptable conclusions" (Kuhn 1992, 7). Some years later, I do not share Kuhn's hostility. The strong program is no longer a demon. During the intervening years many flowers have bloomed, and quite a few withered, in the science studies patch.

In *The Social Construction of What?* (1999a) I devoted chapter 3 to the theme of social construction in the sciences. It defined three substantive and justified differences of doctrine that tend to separate scientists from some of their critics. (It went so far as to suggest where Thomas Kuhn himself might have come out on each of them.) It examined the Edinburgh strong program only in passing, for although Barry Barnes and David Bloor are happy to be grouped among the social constructionists, they hardly use the term "social construction." I wanted exemplars who put the phrase up front in their titles or subtitles. So I chose Bruno Latour and Andrew Pickering, who tend to be regarded as the bad boys by many social students of science, as well as being counted public enemies #1 and #2 by some protagonists in the science wars. I like them because they share with Kuhn and myself a repugnance to analyses in which, to use words from Kuhn's Rothschild lecture, "[n]ature itself, whatever that may be, has seemed to have no part in the development of beliefs about it." Perhaps that reading of the Edinburgh School was permitted a decade ago. Barnes,

Bloor, and Henry (1996) make plain the school's dedication to empiricism, as its adherents understand it. For more specific detail, Pickering's (1996) idea of "interactive stabilization," which involves the sheer cussedness of apparatus as well as the resilience of theories about how the apparatus works, is cacophonous but exhilarating music to my ears. I do not go as far as Bruno Latour (1993) and advocate a parliament of things. I query his intention to minimize the differences between the human and the nonhuman (Latour 1999). He advocates what he calls a "cosmopolitics" in contrast to which I have to own up to old-fashioned humanism (Hacking 1999d). Far from deserving Kuhn-like criticism on the score of "nature" not having a major place in the sciences, this branch of social studies of science seems to me to assign too much agency to nature.

What role should social studies have in historical ontology? This is precisely the sort of methodological question that I find useless. I help myself to whatever I can, from everywhere. If we stick to meta-epistemology for the moment, and use Daston's work as paradigmatic, then of course the events she describes take place in a social matrix, but the point of the inquiry is to understand how the uses of the idea of objectivity are themselves affected and have affected the ways in which we today use it in our discussions and in our organizations. Institutional history is essential, as are many other kinds of history, but one overall project is, in the end, what I can only call philosophical. Its practitioners are engaged in the analysis of concepts, but a concept is nothing other than a word in its sites. That means attending to a variety of types of sites: the sentences in which the word is actually (not potentially) used, those who speak those sentences, with what authority, in what institutional settings, in order to influence whom, with what consequences for the speakers. We first lose ourselves, as befits philosophy, in total complexity, and then escape from it by craft and skills and, among other things, philosophical reflection. My little sketch of the problem of induction, while of course too brief, suggests one (and only one) way to go. I have, however, spent too much time on matters peripheral of historical ontology. Now I shall plunge into its heartland with two examples.

Trauma

Among the thoughts that underlie historical ontology is this: "one cannot speak of anything at any time; it is not easy to say something new; it is not enough for us to open our eyes, to pay attention, or to be aware, for new objects suddenly light up and emerge out of the ground" (Foucault 1971, 44f). Take psychic trauma, for example. That might sound altogether too local an idea to matter to the historical ontologist, who should be preoccupied by general and organizing concepts and the institutions and practices in which they are materialized. To the contrary, trauma has become a remarkable organizing concept. Trauma used to mean a physical lesion or wound. When did it come to mean a psychic wound? People did not simply open their eyes and notice psychic trauma all around them. Dictionaries cite Freud about 1893; one can do better than that, but the point is that this is an entirely new idea of trauma closely connected with the soul, and which has radically transformed our sense of our selves. Compared to trauma, the more familiar Freudian ideas of the subconscious and the complexes may prove to be mere epiphenomena. Traumatology has become *the* science of the troubled soul, with victimology one of its bitter fruits. All of this interest plays into what is at present a moving target, the idea of memory. So here is an example of a way in which the historical understanding of an empirical concept, psychic trauma, may be essential to understanding the ways in which we constitute ourselves. Some of the story of psychic trauma is told in my *Rewriting the Soul* (1995), and a good deal more is elaborated in Ruth Leys's *A Genealogy of Trauma* (2000). Allan Young's *The Harmony of Illusions* (1995) is a stunning archaeology of Post-Traumatic Stress Disorder, even if he would identify his work as medical anthropology. His primary materials were observations, made in (U.S.) Veterans' Administration hospitals, of interviews of American veterans of the Vietnam War. Young now makes the extraordinary suggestion that PTSD, in the current diagnostic manuals, is taking up the space of neuroses. In 1980 American psychiatrists were told that they should never again speak of neuroses. That concept was abolished by their new diagnostic handbook. Of course, it still remains part of common speech. A syndicated cartoon showed a sign in the psychiatric wing of a hospital: "First floor, neurotics. Second floor, psychotics. Third floor, people who *really* think they want to be president" (*Non Sequitur*, 27 May 1999). But Young's provocative thesis is that PTSD is rapidly absorbing all the symptom profiles of the old neuroses, with an added nonoptional extra. The neurotic of olden times must now, as a matter of PTSD logic and definition, have had a traumatic experience. But that definitional requirement is easily met, because no adult human life lacks events that can now be counted as "traumatic"—recounted, told, experienced as, traumatic.

The story of trauma can be looked at as a sequence of events in the history of psychology and psychiatry. But my concern is the way in which the trauma concept figures in the constitution of selves. We can even display this history along the three ontological axes mentioned earlier. First, there is the person as known about, as having a kind of behavior and sense of self that is produced by psychic trauma. Today there is a vast body of "knowledge" in the burgeoning field of traumatology.

Second, in the field of power, we have a congeries of possibilities: self-empowerment; power of victims over abusers; the power of the courts and the legislatures, declaring that statutes of limitations do not apply to those who caused pain long ago, when the pain has been forgotten by the victim; the power of soldiers to claim special pensions and other benefits for wartime trauma. But most importantly, it is the anonymous power of the very concept of trauma that works in our lives.

Let us be more specific. An admirable Canadian charity that I support has been providing funds and helpers in Central America in the wake of the worst storm in two centuries, Hurricane Mitch. An appeal for more support, listing recent good deeds, ends with the words "The remaining funds will be used in post-trauma counseling for children and families." The concept of psychological trauma has always been presented as emancipatory. We need not disagree to see the effects of power that it produces. Those children and families in a flood-ravaged region of Nicaragua will, for the first time, live in a world in which they experience themselves not just as ravaged by floods, but as having suffered trauma.

This is not to say the export of the trauma idea with its embodied practices cannot be resisted. The children who had been inducted into rebellious armies in Northern Uganda are given trauma counseling for the potential effects of post-traumatic stress (Rubin 1998). There is protest against this intervention, with some effect in the field, and preference expressed for indigenous ways of dealing with cruelty, violence, abduction, and physical pain that do not require the recent Western organizations of ideas and emotions. Note that a necessary condition for powerful effects is the knowledge about trauma, the science of trauma, to which four major scientific journals are now dedicated. But that is not sufficient. There must also be "uptake," a trauma "movement," and the material resources to export the knowledge and practices.

The third axis is ethical. At the moral level, events, present or remembered, experienced as trauma, exculpate. A traumatic childhood is used to explain or excuse a later antisocial person, who may also be diagnosed with, for example, "antisocial personality disorder." Traumatic memories create a new moral being. Trauma offers not only a new sense of who others are, and why some may be that way, but it also produces a new sense of self, of who one is and why one is as one is. It takes us into the very heart of what, in traditional philosophy, has been called the theory of responsibility and duty.

I would add only one caution. Foucault did from time to time emphasize the importance of sites, but too often these have been read as reference to sites of action for power: the clinic, the prison. Yes, but there are also material sites, buildings, offices, Veterans' Administration interview rooms, devices to measure electrical and chemical changes supposedly associated with post-traumatic stress. At a more mundane level are the tape recorders and the video tapes playing back interviews to clinicians and even to the veterans themselves. The world of trauma is a very material world, full of essential artifacts that idea-oriented thinkers tend not to notice. If you were an ethnographer, the first things you would describe would be the material artifacts used by traumatologists.

Child Development

Now let us turn to something more agreeable, the notion of child development. It sounds like a purely empirical concept. Yet it has come, in the past 150 years, to determine in the most minute details how we organize our thinking about children. It now swings into action long before birth, but at birth it is deployed, in our civilization, at one of the mysterious moments in life. Not birth itself, which has been with us always, but something bizarre and local. The first fact to be announced after the birth of the baby (whose sex, by now, is likely to be known in advance) is the weight at birth, a number that is doubtless of use, albeit pretty limited use, to the nurse, midwife, or pediatrician. But it is ritually conveyed to family and friends, announced in the workplace, as a holy number, as if it were the essence of the child. It is the signal that from now on the child will develop. Every feature of the child's physical, intellectual, and moral development is to be measured by standards of normalcy, starting with its weight.

Is this a topic for historical ontology? Anecdotally, at least, the answer is a ringing "yes." It was not I who thought of this extension of Foucault's label, but James Wong, the author of a doctoral dissertation on child development (Wong 1995). He suggested to me that many enterprises, including his own, should be called "historical ontology."

Our idea of what a child *is* has been formed by a scientific theory of development. It forms our whole body of practices of child-rearing today, and, in turn, forms our concept of the child. Those ideas and practices form children themselves, and they also form parents. The child, its playmates, and its family are constituted within a world of knowledge about child development. In fact, so certain are we of this knowledge that it can even be used as a registered brand trademark. I recently noticed a subway advertisement for an institution named Invest in Kids. Its ad, which featured a child of color emerging from an egg, asked, "will a child stay in an emotional shell or emerge sunny-side up," already a choice of metaphors that I find, to say the least, equivocal. The ad continues by citing some "hard-boiled facts," namely knowledge about child development. The advertisement includes the trademark of Invest in Kids:

> The years before five
> Last the rest of their lives.™

Child development and psychic trauma are hardly transcendental concepts of the sort that might appeal to Kant. They are, in his terminology, empirical concepts. But they are used for the intellectual and practical organization of a panoply of activities. They are historically situated, and their present versions are highly colored by their predecessors. They seem to be inescapable. Inescapable? The celebrated Dr. Spock tried to undo the regimen of normal development with his maxim that children should develop at their own rate—but *develop* they must, and at a *rate*, if only their own. Spock himself was merely modifying the draconian laws of child development set out by that guru of the interwar years, Dr. Gessell, the household name for a generation of North American mothers—including *my* mother—learning how their infants would develop, and what mothers must do to optimize the world of their children.

These concepts produce a feeling of inevitability. How could we not think in terms of child development if we interact with children at all? Well, I noticed recently when playing with two of my grandchildren, aged two and four, that I really did not think of them that way. They are changing daily. Since I see them less frequently than I would like, I notice change more than their parents. But the changes are totally idiosyncratic, personal, and do not strike me as matters of development. Yes, the children are getting older, and are able to do new things every day. But I do not conceptualize these as "development." But then, I am a grandfather playing, unrelated to the real world. It is parents rather than grandparents who are constituted by doctrines of development.

The only time I got close to thinking about development was one rainy afternoon, playing store-bought games. They were clearly labeled "age 3 and up." Chloe, then 4½, could play these games with only whimsical deviations from the rules, but Charlie, aged two and a bit, who had a lot of fun, could have been trying out for a cameo part in a satirical movie called "Wittgenstein: to follow a rule." So I had to admit, the packaging was correct, "age 3 and up." Shouldn't that be enough to convince me that as a matter of fact children do "develop"? Not so fast. The games we were playing were all thoroughly modern games, that had been designed in order to incorporate and promote certain skills. They were not innocent children's games, but games manufactured in the world of child development.

That world is pervasive, sometimes to the point of parody. My other two grandchildren, Catherine and Sam, only a little older than the two just mentioned, went to an excellent daycare preschool that is obsessively concerned with development. Every week the children came with the name of some new achievement tied around their neck, a bit like Hawthorne's scarlet letter A, in fact sometimes literally a red letter A, as in a card tied round the neck saying, in red, "Wonderful! Can recognize the sound 'A' in the written word 'BAT'." The first lesson learned in this school—a lesson so pervasive that the carers and teachers do not even notice that they are inculcating it—is that each child is a developing entity, so that the child cannot conceive of itself otherwise. And the child who is a bit slow at acquiring the ability to recognize the sound of the letter "A" in "BAT" will learn that lesson—that he is a developer, indeed a slow developer—quicker than the other children who are in other respects quicker than he. Notice that, once again, we are not talking about "ideas." We are talking about institutions, practices, and very material objects: games made of plastic and strings to tie rewards around a child's neck. Without these material and institutional artifacts, many of which litter middle-class homes across North America, there would be no ever-expanding concept of child development.

I have been giving examples of organizing concepts that come into being through quite specific historical processes. They lead us to historical ontology proper. We are directed to what it is possible to be or to do. There is, not surprisingly, a certain vestigial existentialism in this way of thinking. Existence comes before essence; we are constituted by what we do. But our free choices can only be from among the actions that are open to us, the possible actions. And our ways of being, chosen freely or not, are from possible ways of being. At the time Sartre wrote about the classic Parisian *garçon de café*, it was possible for a young man in France to be one. That was not what William James calls a "live" option for me, when I was a screwed-up late-adolescent reading *Being and Nothingness* in Northern Alberta. Conversely, a Parisian lad could hardly have contemplated working in oil fields in the tundra. But at least either of us could have changed places by train, steamer, and more courage than either of us possessed. Those options were not open to many earlier generations, and will be closed off to future ones. Indeed, many options that were open to me are not, I think, open to my grandchildren, who in turn can decide to be hackers, or whatever role will correspond to that in a few years, but which was literally not a way to be a person when I was a young man.

Foucault observes, near the end of *The Order of Things*, that "At any given instant, the structure proper to individual experience finds a certain number of possible choices (and of excluded possibilities) in the systems of the society; inversely, at each of their points of choice the social structures encounter a certain number of possible individuals (and others who are not)" (Foucault 1970, 380). Historical ontology is about the ways in which the possibilities for choice, and for being, arise in history. It is not to be practiced in terms of grand abstractions, but in terms of the explicit formations in which we can constitute ourselves, formations whose trajectories can be plotted as clearly as those of trauma or child development, or, at one remove, that can be traced more obscurely by larger organizing concepts such as objectivity or even facts themselves. Historical ontology is not so much about the formation of character as about the space of possibilities for character formation that surround a person, and create the potentials for "individual experience."

I should emphasize here that there is hardly a grain of so-called relativism in what I have been saying. To bring new possibilities into being is, of necessity, to introduce new criteria for the objective application of the new ideas that permeate our world. Traumatology and child development, to begin with, are rich in what are explicitly called "instruments," a metaphorical use of the word to designate endless objective test protocols, many of which are printed with assessments of their validity in *The Mental Measurements Handbook,* while other handbooks and other more material, nay electrical, instruments are described in texts of physiology.

History and Philosophy

I may seem to have gone a great distance from history and philosophy, as commonly understood. Certainly the Parisian waiter in the café is more the stuff of novels than of science, and the applied geophysics of the 1950s will never make it out of the in-house chronologies of oil corporations and into mainstream history of science. But notice how I emphasize that traumatology and child development do present themselves as positive knowledge, the bearers of general facts and testable truths about the human condition. They are fragments of knowledge in which a person is constituted as a certain type of being: a victim of trauma, a developing child. A person becomes able to act on others in such and such ways. The person becomes a special type of moral agent with both responsibilities and exculpations.

I will be asked: but is not your historical ontology just history? My example of Hume's problem of induction already suggests a philosophical dimension. One reply to the question has already been given: I am engaged in a historicized version of British 1930s philosophical analysis, that is, conceptual analysis conceived of as the analysis of words in their sites. Compare the various historicizings of the thoroughly ahistorical Kant, beginning with Hegel's. Those are assuredly not history, and especially not the history of philosophy. In addition, my concern has long been with how *our* philosophical problems became possible, because I hold that we need to understand that in order to grapple with the problems. Daston, who served as my paradigm for historical meta-epistemology, and who now introduces what she calls applied metaphysics, was trained as a historian and practices her craft. She does have a quality that is not so common among historians: a philosophical sensibility. I am trained as an analytic philosopher, but may have more historical sensibility than many of my colleagues. Not all historians and philosophers can share their enterprises, but some can. Yet even when they do, their overlapping interests differ.

Generally speaking, Foucault's archaeologies and genealogies were intended to be, among other things, histories of the present. Not Whig histories, which show how inevitably we got to here. On the contrary, he emphasized the contingency of the events that led to the predicaments we find pressing or inescapable. At its boldest, historical ontology would show how to understand, act out, and resolve present problems, even when in so doing it generated new ones. At its more modest it is conceptual analysis, analyzing *our* concepts, but not in the timeless way for which I was educated as an undergraduate, in the finest tradition of philosophical analysis. That is because the concepts have their being in historical sites. The logical relations among them were formed in time, and they cannot be perceived correctly unless their temporal dimensions are kept in view. This dedication to analysis makes use of the past, but it is not history.

I must avoid one misunderstanding that comes from a quite different source. Sometimes my readers take me to urge that epistemology should be conducted as historical meta-epistemology, and philosophy itself, or metaphysics, or at least ontology, should be conducted as historical ontology. Of course not. My first methodological statement of any program whatsoever was a fond farewell to Cambridge University, a talk at the Moral Sciences Club in the spring of 1974: "One Way to Do Philosophy." It is summarized in chapter 2 below. I would never advocate any program as anything more than *one way*. I do not do any epistemology aside from theorizing about probable inference, but I certainly do not assert that epistemology has come to an end, or that its end is in sight (Hacking 1980b). Some epistemology—of a totally ahistorical sort—seems to me fascinating and certainly important, while some of it seems too timid and drab and "scholastic." But rather than distribute worthless words of praise on others, let me speak for myself, to illustrate the fact that even one person need not do philosophy in only one way.

My own early work on the foundations of statistical inference (Hacking 1965) was a mix of logic and epistemology. I have only just now, as this essay goes to press, finished an elementary textbook on this topic. I have been teaching it for decades, and I have slaved to make it both lively and philosophically sound (Hacking 2001c). I recently completed a paper on "Aristotelian Categories and Cognitive Domains," and another on the role of Aristotle's category of quality in the twenty-first century (Hacking 2000a, b). Both necessarily refer to ancient texts, and both refer to, among other things, the latest cognitive science. These two papers variously mix amateur textual analysis, logic, philosophical linguistics, and armchair psychology. There is not a trace of historical ontology in either. There are many ways to do philosophy. My wish list in philosophy would barely mention a desire for advance in historical ontology: that will happen in ways that I cannot foresee. One thing that I really do wish is that philosophers of tomorrow would return to the lessons of two twentieth-century figures who never injected a historical word into their primary philosophy. I mean J. L. Austin (not his work on speech acts, but his delicate analyses of explanations for the nuances of meaning), and Ludwig Wittgenstein.

Philosophy and Science

There are many ways of bringing new objects into being that have nothing to do with the sciences. Pop culture and self-help culture are both full of object-making, and there is a lot to be learned there. Here I have not gone beyond the sciences, although my focus, my center of gravity (to use two metaphors from mature old sciences) has been away from optics or physics or other standbys, and toward the human sciences. But the philosophy that I invite you to think about and respond to is far beyond the timid discipline known as the philosophy of science. If "ontology" signals something closer to an older and less professionalized philosophy, so be it, for that was one of my intentions when I chose my title.

In fact, "ontology" turns out to be perfect, for we are concerned with two types of being: on the one hand, rather Aristotelian universals—trauma or child development—and on the other hand, the particulars that fall under them—this psychic pain or that developing child. The universal is not timeless but historical, and it and its instances, the children or the victims of trauma, are formed and changed as the universal emerges. I have called this process dynamic nominalism, because it so strongly connects what comes into existence with the historical dynamics of naming and the subsequent use of name. But it is not my plan to hang a philosophical activity on nomenclature taken from the fifteenth century, and which recalls the glory days of late scholasticism.

I am nevertheless old-fashioned, but chiefly with respect to fashions that emerged in the second half of the twentieth century. For I do profess a belief that I find impossible to defend as a doctrine, but which can still motivate practice. That is, I still would like to act on the obscure conjecture that when it comes to philosophy, many of our perplexities arise from the ways in which a space of possible ideas has been formed. Or, as I put it so long ago, in 1973 (chapter 13), using one of Wittgenstein's metaphors and one of Foucault's nouns-for-a-moment, many of our flybottles were formed by prehistory, and only archaeology can display their shape.

CHAPTER

2

Five Parables

This essay was written for a year-long series of lectures, "Philosophy in Its Context," held at Johns Hopkins University in Baltimore during 1982–3. The lectures, organized by Richard Rorty, Jerry Schneewind, and Quentin Skinner, were supposed to have a slightly subversive tone, and to make philosophers more aware of the ferment that was then going in the writing of history itself, in order to help us rethink how to do the history of philosophy. My contribution was first presented at the University of Bielefeld, Germany, where I was working as part of the "probability group" led by Lorenz Krüger (see Krüger and Daston, 1987). Hence the references, in the first parable, to Dresden—in the still-extant Democratic Republic of Germany. My enthusiasm for Brecht, in the second parable, had been fostered by seeing a number of his plays in East Berlin.

The pen-friend approach to the history of philosophy can irritate me as much as anyone. A few heroes are singled out as pen pals across the seas of time, whose words are to be read like the work of brilliant but underprivileged children in a refugee camp, deeply instructive but in need of firm correction. I loathe that, but my first parable, "The Green Family," expresses just such an anti-historical message. Descartes (for example) lives, or so I say. My second parable is an instant antidote. It is called "Brecht's Paradox" and is constructed around the fact that Brecht, on reading Descartes, could not help exclaiming that Descartes lived in a world *completely* different from ours (or, at any rate, Brecht's).

My third parable, "Too Many Words," is self-flagellating. It is about a fairly radical conception about how the history of knowledge determines the nature of philosophical problems. It was once mine. I repeat it now to

27

repudiate the idealistic and verbalistic vision of philosophy from which it arose.

The last two parables, "Remaking the World" and "Making Up People," are once again complementary and antithetical. In brief, despite all that I have learned from T. S. Kuhn, I think that there is an important way in which history does not matter to the philosophy of the natural sciences, while it does matter to the philosophy of at least some of the human sciences. This will be the hardest of my ideas to explain, but at least for those who prefer theses over parables, there is a thesis there. In some ways it is an old chestnut, but it is roasted, I hope, over new coals.

Parables can be elusive. All five of mine involve different relations between philosophy and its past. The first parable is a reminder that anachronistic readings of canonical old texts can be a fundamental value in its own right. The second one recalls that those same texts can remind us how distanced we are from our past. The third parable, which is quite self-critical, is about an exaggerated use of history for the analysis of philosophical difficulties. The fourth and fifth parables discuss, respectively, history's uses in the philosophy of natural science and in the social and human sciences. Number four draws more on T. S. Kuhn, and number five on Michel Foucault.

The Green Family

A short time ago I visited the phoenix city of Dresden, which, in addition to its collections of European art, is home to a remarkable display of Chinese porcelain. We owe both to the man whom everyone in Saxony calls August der Stark, although technically he is Augustus II (1670–1733), sometime king of Poland, and Friedrich Augustus I, elector of Saxony. He is less admired for his skill as politician and warrior than for his lavish art collections, his prodigious strength, and (in some quarters) for having fathered the largest number of children on historical record. August bought any good porcelain he could lay his hands on. His objects are limited in scope, coming mostly from the period of K'ang Hsi, 1662–1722. In 1717 he built a small palace for his china, and in the same year he traded Friedrich Wilhelm I of Prussia a crack regiment of dragoons for 151 vases, still known as the *Dragonenvasen*. Although he did indeed wield his sword, not all that effectually, he was no Prussian. August der Stark chiefly made love, not war. He put his research and development money not into cannon but chemistry, funding the rediscovery of the ancient Chinese secret of porcelain manufacture, so that Meissen in Saxony became the first European porcelain factory. (This was of commercial as well as aesthetic interest, for in those days porcelain was the main manufactured commodity imported into Europe.)

I know little about porcelain. I report without any claim to discernment that in Dresden my eye was especially caught by work in the style called "The Green Family." New techniques of glazing were developed in one of the great exporting regions. The results were stunningly beautiful. I do not single out August der Stark's pieces as the highpoint of Chinese art. Slightly later work is often more esteemed in the West, and I know well that very much earlier work has a grace and simplicity that moves the spirit more deeply. I use the green family rather as a parable of changing tastes and enduring values.

August der Stark may have loved his china to the point of building a palace for it, but it was dismissed by later cognoscenti as of no more value than a collection of dolls. For a century it languished in a crowded cellar, where on dull days you could only barely make out the looming shapes of some of the larger pieces. One man in particular guarded these obscure treasures, Dr. Gustav Klemm, and he traded duplicate pieces with other dusty curators to expand what would become the noblest collection of this kind of work in Europe. Only towards the end of the nineteenth century was it returned to light. Then it came out to amaze and delight not only scholars but transients such as me. During World War II, the china went into the cellars again, and survived the Dresden fire-bombing. Then all the Dresden collections went to Moscow for care and custody. They returned in 1958 to be housed in the noble rebuilt rooms of the Zwinger Palace.

One could use this adventure to tell two opposite stories. One says: here is a typical human tale of wealth, lust, changes in taste, destruction, survival. Only a sequence of accidents created the Chinese export trade of objects suited to a certain European fashion for chinoiserie around 1700, and then brought some characteristic examples under one lavish roof, saw them lapse from public taste, witnessed a revival, a firestorm, and a return. It is a mere historical fact that Leibniz (for example) doted on Chinese work, for such was the fashion of his time. Likewise I, more ignorantly, gape at it too, conditioned by present trends. It was not, however, for Wolff, Kant, or Hegel to admire. In short, there were periods of admiration and times when these pieces were despised, unlit, unloved. It will be like that again, not only in Europe, but also in the land of their manufacture. In some years they will be condemned as an example of early subservience to the bourgeoisie of Europe and its colonies (the green family was a big hit with the planter families in Indonesia). In other years it will come out of Chinese cellars and be invested with an entirely different aura. Evidently there is no intrinsic value in this stuff, it goes up and down in the scale of human admiration as the wind blows.

Relativists seldom state their position so crassly, but that is roughly what they think. No one pretends that the conclusion, "there is no intrinsic value in this stuff," follows from the events described in my example, but I wish to urge, against that conclusion, a slightly more empirical claim which is, I think, supported by the historical facts. I hold that no matter what dark ages we endure, so long as cellars save for us an adequate body of the green family, there will be generations that rediscover it. It will time and again *show itself.* I do not need to be reminded that porcelain will show itself only under certain conditions of wealth, pride, and human eccentricities (such as the bizarre practice of crossing disagreeable borders to wander around a strange institution that we call a museum).

I claim no intrinsic value for the green family to be found in heaven, but only an essentially human value, one tiny instance of an inherently human bundle of values, some of which manifest themselves more strongly at one time, some more strongly at another. Achievements created by humans have a strange persistence that contrasts with fashion. Most of the junk that we create has no such value. A sufficiently broad experience of the older private European collections—where objects are kept more for reasons of historical piety than of taste—assures us that being museumized is almost irrelevant to worth. August's collection is special, as its systematic survival and revival bear witness.

What has this to do with philosophy? The resurgence of historicism in philosophy brings its own relativism. Richard Rorty captured it in his powerful book, *Philosophy and the Mirror of Nature* (1979). I was happily inoculated against that message. Just before *Mirror* appeared, I had been giving a course introducing undergraduates to the philosophers who were contemporaries of the green family and August der Stark. My hero had been Leibniz, and as usual my audience gave me pained looks. But after the last meeting some students gathered around and began with the conventional, "Gee, what a great course." The subsequent remarks were more instructive: "But you could not help it . . . what with all those great books, I mean like Descartes . . ." They loved Descartes and his *Meditations.*

I happen to give terrible lectures on Descartes, for I mumble along saying that I do not understand him much. It does not matter. Descartes speaks directly to these young people, who know as little about Descartes and his times as I know about the green family and its time. But just as the green family showed itself to me, directly, so Descartes shows himself to them. My reading list served the function of the Zwinger gallery: it is the porcelain or the reading itself, not the gallery or lecture room, that does the showing. The value of Descartes to these students is completely anachronistic, out of time. Half will have begun with the idea that Descartes and Sartre were contemporaries, both being French. Descartes, even more than Sartre, can speak directly to them. Historicism, even Rorty's, forgets that.

A novice needs food, then space, then time, then books, and then an incentive to read, and often that is hardly enough, for just as with the green family, Descartes will have his ups and downs. In London 150 years ago, Spinoza was the rage and Descartes ignored. Neither goes down well in Dresden or Canton today. Both will be much read there in the future, if physical and human conditions permit, or so I say.

As for our more immediate surroundings, any of ten thousand lecture courses would serve as the gallery for Descartes to show himself. It may be my bumbling attempt to locate Descartes in the problematic of his day; it may be Rorty's rejection of epistemology; or it may be any one of the standard penfriend-across-the-seas-of-time courses. I give no argument for my conviction, but invite only experience. I mimic G. E. Moore holding up his hand before an audience of jaded skeptics. Most of us are too jaded even to remember the initial way in which Descartes spoke to us. That is the point of my parable. I gave, from my own recent past, a parallel to just that first speaking. I invite readers to invent or recall their own personal parallel. But if you resist, let me point it out once more: Hegel dominated the formation of Dewey, and perhaps that of Peirce, and also that of the upstarts Moore and Russell who laid waste to him within a few years. Hegel has, however, long lain fallow among those who read and work in English. Yet I need only mention Charles Taylor (whose expositions have much to do with the new anglophone practice of reading Hegel) to remind you that Hegel is back. The francophone was, a little earlier, even more hindered when attempting to read Hegel, until Jean Hypolyte provided the gallery within which Hegel would once again show himself. But even Michel Foucault, although he may be seen in print as the denier of the substantiality of "the text," was willing in conversation to admit with glee, when asked for his reaction to the *Phenomenology of Spirit*, that it is *un beau livre*. As indeed it is. That is what it is for a writer such as Hegel to speak directly, once again, first to the French, and later to us, after decades of oblivion.

Brecht's Paradox

Having stated some conventional wisdom, I must at least record the opposing wisdom. I do find it very hard to make sense of Descartes, even after reading commentaries, predecessors, and more arcane texts of the same period. The more I make consistent sense of him, the more he seems to me to inhabit an alien universe. That is odd, for he formed French philosophical writing and continues to provide one of its dominant models. I shall not here argue my problems using pedantic scruples. Instead I shall take a few notes written down by Bertolt Brecht early in 1932, when he, too, had been reading Descartes with consternation.

Brecht is useful because his reaction is so direct. "This man must live in another time, another world from mine!" (Brecht 1967, VIII, 691). He is not troubled with niceties. His complaint is a robust astonishment at Descartes's central proposition. How could thinking possibly be my guarantee of my existence? What I *do* is what assures me of existence: but not just any doing. It is doing with purpose, especially those acts that are part of the work that I do. Brecht is a writer. His labor is writing. He is well aware of the paper in front of him. But it is not *that* awareness which (in the manner of Moore) makes him certain of its existence. He wants to write on the paper, and does so. He possesses the paper with his inscriptions, he changes it. Of that he can have no doubt. He adds, a trifle ironically, that to know anything about the existence of the paper, without manipulating it, would be very difficult.

Brecht notoriously writes from an ideology. His next comment is headed, "Presentation of capitalism as a form of existence, that necessitates too much thinking and too many virtues." It is in praxis and not in theory that he and his being are constituted. Implicitly turning to Berkeley, he remarks that one can perfectly well doubt whether a tree over there exists or not. But it would be a bit troublesome if no trees or the like existed, for then we would be dead for lack of oxygen. *That* truth may be known by theory, but it is the practical interaction with trees that is at the core of that certainty.

Some will feel that it is Brecht who lives in another world, a world less familiar than that of Descartes. You may dissent from Brecht's seemingly simple-minded ideology and still feel his cry of astonishment at that famous Cartesian utterance. I am not saying that Pyrrhonism is unthinkable. People go through intellectual operations that lead them to skeptical utterances, and then go through other operations that have the form of relieving them from skepticism. I have no quarrel with that. I am not urging those linguistic "paradigm case" arguments of a couple of generations ago, in which it was claimed that one could not coherently use English to express skeptical problems. Brecht directs me to a more central worry. How could someone with the deepest seriousness make existence depend upon thought? How could someone relieve real doubt by a chain of reflections which culminates in "even when doubting, I think, and when thinking, I am?" The step to *res cogitans* seems transparent compared to that first thought. Curiously, Hintikka (1962), made a quasi-Brechtian hermeneutic move when he claimed that the *cogito* is to be heard as a performative utterance in the sense of J. L. Austin. I can see that in a rather special circumstance of speech (and Austin always attended to the circumstances!). A modern orator, whose labor is talking, may talk to prove he exists. We have all heard people whom we sarcastically describe in just those terms. But that is not what Descartes was up to, nor are readers of Hintikka usually persuaded by the "performative" interpretation of the *cogito*.

I am not drawing attention to concepts in Descartes that have been transmuted ("substance") or which have died (*"realitatis objectivae,"* a term well translated by Anscombe and Geach (Dascartes 1964) as "representative reality"). We can, with pain, reconstruct those concepts. Brecht is protesting against something at the very core of Descartes. No being of my time, asserts Brecht, can seriously intend the basic Cartesian sentence.

I agree. I have also said in my first parable that generation after generation loves the *Meditations* and feels at home with the text. I think that is a paradox about history and philosophy without resolution. "You can do the history better"—"the students are taken in by Cartesian prose style, they only think they understand it and empathize with it"—those are mere comforting kinds of talk that fail to grasp the seriousness of the Brechtian reaction or fail to grasp the seriousness of the students to whom Descartes speaks directly. Naturally, you do not need to use Brecht to make this point. I thought it useful to remind ourselves that while we philosophers beat around the bush, an alert and inquisitive outsider can at once go to the heart of what is unintelligible about Descartes.

Too Many Words

Brecht connects the rise of capitalism with twin vices: too many virtues, too much thinking. Those are not our vices. Our problem is too many words: too much confidence in words as the be-all, the substance of philosophy. Perhaps Richard Rorty's *Philosophy and the Mirror of Nature,* with its central doctrine of "conversation," will some day seem as linguistic a philosophy as the analysis emanating from Oxford a generation or two ago. To recall what that was like, it is best to think of routines rather than the occasional inspiration of a master such as Austin. We read in a book on Kant's ethics, for example, that "A discussion which remains strictly within the bounds of ethics would have no purpose beyond that of analyzing and clarifying our moral thinking and the terms we use to express that thinking." The author, A. R. C. Duncan (1957, 12), then quotes Henry Sidgwick's definition from page 1 of the classic *Methods of Ethics* (1874): "the study of what is right or what ought to be, so far as this depends upon the voluntary acts of individuals." Duncan says that he and Sidgwick have the same conception of ethics. Alas poor Sidgwick, poor Kant, who thought they were studying what is right or what ought to be! We might speak of the linguistic blindfold here, a blindfold that allows one to copy a sentence from page 1 of Sidgwick without being able to read it. Gustav Bergmann wrote of "the linguistic turn" in philosophy, an evocative phrase that Rorty (1967) used as the title of an anthology of the period. As Rorty's remarkable collection shows, the linguistic turn was compelling, and in retrospect seems to have been too compelling. There are, however, subtler linguistic blindfolds than ones that make us read Kant as a philosopher of language. To avoid discourtesy I shall tug at my own. It shows up in a book such as *The Emergence of Probability* and a solemn lecture to the British Academy about Leibniz, Descartes, and the philosophy of mathematics, reprinted as chapter 13 below. I had been reading Foucault, but, significantly, I had chiefly been reading *Les Mots et les choses* (1970), a work that does not so much emphasize *mots* at the expense of *choses,* as make a strong statement about how words impose an order on things.

It is easy to state a series of premises leading up to my historic-linguistic turn. Most of them will seem commonplace until they are totted up. They once stood for my methodology. I stated them as such in a sort of valedictory talk to the Cambridge University Moral Sciences Club in the spring of 1974. It was called "One Way to Do Philosophy."

*   *   *

1. *One kind of philosophy is about problems.* This may not be an eternal truth. The idea that philosophy (perhaps all philosophy!) tries to solve problems may have become fixed in English as late as 1910. In the winter of that year, G. E. Moore gave some public lectures in London under the title *Some Main Problems of Philosophy.* These lectures at Morley College, London, "during the Winter of 1910," were published as Moore (1953). During the years 1909 and 1910 William James almost finished his last book, *Some Problems of Philosophy* (1911), which includes a list of 21 problems. And Bertrand Russell published what has been, to this day, a nonstop bestseller, *The Problems of Philosophy* (1912), cheerfully passing from the modest *"Some"* of his predecessors to the imperious definite article: *"The"* problems.

2. *Philosophical problems are conceptual.* They arise from facts about concepts and from conceptual confusion.

3. *A verbal account of concepts.* A concept is not an abstract nonlinguistic entity grasped by our minds. It is to be understood in terms of the words that we use to express the concept, and the contexts in which we use those words.

4. *Words in their sites.* A concept is no more than a word or words in the sites in which it is used. Once we have considered the sentences in which the word is used, and the acts performed by uttering the sentences, and the conditions of felicity or authority for uttering those sentences, and so on, we have exhausted what there is to be said about the concept. A strict version would say we have exhausted the concept when we have considered *(per impossibile)* all the actual specific utterances of the corresponding words. A less strict version would allow us to contemplate circumstances in which the word could be used, but in fact is not. Rigor inclines me towards the strict version, but the loose version is more popular.

5. *Concepts and words are not identical.* This is because, in addition to synchronic ambiguity, the same words may, through various kinds of change, come to express different concepts. But concepts are not to be multiplied beyond necessity. Evidence for difference in concept is provided by difference in site: the word is used by different classes of people to do different things. I still admire one theory of how to do this, which is not often thought of in this connection: that of Paul Ziff's *Semantic Analysis* (1960). In parity, we must admit that at different times the same concept may be expressed by different words within the same community. A Ziffian inclination makes me more cautious about this than are most people; I take seriously Fowler's *Modern English Usage* (1926, 591) and its claim that

British English knows only one exact synonym, "furze" and "gorse." Even today, when I find that the word "determinism" begins in German around 1788, and that its usage in terms of efficient causes rather than predeterminating motives begins in all European language around 1860, I am inclined to say that a new concept comes in with this use of the word (Hacking 1983b).

6. *Revolutions.* Ruptures, mutations, epistemological breaks, cuts—whatever metaphor you wish—occur in bodies of knowledge. Typically, a concept, category, or mode of classification may not survive a revolution intact. Even if we preserve the same word, it may express a new concept superseding an old one. We need not succumb to the excesses of incommensurability here. We need not suppose that post-revolutionary speakers have trouble understanding pre-revolutionary ones who stick to the old ways. But it does follow from this, plus the preceding premise, that concepts may have beginnings and endings.

7. *Problematic concepts.* At least one important class of conceptual confusions arises with concepts that came into being with a relatively sharp break. There is a trivial way that can happen, simply because people have not had time to work things out.

8. *Persistent problems.* There is also the less trivial cliché that some philosophical problems persist throughout the life of a concept. Some problems are as old as the hills, but others are specific and dated, and we may even have the view that some died so effectively so long ago that not all the artificial hermeneutic resuscitation in the world will bring them back to life again. We also know the flybottle phenomenon of the same bundle of arguments being proffered again and again, from generation to generation. Now we are near the end of our journey and pass to sheer speculation that the problem arises because of whatever it was that made that concept possible. It is as if a problematic concept had an unhappy consciousness.

9. "This *unhappy, inwardly disrupted* consciousness, since its essentially contradicted nature is for it a single consciousness, must forever have present in the one consciousness the other also; and thus it is driven out of each in turn in the very moment when it imagines it has successfully attained to a peaceful unity with the other." (Hegel, 1977, 126).

Item (9) is not a premise but a project whose influence has been ample. Marx and Freud are the giants spawned by Hegel, but philosophers know the model too. In analytic philosophy it is as strongly connected with therapy as it is in Freud. The most sustained therapists were the linguistic analysts who thought that once linguistic confusions had been removed, philosophical problems would disappear. Then there were the nonlinguistic analysts, of whom John Wisdom is the most notable, who made explicit comparisons with psychotherapy. Wittgenstein had some influence on the formation of Wisdom's ideas, but I find less "therapy" mentioned in Wittgenstein's own work than many other readers do. The Hegelian project, whatever its provenance, leads on to my final premise. It is the most improbable one.

10. *Concepts have memories,* or at any rate, we in our very word patterns unconsciously mimic the phylogeny of our concepts. Some of our philosophical problems about concepts are the result of their history. Our perplexities arise not from that deliberate part of our history which we remember, but from that which we forget. A concept becomes possible at a moment. It is made possible by a different arrangement of earlier ideas that have collapsed or exploded. A philosophical problem is created by the incoherencies between the earlier state and the later one. Concepts remember this, but we do not: we gnaw at problems eternally (or for the lifetime of the concept) because we do not understand that the source of the problem is the lack of coherence between the concept and that prior arrangement of ideas that made the concept possible.

The therapy model would teach that we should solve or resolve our problems by undertaking their prehistory. I strongly dissociate myself from that model. It is extraneous to the unhappy consciousness story. About 25 years ago an eclectic Norwegian psychiatrist remarked to me in conversation that Freud was wonderful for *explaining* mental phenomena, from slips through dreams to neuroses. The explanations were often splendid, the best in the market, although so far as curing people goes Freud is neither particularly good nor bad. The remark about cure has its tedious partisans pro and con. The remark about explanation was, for me exhilarating. Partly because of positivist training, I was not supposed to believe in explanations that did not have corresponding predictions. Now I could at once admit that Freud's and Freudian explanations of dreamwork and of much odd behavior were simply wonderful. But don't count on cure.

This negative premise (don't expect therapy) concludes the basis for my model of the *explanation* of (some) philosophical problems. One had to understand the prehistory of problematic concepts and what made them possible in order to grasp the nature of the philosophical problems. One would explain the problems. This need have no effect on whether the problems remained troubling to you. Those who look for solutions of philosophical problems will get no help from their explanation.

On the other hand, an explanation of the concept "philosophical problem" (according to premise [1], a dated concept in the sense of premise [5]), would, I hope, make one more uncomfortable about the very idea of solving philosophical problems.

I can caricature these premises as a pinch of this and a pinch of that, but until we get up to the very end, *they were the commonplaces of a perfectly conventional training in analytic philosophy.* Even at the end, where there was more historicizing than traditional philosophical analysis wanted, the extra ideas were scarcely novel.

Why do I no longer like these premises? At first, not for their emphasis on language or the past. Instead, it is because, as many could have forewarned me, of the opening premise. One was in the business of "solving" philosophical problems. Despite a gallant attempt to do that in connection with probable reasoning, and a briefer flirtation with that approach in the philosophy of mathematics, I was not doing that. But had I not succeeded in the task of explaining the existence and persistence of the problems? Well, no one else likes the explanations as much as I do: a good warning!

I still like the explanations, but now realize I was doing something else, at least in the two cases with which I began, probability and mathematics. I was embarking on what in chapter 1 I call historical meta-epistemology. I was also beginning to think about what in chapters 12 and 13 I call styles of reasoning.

Once you become suspicious of the first premise, that philosophy is about problems, none of the rest is very stable. In one way, though, the premises are terrifyingly stable, for they are part of the idealist gambit that so permeates Western philosophy. Philosophy is about problems, problems arise from words, solutions must be about words, and philosophizing ensues. Occasionally someone yelps. An example is C. S. Peirce, the only able experimenter in our canon, who when he saw what verbalists had done to his word "pragmatism," yelped "ic" and invented the word "pragmaticism." Pragmatism is nominalist and idealist, both, but Peirce's pragmaticism, as he cantankerously averred, is realist all the way. Although it has views about how words have meanings, it does not reduce philosophy to words. Nor does Ludwik Fleck, so utterly sensitive to styles of reasoning, for the experimenter cannot afford idealism nor its present form of verbalism. An instructive task for a more critical author than myself would be to check out if every post-Copernican revolution honored by Kuhn had not been triggered by work in the laboratory: deeds, not thoughts; manipulation, not thinking.

I have laid bare one sequence of premises leading up to one way of doing philosophy historically. Internally, within this sequence of parables, it has at least one other role. It suggests to me that a well-articulated methodology may lead one to interesting work to which the methodology is largely irrelevant.

Remaking the World

No one from his generation has had a more dramatic impact on the philosophy of science than T. S. Kuhn. Any discussion of the relation between history and philosophy of science will begin with *The Structure of Scientific Revolutions* (1962). This is odd, because he wrote entirely about natural science, indeed about the physical sciences. There is a time-honored opinion that history matters to the very content of the human sciences, while it does not matter much to the natural sciences. If Kuhn had succeeded in historicizing our understanding of natural science, his achievement would have been revolutionary. I want to show why he did not succeed, and to give another twist to the old idea about a difference between natural and social science. This is in no sense a criticism of Kuhn. I believe that the totality of the work of this historian places him among the major philosophers of the twentieth century. Philosophers usually respond only to *Structure*. His work on experiments, measurement, and the second scientific revolution (all published in *The Essential Tension,* 1977) are of comparable importance. His last historical book—on Max Planck and the first quantum theory (1978)—describes the sort of revolution that *Structure* is all about, and it is a notable achievement. Yet it is possible to learn from Kuhn in the most thorough way possible, and still to hold that there is a sense in which he did not succeed, and could not have succeeded, in historicizing natural science.

My distinction comes out at the level of one of the older philosophical disputes. It concerns nominalism. The most extreme version of nominalism says that we make up the categories that we use to describe the world. That is a most mysterious doctrine, which is perhaps why, like solipsism, it is almost never maintained. The problem is that we cannot understand why the world is so tractable to our systems of naming. Must there not be some natural kinds in the world for our invented categories to latch on to? Does that not refute strict nominalism?

I hold that Kuhn has importantly advanced the nominalist cause by giving some account of how at least an important group of "our" categories come into being in the course of scientific revolutions. There is a construction of new systems of classification going hand in hand with certain interests in describing the world, interests closely connected with the "anomalies" on which a community focuses in times of "crisis." At the same time, this cannot lead us to a *very* strict nominalism, for the anomalies "really" do have to seem to be resolved in order for a revolutionary achievement to be recognized. Removal of anomaly is never enough, Kuhn has taught, because all sorts of social conditions are needed for a revolution to "take." But reality has to go some part of the way—more than a wilder, stricter nominalism would allow.

My contrast with the social sciences is as follows. In natural science, our invention of categories does not "really" change the way the world works. Even though we create new phenomena which did not exist before our scientific endeavors, we do so only with a license from the world (or so we think). But in social phenomena we may generate kinds of people and kinds of action as we devise new classifications and categories. My claim is that we "make up people" in a stronger sense than we "make up" the world. The difference is connected with the ancient question of nominalism. It is also connected with history, because the objects of the social sciences—people and groups of people—are constituted by a historical process, while the objects of the natural sciences, particular experimental apparatus, are created in time, but, in some sense, they are not constituted historically.

It must be clear that I am groping for a complex distinction between social and natural science. Perhaps I should warn against the most superficial distinction of all. It is curious, even comical, that physical scientists have paid little attention to Kuhn. Science journalists may now fill their articles with the word "paradigm," but it is not a word that plays any role in reflection about serious research. It is quite the opposite in the social and psychological sciences. Kuhn's *Structure* had hardly appeared in print when presidential addresses to annual meetings of the American Psychological Association and the American Sociological Association avowed their need for paradigms. It has always seemed to me that Kuhn was a good deal clearer about his use of his famous word than most of his readers, including presidents of learned societies. When I claim that there is a sense in which Kuhn has not succeeded in historicizing physical science, it is not because his terminology has had more of a fad in the social sciences. Quite the contrary: it may be that the impact of Kuhn on social sciences is a sign of their lack of self-understanding.

Let us first recall philosophical reaction to Kuhn's book. He was accused of a scandalous undermining of rationality. "Normal science" did not seem to have any of the virtues that a previous generation of positivists ascribed to science. Even worse, revolutionary change was not cumulative, nor did it occur because there was good reason for making the change, sound evidence for the new post-revolutionary science. Part of the philosophical guild defended its entrenched rights, and protested that history could never teach us anything about scientific rationality. The historian might exhibit some events in the history of science, but the philosopher would always be required to say whether those events were rational or not.

Thus the first wave of philosophical reaction was on the score of rationality, and people still do debate Kuhn's contribution, if any, to the methodology of science. He himself was a bit bemused by this reception, as is shown by his 1973 lecture, "Objectivity, Value Judgment, and Theory Choice" (Kuhn 1977b). He subscribed to the traditional values after all—theories should be accurate, consistent, broad in scope, simple, and fruitful in new research findings. He insisted that these desiderata were not in general decisive. Moreover, the relative weights given to these considerations vary from research group to research group, from discipline to discipline, and from one era of science to another. Finally, the sheer rough and tumble of research is too messy for there to be any systematic algorithm. Kuhn was, however, no irrationalist demeaning these common-sense values, and I think the rumor of a "rationality crisis" provoked by Kuhn was exaggerated.

Another theme of Kuhn's was less discussed, at first, than rationality: an anti-realism, a strong temptation, it appears, towards idealism. Not only are revolutions "changes in world view"—not a very daring statement, but Kuhn is "tempted" to say that after a revolution one "lives in a different world." Some twenty years after the book was published (a period during which Kuhn completed his monumental study of the onset of quantization), he returned to that theme. People do see the world differently: what better evidence than that they draw it differently! He illustrated this with the first drawings of Volta's electric batteries (Kuhn 1987). When we examine them closely, we want to say that the cells cannot have been made like that, for they simply would not work. The voltaic cell, I may add, is no minor invention, but one of the fundamental tools of all science. It came into being in 1800, coinciding with the revival of the wave theory of light, of infra-red radiation, and much else that had no immediate place in Newtonian physics. Volta's invention was fundamental because it provided a steady current of electricity, and hence deflected the magnetic compass. Therefore it created a new epoch, that of electromagnetism.

Kuhn's "temptation to speak of living in a different world" suggests that he is an idealist, one who holds, in some way, that the mind and its ideas determine the structure of our world. I think he is no idealist, and urge that we should think not of the post-Kantian realism/idealism dichotomy, but of the older, scholastic, realism/nominalism distinction. Kuhn is not among those who challenge the absolute existence of scientific entities or phenomena, nor among those who query the truth conditions for theoretical propositions. Instead, he believes that the classifications, categories, and possible descriptions that we deploy are very much of our own devising. But rather than leaving this as a mystery about how human categories come into being, he makes the creation and adjustment of schemes of classification part of his definition of a revolution:

> What characterizes revolutions is, thus, change in several of the taxonomic categories prerequisite to scientific description and generalization. That change, furthermore, is an adjustment not only of criteria relevant to categorization, but also of the way in which objects and situations are distributed among pre-existing categories. (Kuhn 1987, 20)

I read that as a species of nominalism, and name it revolutionary nominalism, because the transitions in systems of categories occur during those revolutionary breaks with the past whose structures Kuhn proposes to describe. (My own subsequent gloss on Kuhn's identification of revolution and taxonomic change is given in Hacking 1993a.)

This nominalism is also, of course, a historicized nominalism, because it gives a historical account (or is it only a historical metaphor?) of the genesis and transformation of systems of naming. It also has the great value of being local rather than global, for although Kuhn includes big events among his revolutions (Lavoisier, Copernicus), he insists that most revolutions apply only within a small community of, say, one hundred main researchers.

Kuhn's revolutionary nominalism invites histories of category change, but it may seem that the objects of the sciences, although described by changing systems of categories, are not themselves historically constituted. Yet what are the objects? Do they include voltaic cells, for example? Do they include such phenomena as the deflection of a magnetic needle by a steady electric current, or Faraday's more ingenious devices, the electric generator and the electric dynamo? These are not eternal items in the inventory of the universe, but came into existence at very specific times. Nor am I content to say that the inventions are dated, while the phenomena and laws of nature that they employ are eternal. One of the chief activities of the experimenter in the physical sciences is quite literally to create phenomena that did not exist before (Hacking 1983a, ch. 16). Moreover, most of physical science (as opposed to astronomy) is about phenomena that did not exist until people brought them into being. What physicists have from the 1870s been calling "effects" (the photoelectric effect, the Zeeman effect, the Compton effect, the Josephson effect) are mostly phenomena which do not exist, at least in a pure state, anywhere in unpolluted nature, yet they are arguably what physics is, or has come to be, *about*. There is a case (of sorts) for saying that the very objects of physical science are not merely recategorized and rearranged, as Kuhn says, but brought into being by human ingenuity.

If I go to this extreme, is not my proposed distinction between human and natural science in ruins? Is it not the case that the objects of natural science become "historically constituted"? I do not think so. Indeed, I developed a return to serious consideration of experimental science precisely to urge a good many realist, anti-idealist, anti-nominalist conclusions. I claim, in the "representing" half of *Representing and Intervening* (1983a), that in principle no debates at the level of theorizing will settle any of those realism/anti-realism debates in the philosophy of natural science. I urge, in the "intervening" half, that recognition of the facts of experimental life and of changing the world leads powerfully to scientific realism. You will detect one source of my admiration for Brecht's direct materialism that puts "manipulation" rather than "thinking" as the source of realism. My "experimental realism" no more invites nominalism than does Brecht's materialism. The physical phenomena that are created by human beings are rather resilient to theoretical change. Kuhn's own example of the voltaic cell serves me well.

Kuhn writes that Volta saw his invention on analogy with the Leyden jar.

Volta's description of it is strange, and we cannot credit his drawings, for they build in the wrong analogies. But the thing worked. Current did flow. Once that had been done physics never looked back. Likewise, the photoelectric effect was perhaps first produced in 1829 by Becquerel. Various photoelectric manifestations were induced throughout the nineteenth century. One can construct a Kuhnian argument that the effect was not properly "discovered" until the time of Lenard—1902—or even Einstein and the theory of photons—1905. Certainly once we had the theory we were able to use the phenomena we had begun to create. Automatic doors at supermarkets, and television, were not too far behind. But if (as some have urged) the photon approach needs drastic revision or revolutionary rejection, the supermarket doors will still go on working. Phenomena are resilient to theory. Elementary physics may teach a completely different story about how they work, but work they will. Even if, to re-quote Kuhn (1987), "there is an adjustment not only of criteria relevant to categorization, but also of the way in which objects and situations are distributed among pre-existing categories," the phenomena which we have created will still exist and the inventions will work. We may lose interest in them. We may replace them by more useful or interesting phenomena. We might lose the skills needed to produce a phenomenon (no one can work brass today the way that a nineteenth-century laboratory assistant could work brass, and I am sure most of the old skills for polishing lenses are now extinct). I am the last philosopher to forget the radical changes in experimental technology. I still hold that the objects of the physical sciences are largely created by people, *and* that once created, there is no reason except human backsliding why they should not continue to persist.

Thus I claim that Kuhn leads us into a "revolutionary nominalism" which makes nominalism less mysterious by describing the historical processes whereby new categories and distributions of objects come into being. But I assert that a seemingly more radical step, literal belief in the creation of phenomena, shows why the objects of the sciences, although brought into being at moments of time, are not historically constituted. They are phenomena thereafter, regardless of what happens. I call this "experimental realism."

Never shy to add a few more "isms" to our ismically troubled world. I would say that my position is strikingly similar to that evolved by Gaston Bachelard's (1953) "applied rationalism and technical materialism." No other philosopher or historian so assiduously studied the realities of experimental life, nor was anyone less inclined than he to suppose that the mind is unimportant (his applied rationalism). Fifty years ago he was teaching that epistemological breaks occur in science (for example, "the photoelectric effect represents an absolute discontinuity in the history of the sciences"). At the same time he believed in scientific accumulation and *connaissance approchée*. What we accumulate are *experimental techniques* and *styles of reasoning*. Anglophone philosophy of science has too much debated the question of whether theoretical *knowledge* accumulates. Maybe it does not. So what? Phenomena and reasons accumulate.

Having thus made a slight obeisance towards Bachelard, I pass to one of his spiritual descendants, namely, Michel Foucault. I shall try to be aware of one of Addison's warnings in *The Spectator*. "A few general rules, extracted out of the French authors, with a certain cant of words, has sometimes set up an illiterate and heavy writer for a most judicious and formidable critic" (*Spectator* 291, Saturday, 2 Feb., 1711).

Making Up People

At the end of a recent review of Rorty's *Consequences of Pragmatism* (1982), Bernard Williams first quotes Rorty quoting Foucault, "the being of language continues to shine ever brighter on the horizon." He then goes on to say that unless we keep sense

> that science finds ways out of the cell of words, and if we do not recover the sense that pursuing science is one of our essential experiences of being constrained by the truth, we shall find that the brightness of language on the horizon turns out to be that of the fire in which the supremely bookish hero of Canetti's *Auto Da Fé* immolated himself in his library. (Williams 1990, 37)

Such games of meta-meta-quoting invite a little burning, but I have two reasons for quoting Williams. The minor one, something of an aside, is that Williams himself may be trapped within the cell of words. The way out of Williams's cell is not to be constrained by the truth, but to create phenomena. Only within a theory-dominated verbalistic philosophy of science is "pursuing science one of our essential experiences of being constrained by the truth." Let us take an example of an important discovery from the 1980s. The event in question bore out some guesses made by Fermi many years before. He thought that there must be a particle, a weak elementary particle or boson W, which was in some sense the "carrier" of weak neutral currents (just as the electron carries ordinary charged currents). Around 1970, people were trying to find W, but then the high energy physics community switched to study weak neutral currents themselves. They regarded W as a mere hypothetical entity, a figment of our imagination. Only early in the 1980s was the search resumed, at very much higher energy levels than Fermi had thought necessary. Finally, in January 1983, CERN announced it had located W in proton-antiproton decay at 540 GeV. There is a complex history of science story to tell about the shift away from a search for W and then back. There certainly were constraints, but not "constraints of truth." I do not suppose there is a true theory of truth, but there is an instructive one, namely the redundancy theory, which says that "p is true" says no more than p. If something verbal constrained the earlier experimenters, it was a p, not the truth of p. What really constrained research workers was a need for greater energy sources; one had to wait for the next generation in order to create the sought for phenomena involving proton-antiproton decay. There were constraints all over the place, but none of them were constraints of truth, unless by vicious semantic ascent we express the constraints using the redundant word "true."

The redundancy theory of truth is instructive but defective. I refer not to its formal defects, but to its philosophical ones. It makes it seem as if "is true" is merely redundant, but harmless. I think that it does invite semantic ascent, and takes us up the ladder to that cell of words in which philosophers, not excluding Williams, confine themselves. If there is an interesting theory of truth to discuss at the moment, it will lie in Foucault's own "suggestions to be further tested and evaluated":

> "Truth" is to be understood as a system of ordered procedures for the production, regulation, distribution, circulation and operation of statements.

> "Truth" is linked in a circular relation with systems of power which produce and sustain it, and to effects of power which it induces and which extend it. (Foucault 1980, 133)

We should, if we have a philosophical interest in truth, care about how statements come into being as candidates for being true or false, and as possible objects of knowledge. But even here "truth" is redundant, for we are concerned simply with how statements come into being.

So much by way of aside. What of Williams's critique of Foucault? My second thoughts on *The Order of Things* notwithstanding, Williams's remarks seem curiously misplaced. Foucault's books are mostly about practices and how they affect and are affected by the talk in which we embed them. The upshot is less a fascination with words than with people and institutions, with what we do for people and to people. He does have a noble obsession with what he takes to be oppression: the asylum, the prison, the hospital, public hygiene, and forensic medicine. His view of these practices may be entirely wrong. Some say that he has already done untold harm to wretched disturbed people who are released on the streets of the American metropolis because Foucault has convinced doctors that the disturbed ought not to be constrained. But one thing is clear. Foucault has not been locked in a cell of words. Moreover, it is precisely his intellectual work, his philosophical work, that directs our attention away from our talk and on to our practices.

I am not denying that Foucault is verbal. Few people have read one of his first books, about the surrealist Raymond Roussel (Foucault, 1986). Roussel seems to be the very epitome of the man in the cell of words. One of his books is *How I Have Written Some of My Books* (Roussel, 1977). He says he would try to find a sentence such that, by changing one letter in one of the words, you change the meaning of each of the words in the sentence, as well as the grammar. Then you write down the first sentence at the front of your novel, and carry on until you end your book with the second sentence. In 1910 he wrote a book, *Impressions of Africa* (1969), and then toured Egypt to make sure nothing in the book was true. He came of good stock. His mad rich mother chartered a yacht to make a voyage to India. When she got near the coastline she screwed up her telescope, said, "Now I have seen India" and sailed home. Roussel killed himself. This can all be read at one level as the hyperparisian linguistic obsession. But a caricature, even if lived seriously, may also be read as directing us to the exact opposite.

Whatever be the point of the Roussel phase, let us consider the main sequence of Foucault's work, the madhouse, the clinic, the prison, sexuality, and in general the intermeshing of knowledge and power. I have remarked that Kuhn says nothing about the social sciences or knowledge of human beings. Likewise Foucault says nothing about the physical sciences. His remarks about what we charmingly call the life sciences are chiefly, although not entirely, directed at how we interfere with human lives. I have heard

Foucault criticized for being scared of physical science. Let us instead consider the hypothesis that there is something fundamentally correct about the division of labor, Kuhn to the physical sciences, and Foucault to human affairs.

I shall focus on only one thing, making a specific contrast with Kuhn's revolutionary nominalism. The problem with scholastic nominalism, I said, is that it leaves our interaction with, and description of, the world a complete mystery. We can well understand why the word "pencil" nicely sorts out some objects. We manufacture pencils; that is why they exist. Nominalism about human artifacts is no problem. It is nominalism about grass, trees, and stars that is the problem. How can our words fit the earth and heavens, if there are not, prior to us, grass, trees, and stars? A strict and universal nominalism is a preposterous mystery. What, however, about categories applying to people?

People are alive or dead, tall or short, strong or weak, creative or plodding, foolish or intelligent. These categories arise from the nature of people themselves, although we are by now well aware how "intelligence" can be warped by quotients. But consider the categories so much worked over by Foucault, involving madness, criminality, and other kinds of deviancy. Consider even his assertion (which I do not quite believe) about what a soldier was in medieval times, and what he became with the new institutions of discipline and uniform: soldiers themselves became different kinds of people. We may begin to grasp at a different kind of nominalism, which I call dynamic nominalism. Categories of people come into existence at the same time as kinds of people come into being to fit those categories, and there is a two-way interaction between these processes.

This is not very sensational, as most of the interesting things about us are what we choose to do, or try not to do, how we behave or misbehave. I subscribe to G. E. M. Anscombe's view in *Intention* (1957), that by and large intentional action is action under a description. So there have to be descriptions. If we can show that descriptions change, some dropping in, some dropping out, then there simply is a change in what we can (as a matter of logic) do or not do. One can reread many of Foucault's books as in part stories about the connection between certain kinds of description coming into being or going out of existence, and certain kinds of people coming into being or going out of existence. More important, one can do this kind of work explicitly oneself. I study the dullest of subjects, nineteenth-century statistics. It turns out to be one aspect of what

Foucault calls a "biopolitics of the population" that "gave rise to comprehensive measures, statistical assessments, and interventions aimed at the
entire social body or at groups taken as a whole" (Foucault 1978, 139).
What do I find at the beginning of the great avalanche of numbers, around
1820? Nothing other than the statistics of deviancy, of madness, suicide,
prostitution, vagrancy, crime against the person, crime against property,
drunkenness, *les miserables.* These vast arrays of data are called *analyse morale.* We find constant subdivisions and rearrangements of, for example,
the mad, as the counting progresses. We find classifications of over 4,000
different criss-crossing motives for murder. I do not believe that mad people of these sorts, or these motives for murder, in general existed until
there came into being the practice of counting them (Hacking 1982a).

Constantly new ways of counting people were devised. New slots were
created into which people could fall and be counted. Even the decennial
censuses in the different states amazingly show that the categories into
which people fall change every ten years. This is partly because social
change generates new categories of people, but I think the countings were
not mere reportings. They were part of an elaborate, well-meaning, indeed
innocent creating of new kinds of ways for people to be, and people innocently "chose" to fall into these new categories.

I have no idea what such a dynamic nominalism will amount to. Let us,
however, consider its implications for history and philosophy of the human sciences. Like Kuhn's revolutionary nominalism, Foucault's dynamic
nominalism is a historicized nominalism. But there is something fundamentally different. History plays an essential role in the constitution of the
objects, where the objects are people and the ways in which they behave.
Despite my radical doctrine about the experimental creation of phenomena, I hold the common-sense view that the photoelectric effect is timeless
at least to this extent: if one does do certain things, certain phenomena will
appear. They never did appear until the nineteenth century. We made
them. But what happened when in mid-twentieth-century we used the
photoelectric effect to open supermarket doors was constrained by "the
world." The categories created by what Foucault calls anatomopolitics and
biopolitics, and the "intermediary cluster of relations" between the two
politics, are constituted in an essentially historical setting. Yet it is these
very categories in terms of which the human sciences venture to describe
us. Moreover, they bring into being new categories which, in part, bring
into being new kinds of people. We remake the world, but we make up

people. Just before the warning about heavy writing and of French cant, with which I closed Parable 4, Addison wrote, "it is very certain that an author, who has not learned the art of distinguishing words and things and of ranging his thoughts and setting them in proper lights, whatever notions he may have, will lose himself in confusion and obscurity." I think that we shall lose ourselves in confusion and obscurity for some time yet, in the so-called social and human sciences, because in those domains the distinction between word and thing is constantly blurred. It is precisely experimental methods that I take to be essential to the physical sciences and which, I claim, make Kuhn's historicized revolutionary nominalism fall short of a strict nominalism. The experimental methods of the human sciences are something else. The lack of a sharp distinction between word and thing is at the root of Wittgenstein's famous concluding remark in *Philosophical Investigations,* that in psychology (and the like) "there are experimental methods and *conceptual confusion.*" Here Foucault's "archaeology" may yet prove useful, not in order to "display the shape of the flybottle" but at least to grasp the interrelations of power and knowledge that literally constitute us as human beings. That would be the strongest impact of history upon philosophy. But until we can do that job better, it will have to remain one more parable, deliberately open, like all parables, to far too many interpretations.

3

Two Kinds of "New Historicism" for Philosophers

This essay was a contribution to a conference called "History and . . . ," organized by Michael Roth and held at the Claremont Colleges in southern California in 1988. The idea was that contributors to a number of fields, such as
musicology or anthropology, should discuss the relationship of their work
to history, and most particularly to the "new historicism" that had been
sweeping our ranks from Berkeley, California. The first section of the chapter, "The Mandate," describes what Michael Roth suggested that speakers
should do—based on quotations from his original letter of invitation, dated
11 March, 1986.

Could philosophical analysis have anything to do with the activity that
Michel Foucault called the history of the present? Yes, I say. No, says almost
everyone else. So I have some explaining to do.

Philosophical analysis is an activity, a way of doing philosophy, defined
in part by its practitioners. They used to think of it as analyzing concepts,
and then turned to words. I think of J. L. Austin, C. D. Broad, Paul Grice,
G. E. Moore, Bertrand Russell, Gilbert Ryle, Ludwig Wittgenstein, but of
course there are many very much younger, very much American, and very
much alive analysts today. The men whom I have mentioned knew, in
some cases, a great deal about the past and in particular about ancient philosophy. Some felt intellectual kinship with Aristotle. But a sense of the
past played little role in their most creative work. Analytic philosophy is
widely regarded as the very antithesis of historical sensibility. It needn't be,
or so I contend.

I have no desire to make peace among different traditions. Attempts to
reconcile continental and analytic philosophy are at best bland, lacking the

savor or pungency of either. I should add that in connecting philosophical analysis with certain techniques used by Foucault I am not making a point about recent French thought in general. I am discussing one kind of use of the past, represented by some of Foucault's books. Finally, although I in no way dissociate myself from analytic philosophy as at present practiced in America, my list of heroes in the second paragraph shows my connection with those roots primarily concerned with the analysis of concepts. There are other roots, those of the Vienna Circle, that, at least after Moritz Schlick, seldom influence my kind of work.

My title speaks of two uses of history. One I've just mentioned: philosophical analysis and the history of the present. But I was invited to discuss something more general: philosophy under the rubric "History and. . . ." The invitation alluded to the ways in which Richard Rorty has combined history and philosophy. That, then, is the other use of history for philosophy to which my title refers.

The Mandate

"Our various papers," so went my invitation, "will not consist of case studies or histories of the disciplines." We were asked to "concentrate on the ways in which the kind of knowing in which each field is engaged is affected by consciousness of and connections with the past." In the next section I state, for the record, the obvious fact that most philosophy written in English is *not* much affected by consciousness of or by connections with the past.

"How is the new historicism, or philosophy as conversation, connected with philosophy as problem-solving?" "Problem solving" must refer to analytic philosophy in the twentieth century, for the self-description of philosophy as a problem solving is at best minor in other traditions. "Philosophy as conversation" adverts to a theme of Richard Rorty's book, *Philosophy and the Mirror of Nature* (1979). And "new historicism" must denote a historicism that has recently appeared or reappeared in philosophy written or spoken in English. Hence my mandate was to focus on recent events connected with philosophy and history in an English language milieu.

"New historicism, or philosophy as conversation": philosophy as conversation is not, for me, identical to the new historicism. I shall insist that it denotes only one kind of new historicism. But what's historicism? Some-

thing like this: the theory that social and cultural phenomena are historically determined, and that each period in history has its own values that
are not directly applicable to other epochs. In philosophy that implies that
philosophical issues find their place, importance, and definition in a specific cultural milieu.

That is certainly Rorty's opinion, and, aside from some qualifications
stated below, it is mine too. He reaches a subversive conclusion about the
nature of philosophy by analyzing the philosophical tradition in which he
himself grew up. He holds that traditional topics of mind and matter, of
the foundations of knowledge, and refutation of skepticism, freedom of
the will, and the problem of universals—the kit and caboodle of metaphysics and epistemology—had a place in earlier pieces of European history but are now defunct. Philosophy shall absent itself from a post-philo-
sophic age. I am perhaps out of step when I see this less as a new
historicism than as an example of a historicism that is recurrent among
philosophers. I shall say something about that in "Undoing." It is an old-
fashioned historicism that pays little attention to the complex inter-
weavings of past and present. But perhaps that is what is intended: a fly-
by-night encounter with the past, more story than history.

It does matter that philosophy as conversation is not the only sort of
"new" historicism around. In "Taking a Look" I describe another kind. The
individual concepts traditionally of interest to philosophers are not, for
this school of thought, timeless objects. Instead, "normalcy," "chance,"
"cause," "person," "evidence," "guilt," or "abuse" are structures whose roles
and power have been determined by specific histories. This is a local historicism, attending to particular and disparate fields of reflection and action. It discourages grand unified accounts, but it does demand taking a
look at lots of little facts. Rorty's use of history is in contrast global, drawing conclusions about the whole of philosophy and indeed everything else,
for chemistry and literary criticism are alike ruled part of conversation.

Antihistory

The invitation mentions that "in the wake of structuralism's and function-
alism's celebration of the synchronic, the significance of historical knowing
is far from clear." This remark is germane to some disciplines, but there has
been no significant interaction between structuralism and American philosophy. The exception proves the rule. Noam Chomsky's ideas about gen-

erative grammar, Cartesian linguistics, and innate mental structures did attract young philosophers of language. He has also been recognized as a structuralist. I say he proves the rule that structuralism had no impact on American philosophy, because the selfsame philosophers who took up his work thought of it as readily fitting into ordinary analytic philosophy. They were astonished to hear it given the alien name of structuralism.

Structuralism has emphasized the synchronic. Analytic philosophy could so readily engage Chomsky's grammar not because it is synchronic, but because it is achronic. Thus it is like many other philosophical reflections that have no temporal dimension. The few "professional" historians among philosophers have commonly declined to be historicist when doing philosophy. Hume's *History of England* made him the first man to earn a good living from the sales of his books. For years Leibniz was paid to do historical hackwork. But Leibniz's philosophy is nonhistorical. Hume's is positively antihistoricist—as befits the original Whig historian. The old historicism in philosophy was the work of amateurs like Hegel, and it is amateurs (like Rorty or myself) who practice new historicisms today.

I shall be talking about how some kinds of history matter to some ways of doing philosophy. But I would be disloyal to many of my friends if I did not report what they believe: "There's history, and then there's philosophy. There's the history of philosophy (and the philosophy of history) but philosophers today need be no more conscious of their history than any other kind of thinker!"

This attitude is not some freakish disposition of analytic anglophones. Popular tradition says philosophy is about the eternal verities. A dictionary says that philosophy is the rational investigation of being, knowledge, and conduct. Philosophers have wanted to know what kinds of things there are, how we find out about them or what we can know, and what we ought to do. To say it a third time in Greek, philosophers do metaphysics, epistemology, and ethics. These are thought of as timeless inquiries. That sort of thinking spills out into several distinguishable attitudes, each well represented by able young American philosophers. I shall sketch them in order of decreasingly virulent antihistoricism.

Present-Timeless. We want to understand things such as duty, reason, causation, personal identity, existence, truth, and the difference between the universal and the particular. We try to understand excuses for not doing what one promised to do; we need to understand promises and how or why they bind. We need to know the differences between explanations in history, in the deterministic sciences, in the statistical sciences, and in matters of personal behavior. We may salvage some good ideas from dead thinkers (says Present-Timeless), but consciousness of the past is irrelevant except as a warning against pitfalls and bad mistakes. Hence we have no historicist sensibilities. As teachers of philosophy, we would be happier if the interesting bits of the history of our subject were taught partly in the Western Civilization and Culture Series, and the rest taught elsewhere as a specialist subject, no more part of philosophy than the history of science is part of science, or the history of art part of art.

Pen Pals. A milder position notes the persistence of certain philosophical interests. Older philosophers set the stage and made permanent contributions. It is a slightly surprising matter of fact that many of their concerns remain vital. We profit by reading and analyzing their ideas, clarifying their conclusions, refuting their errors. Old philosophers are to be studied as pen friends: one-way discussants across the seas of time. We don't care about them because of their role in *their* day. The problems peculiar to fourth-century Athens or seventeenth-century Amsterdam don't matter to us. We care about only the old books that speak to us. (A *Pen Pal* can also be a [moderate] *Present-Timeless.* For a good example, take a sequence of five excellent books by Jonathan Bennett which alternate between the two: *Rationality* (1964), *Locke, Berkeley, Hume: Central Themes* (1971), *Linguistic Behaviour* (1976), *A Study of Spinoza's Ethics* (1984), *Events and their Names* (1988).)

Doing-and-Sharing. A yet gentler suggestion: philosophy is not a kind of knowing but an activity. Despite our practice of writing books, Socrates should be our archetype. One kind of apprenticeship that distinguishes philosophy is the reading of canonical philosophers and discussing their work—with a teacher. Do not blush at philosophy's perennial themes. Unlike the natural sciences, it is not in the progress business. And do not be misled by the fact that philosophical minds have long been turning inchoate conceptual messes into natural sciences; that is a hobby that comes with the trade, and when it works a new kind of professional is created, not a revamped philosopher. No matter how many topics it creates and then evicts into the province of science, philosophy will continue to deal with fundamental aspects of the human condition and the human mind. Dead philosophers speak to us not because, as *Pen Pal* thinks, they got a foot in the door of some difficult problem that helps us pry it open further. They speak to us directly about matters of joint concern.

Getting-Inside. Our *Pen Pals* hear whatever they want to hear. It is no criticism that they take the words of the dead philosopher totally out of context (if that's what they want to do). Let one be Whig in his reading an the other Tory. What the dead philosopher himself meant is of no moment to either reader, for a *Pen-Pal* values only what helps him to do his own philosophizing. But *Doing-and-Sharing* has a difficulty. If we are engaging in a discourse with the dead, we had better understand them. Even if they do speak to something mysterious called the human condition (read "Western tradition"?) they speak in the words of their day, in their settings. We must become engaged in the interpretation of texts. We must work our way into a circle of meanings. We must become hermeneutical.

This four-fold classification is evenhanded. It caricatures all parties. Caricature, yes; but those parties are out there in abundance. I thought it improper to proceed to history-and-philosophy without putting that on record.

My sketch glides over one question that does trouble me. It was posed in my invitation. I shall neglect it, although it was part of my mandate. "In what way does a precontemporary philosopher's ability to speak directly to some of us alter our notions about the importance, or irrelevance, of historical understanding to philosophical understanding?" I don't know the answer. More candidly, the fact that dead philosophers can speak directly doesn't *alter* my notions at all. But I would like to understand the phenomenon better. I find it *astonishing.* I put my perplexity as vividly as I could in the first two parables of chapter 2 above. I think it is paradoxical that Descartes can speak directly to sophomores whose conception of the world seems to be distressingly achronic—yet the better you know the text the more you realize that only the most arduous hermeneutical scholarship can make much sense out of it at all.

A mild version of this paradox lies in the fact that all four ways of not doing history are OK. All are honorable ways in which to be a philosopher. Do not think, however, that the path from *Present-Timeless* to *Getting-Inside* takes us to a more and more historicist practice of philosophy. It does involve the use of more and more old sentences. *Pen Pal* takes the ones he likes. *Doing-and-Sharing* should attend to all the sentences in some major texts of certain great authors. *Getting-Inside* must enter the entire discourse which a text exemplifies. Yet by the end of the process I would have a certain sympathy with the cross interjection of a particularly anti-historical *Present-Timeless.* He says that there is nothing peculiarly philosophical about the task of interpreting texts. We (continues *P.-T.*) are members of the republic of letters. So we do care about a rereading of the *Laches*. We care equally about the re-presentation by Octavio Paz and others of the sumptuous poetry of Sister Juana Ines de la Cruz.

Undoing

Philosophers have never lacked zest for criticizing their predecessors. Aristotle was not always kind to Plato. Scholastics wrangled with unexcelled vigor. The new philosophy of the seventeenth century was frankly rude about the selfsame schoolmen. But all that is criticism of someone else. Kant began something new. He turned criticism into self-reflection. He didn't just create the critical philosophy. He made philosophy critical of philosophy itself.

There are two ways in which to criticize a proposal, doctrine, or dogma. One is to argue that it is false. Another is to argue that it is not even a candidate for truth or falsehood. Call the former *denial,* the latter *undoing.* Most older philosophical criticism is in the denial mode. When Leibniz took issue with Locke in the *Nouveaux Essais,* he was denying some of the things that Locke had said. He took for granted that they were true-or-false. In fact, false. Kant's transcendental dialectic, in contrast, argues that a whole series of antinomies arise because we think that there are true-or-false answers to a gamut of questions. There are none. The theses, antitheses, and questions are undone.

Kant was not the first philosophical undoer. The gist of Bacon undoes the methodology of scholastic thought. But Kant is assuredly the first celebrated, self-conscious, systematic undoer. Pure reason, the faculty of the philosophers, outsteps its bounds and produces doctrines that are neither true nor false.

Kant occasionally adverts to this or that famous thinker ("the good Berkeley"), but little in his three Critiques is historical. He is close kin to *Present-Timeless* and *Pen Pal.* But Kant, the last great philosopher of the Enlightenment, lived when the romantic era in Germany had begun. The conception of language not as mental but as a public object with a history—an idea that we associate with Hamann, Herder, and Humboldt, whom I discuss in chapter 8 below—was being established as Kant aged. The philosophy of language became historical like much else. Life, culture, and one's identity as a person and moral agent were seen as essentially embedded and indeed as constructed in a historical tradition.

Undoing thus became historicist, but not just with the likes of Hegel;

one thinks, for example, of Comte's post-Kantian historicist positivism. Comte's kind of progress is the suppression of defective earlier stages of human consciousness—the abandoning of beliefs that in reality lack truth value. They are replaced by a cast of propositions that really are up for grabs as true or false. It is as if Comte thought that revolutionary history could replace the transcendental analytic.

But it is not Kant, let alone Comte, that we think of when we mention *historicism, progress, undoing.* We think of Hegel. No one thinks of Hegel and Comte in the same sentence anymore, so it is well to have another classification, this time three-fold, into which these people and others fit naturally enough.

The history of philosophical doctrines: a sequence of propositions was advanced over the centuries, one or more of which might in essentials have been true, but most of which were false. *And* we are progressing, for we are winnowing away false notions while adding true ones. Comte is the post-Kantian version of this. Early doctrines are rejected as neither true nor false. A new method is offered to pick out what is true within the true or false.

Undoing by antinomies: two theses opposed to each other both possess seemingly compelling arguments. Each is based on presuppositions shown to be untenable by the critical philosophy. Neither is true or false. *And* with this discovery we are progressing, indeed making a decisive conceptual step akin to that of Copernicus. But our progress is partly one of limitation, through the Kantian realization that many of our aspirations to knowledge were misconceived.

Historicist undoing: ideas are presented as thesis countered by antithesis in a historical setting. They are superseded by a replacement of both by synthesis. In consequence neither thesis nor antithesis can strictly be regarded as true or false. Such a sequence is not the passive discovery of truth and elimination of error. Nor is it Comte's revolutionary discarding of what was neither true nor false. Nor is it Kant's undoing by limiting the possibilities of pure reason. The process of thought in the course of human history is itself proposed as the making of Truth and Possibility. It is more than the manifestation of Man. It is Mind Making Itself. Hegel married rampant historicism to Kant's practice of undoing. *And* the ring that bound the two together was progress. This progress was not merely something that was happening (how lucky we are to be alive in these times, and so forth). The process of history was essentially Progress, Mind superseding its past to make of itself the future.

There are three handy dimensions to this banal trio of *undoing, historicism,* and *progress.* Some twentieth-century philosophies can be graphed upon this framework. To take only some trite labeling for figures not yet mentioned:

- Undoing, progress based on a bold new method, but no historicism (Logical positivism).
- Undoing, some historicism, and lots of progress (Dewey).
- Undoing, lots of historicism, the whole idea of progress untenable thanks to historicist reflection, but if we could restart everything, after reflective total undoing, that would be something (Heidegger).
- Undoing, no historicism, pessimism and probably no progress (Wittgenstein).

Everything interesting is omitted in such a scheme, but it enables me to leap back to my mandate. How, I was asked, do I "see philosophy being affected by its recent attempts to come to terms with its past. How is the new historicism, or philosophy as conversation, connected with philosophy as problem-solving?" When we hear of philosophy's "recent attempts to come to terms with its past," and "philosophy as conversation," we know that the reference is to Richard Rorty's *Philosophy and the Mirror of Nature.* Where is Rorty on my set of coordinates? I put the question this way to remind us that his work is not anomalous: it has a place in a well-orchestrated if simple-minded schematism.

Rorty is a historicist undoer, and in a sense he believes that progress has been made (thank goodness philosophy's over). That's not novel. It is *what* he undoes historically that makes him profoundly original. No matter how loosely we construe membership in an analytic and primarily anglophone tradition, Rorty was the first member to apply the technique of historicist undoing to that tradition. He clearly feels an affinity for Dewey, but Dewey's prose was never so trenchant as Rorty's, nor did he have the same analytic tradition both to deploy and to undo. That is one reason to call Rorty, not Dewey, the source.

Rorty sees philosophy as constantly foundational, as setting itself up as judge over the other fields of human thought and activity. Analytic philosophy—within which Rorty not only includes but emphasizes logical positivism—was a final stage in an attempt to provide foundations and to provide criteria of good and bad thought. Its apparatus, notably the analytic/synthetic distinction, falls into disarray. Correspondence theories of truth collapse. The very concept of being true to a real world of facts becomes idle, and various sorts of realisms and antirealisms become Mickey Mouse. The paraphernalia of analytic philosophy came to be seen as such, as rigamarole. A thrust in that direction can be extracted from the best thinkers, from Sellars, Davidson, Goodman. If there is a name for what's left, it is pragmatism. "James and Dewey," writes Rorty in the Introduction to *Consequences of Pragmatism,* were "waiting at the end of the dialectical road which analytic philosophy traveled," and now wait for Foucault and Deleuze (Rorty 1982, xviii).

I would emphasize that Rorty's undoing is undoing by tracing the path of programs and projects in philosophy. He is not much concerned with the concepts and how they are constructed. It is seldom an undoing by asking into the origin and formation of concepts. There is his important discussion of the "invention of the mind." He has some things to say about "knowledge." But the book is interestingly non-Kantian, non-Hegelian, and, I venture with trepidation, non-Heideggerian; certainly non-Wittgensteinian. He does not say of the dead philosophers whom he condemns to the past that their doctrines can now be seen as neither true nor false. He is saying that they are wrong, or have come to be wrong because of other historical developments.

Rather surprisingly, Rorty's way of undoing is more in the spirit of the Vienna Circle than of Kant or Hegel or Heidegger. It is plain, bluff, middle-American. It differs from the Vienna Circle in that there is no progressive theme of a new method in philosophy. The theme is retrenchment. Let us tolerantly put the past aside, have no new philosophy as such, encourage stability, and engage in conversation without threat, without revolution, above all without programs. "Every generation finds its philosopher," I hear some cynic muttering, "and middle America in the eighties found its own."

One reason for the enthusiastic reception of his book was that all the British and American students who had felt angry, oppressed, and impotent in the face of a hegemonic analytic philosophy were told, almost from the inside, that it had committed suicide. That is also one reason why the book was greeted, in other quarters, with resentment. Rorty himself makes humane pleas for pluralistic tolerance in these matters. Sharing Rorty's pluralism, I find the ephemera of acceptance and resentment unimportant—certainly to my present mandate. But I was asked how "philosophy as conversation connected with philosophy as problem-solving." Officially, not at all. This is made especially plain in "Philosophy in America Today," the last essay in *Consequences of Pragmatism* (1982, 211–30). Rorty states as a matter of brute fact that there is no shared recognition of problems, and that a problem for a Cornell Ph.D. may not be seen as a problem or even as philosophy at UCLA. And that is within mainstream establishment analytic philosophy. He also talks of "programs which seem to have a shorter and shorter half-life" (216).

I do think that specific programs of research and inquiry in philosophy have short half-lives. I think that has been true through much of Western philosophy, unless you take "rationalism" or "nominalism" or another such jargon "ism" as a program. Problems—"the problems of philosophy"—seem to me something else. Perhaps we suffer from equivocation. I am sure that there are people now or recently at both Cornell and UCLA thinking and talking and writing about the problem of free will. *The* problem is the same in both places, although in one place a person will be wrestling with a complicated logic of tense and modalities intended to represent freedom—that will be the UCLA problem and program, say. At Cornell, perhaps, it would be an examination of common law and its attributions of responsibility. Of course the members of this pair of programs and problems share little—except that both address the problem of free will.

I must tread cautiously here. I do not think that philosophy is only or even mainly for solving problems. Problem-solving may have been an ephemeral feature of philosophy. I do not deny that Plato had problems, that Hume gave us what we now call the problem of induction, or that Kant made us focus on problems about knowledge, existence, duty, and God. I proposed in chapter 2 (albeit with a slight air of self-mockery) that our fixation on problems as the subject matter of philosophy was cemented only at the beginning of the twentieth century, with titles by G. E. Moore, William James, and Bertrand Russell. The three "problems" books by those three authors examine different problems, but there is an enormous overlap. On what? Let William James the pragmatist speak. *Some Problems of Philosophy* was written in 1909–10. The text was not quite finished, and it is possible that the title is not William's but was imposed by his son Henry, who edited the material for publication. At any rate, William James was quite selfconscious about problems. He thought that pragmatism was defective just because it did not address the problems of philosophy; "it is much like an arch built only on one side" (James 1911, 27). And of course a historical ontology that contented itself with explaining the nature of problems would equally be an arch built only on one side.

What are these problems? "No exact definition of the term 'metaphysics' is possible, and to name some of the problems it treats of is the best way of getting at the meaning of the word" (29). James proceeds to list twenty-one problems. For example, "What are 'thoughts,' and what are 'things'? and how are they connected?" (29). "In knowledge, how does the object get into the mind? Or the mind get at the object?" "We know by means of universal notions. Are these also real? Or are only particular things real?" (30). He also includes among his problems the issue of objective validity (or not) of moral and aesthetic judgments.

I would not express James's twenty-one problems with quite the words that he thought to use for the students of 1910. But they are almost all with us, including the three I've quoted. I won't quarrel with a romantic who says they are all in Plato. That's 2300 years ago. The half-life of problems is short? I'm guessing we're nowhere near the half-life of these issues yet.

Nor is Rorty himself uninterested in certain traditional "problems of philosophy." On several recent occasions he has taken Bernard Williams to task for, in effect, saying that there is a fundamental difference between ethical discussion and scientific research (Williams 1985, 139). We cannot dismiss this interest of Rorty's as a passing whim. I have had the honor to hear him lecture on the topic in both Charlottesville, Virginia, and Jerusalem; the arguments have been published (Rorty 1988). There are hallowed, traditional names for what is at issue between Rorty and Williams, for example, "the fact/value distinction."

People have been a long time asking, in all sorts of idioms, whether there is such a distinction. If there is, what is it? Does it lie in objectivity? In method? In reference? Are there intrinsically different ways of settling disputes? Or is it all a matter of degree? Is one relevant difference that between verifiability and meaninglessness, as the Vienna Circle urged? Is it the case that the moral concepts that we have of people are in significant ways distinct from the nonethical concepts that we apply to things?

We return, in short, to variations on one of William James's problems. What's notable is that when Rorty takes up a problem of philosophy, no hint of a historical consideration is adduced. Problems appear to be addressed in the old antihistorical analytical way. Rorty may be more true to James than he noticed. *Philosophy and the Mirror of Nature* may also be "much like an arch built up on only one side." A return to problems may be building up the other side—but not in a historicist way.

Taking a Look

Now I turn to a combination of history and philosophy that is in some ways the exact opposite of Rorty's. It does not apply history to the whole sweep of philosophy, but does conceive of many philosophical problems as being essentially constituted in history. I sometimes think of the projects as Locke plus history.

Locke's *Essay Concerning Human Understanding* is as nonhistorical a work as we could imagine, yet its project is amenable to historicization. It is about the origins of ideas and the origins of knowledge. Many readers find that it emphasizes foundations for human knowledge. The book aims, on that reading, at overcoming any skepticism residual after Descartes. It also does its professed work as "underlabourer" to the Fellows of the Royal Society of London. It is a perfect example of what Rorty takes to be the core project of modern philosophy (that is, Western philosophy from Descartes to almost now): epistemological foundations.

Where others rightly spot foundations, I also see a quest for analysis and genesis. Locke thought that we understand concepts and knowledge better when we understand what puts them in place, what brings them into being. I call this the Lockean imperative: to understand our thoughts and our beliefs through an account of origins. The fancy name is to be set beside another one, "genetic fallacy," according to which it is foolish to expect that the content of an idea, or the credibility of a proposition, can in any way be illuminated by our routes to it. I think that "genetic fallacy" is insubstantial name-calling.

Locke is the model empiricist: our ideas and our knowledge originate in experience. But his methodology is rationalist. His book is one great thought experiment. Aside from anecdotes, he almost never takes a look. This is true of the entire tradition of the *idéologues*—Berkeley, Hume, Condillac, Maine de Biran, take your pick. A transition occurs only at the end of the line, namely, Condorcet, and in the work of his great historicist admirer, Auguste Comte, the man who invented the very word "positivism."

Positivism began as a historicist doctrine. It was a theory about the successive transformation of knowledge. The *Cours de philosophie positive* does more than take a look at the evolution of knowledge (Comte 1830–1842). It bores us by being all too comprehensive. In contrast, what philosophers now commonly call positivism, that is, logical positivism, urged that we attend not to "the context of discovery" but to the "context of justification" (Reichenbach 1947, 2). To think that the context of discovery meant anything to what was discovered was to commit the genetic fallacy. Logical positivism was better named logical empiricism. Positivism was historicist, as Comte understood it, but empiricism definitely is not.

Logical positivists admired the natural sciences. Their antihistorical notion of knowledge became standard among anglophone philosophers of science. It was battered by Kuhn's famous opening sentence: "History, if viewed as a repository for more than anecdote or chronology, could produce a decisive transformation in the image of science by which we are now possessed" (Kuhn 1962, 1). Kuhn proposed to take a look.

Kuhn's theses, his style, and the needs of readers at the moment turned *The Structure of Scientific Revolutions* into a compulsive best seller. It also got a lot of other people to examine how the most seemingly adamant, well tested, but abstruse items of human knowledge get there. Comte, who had bitterly campaigned for the creation of a chair of the history of science at the Collège de France some 125 years earlier, might have felt justified. But not happy: for many of Kuhn's readers began to reach skeptical conclusions about the very nature of science. That seemed to scare empiricist philosophers. Yet Kuhn was following the empiricist adage—"take a look."

Kuhn is too well known to need discussion, but the present generation of post-Kuhnian students of science isn't, yet. It takes *social construction* as its motto. In the matter of taking a look it has been courageous. We have Bruno Latour, trained as an ethnographer, who became a participant observer in a biochemistry laboratory, breaking a lot of glass in the process, and coauthoring *Laboratory Life, the Social Construction of Scientific Facts* (Latour and Wodgar 1979). We have Andrew Pickering venturing into the holiest of holies, high energy physics, incidentally providing a first-class "objective" account of what has happened in the subject over two decades, but concluding with a philosophical thesis encoded in his title, *Constructing Quarks* (Pickering 1984).

It is unimportant how one labels work like this. History? (Historians of science don't like that.) Anthropology? (New tribes to study: denizens of the laboratory.) Sociology? (These workers practice nothing remotely like American sociology.) Microsociology, chronologically recounted? ("Microsociology" was one of Latour's buzzwords.) Nothing fits well. No matter. In the present institutionalization of America, these people by and large get co-opted into philosophy or paraphilosophy departments. Kuhn, once adamant that he was a member of the American Historical Association and not of the American Philosophical Association, came to work at M.I.T. in "Linguistics and Philosophy" and served as president of the Philosophy of Science Association.

It is true that the people I have mentioned have tended to include something other than philosophy in their training. They have not been generated by the vast machinery of the philosophy departments that they later join and sometimes adorn. Perhaps it is precisely because they know something about something, that they are so given to what I nonchalantly call "taking a look." Nevertheless their motivation is none other than the Lockean imperative. And the general conclusions at which these workers drive are original but mainstream philosophy. Here are two examples, one about knowledge, one about kinds. Each is based on either Latour or Pickering.

The *knowledge* about a particular tripeptide produced by the hypothalamus of mammals or the *established hypothesis* of quarks is best described not in terms of *discovery,* but in terms of *social construction.* This is not to say that these authors think that the product of the construction is not "really" a fact (now)—only that the unthought world doesn't come in facts. The factization of the world is a human activity.

The *kinds* in terms of which the world is described (and the corresponding ideas, concepts, categories, classifications, or what have you) are not kinds with which the world is ready-equipped, and which we elicit by probing. They too are constructed. It needs no insight to locate the philosophical thrust. These authors are addressing the problem of universals. They are propounding a somewhat novel historicist nominalism. Its roots are in the Lockean imperative to investigate the origin of ideas. The conclusions would, I hope, have cheered Locke, if not the Fellows of the Royal Society. But the procedure is unLockean, in that it takes a look at how the concepts did come into being in real life.

Note that *one* of the things that writers such as Pickering and Latour are doing is conducting historical inquiries, even if they are taking a look at rather recent events. In the same spirit, Simon Schaffer and Steven Shapin (1986) study the seventeenth-century battle over the experimental method of reasoning. In *Leviathan and the Air Pump: Hobbes, Boyle and the Experimental Life* they tell how a new style of scientific reasoning was put in place. These histories, whether they be of the 1970s or the 1650s, are not done out of curiosity about the past. They are intended to show something about our present reality, our present reasoning, our present modes of research. They may, not unfittingly, be called histories of the present.

Such workers put historical substance on the bare scaffolding of Nelson Goodman's *Ways of Worldmaking* (1978). Where Goodman wrote pithily about versions of the world and right and wrong categories, these men say *what* the versions and categories are and *how* they come into being. Note that the conclusions about knowledge and about kinds directly address two of William James's twenty-one problems.

The conclusions of a Latour, a Pickering, or a Schaffer and Shapin will not seem striking to some established philosophical schools that are skeptical about the natural sciences. "Just what we expected all along," say the know-nothings, briefly forsaking logorrhoea: "the scientists make it all up." Such *a priori* antiscientism appeals only to the ignorant. The books I've mentioned are something else. They are based on a very serious working knowledge of the very sciences about which they are, in a certain sense, skeptical. The nominalism of authors like this is combined with a high level of *facticity* (or is it just plain curiosity?).

It was not my intention to advertise recent historicist work in the philosophy of science. For me it leads on to another observation. It is remarkable that this ferment should chiefly be happening in connection with natural science. We can see how that came to pass. There are three reasons. First, after Kuhn, a snowball. Second, if you're going to be iconoclastic and constructionalist, the idols to bash are those of natural science. Third, the Lockean imperative, unstated but present. Genetic accounts of ideas and knowledge have always tended to focus on the concerns of Locke's old friend, the Royal Society.

But what about arenas where we would be more likely to find concepts molded by history? Arenas where what pass for facts bear on human nature and behavior? What about conduct, ethics, morality? We are curiously lacking, particularly in English, any serious philosophical-historical consideration of moral kinds and moral knowledge.

Perhaps philosophy of natural science was lucky. Tired old cultural relativism in morality has been with us (it feels) forever. No jejune relativism had comparable currency among those well acquainted with a natural science. Then Kuhn came bounding in with what many of his readers took to be all the trappings of "relativism" in science, "mob psychology" and the like. Two decades later we had work of the sort I've just touched upon.

Compare the abstract topic headings of metaphysics and ethics. We have reality, truth, fact, . . . on the one hand, and right, good, justice, . . . on the other. In the natural sciences we have been taking a look at the material circumstances under which truth, reality, and fact are constructed from case to case (with no obligation to tell the same story in every case). This meant investigating not truth, reality, and fact, but truths, real things, and facts. In ethics, especially in English, there has been too much fixation on the abstract, on the good, the right, and the just.

J. L. Austin tried to get us to focus on what is small and alive rather than grand and abstract—as in "A Plea for Excuses" (1970). Unfortunately, subsequent writers mostly picked up on his study of speech acts rather than his fine attention to the nuances of ordinary language. Even fewer philosophers paid heed when a novelist-philosopher like Iris Murdoch told moralists to examine "thick" concepts rather than abstract notions. Indeed, I may have been the only philosopher to write a long, admiring, and caring review of her *Metaphysics as a Guide to Morals* (1992; Hacking 1992c).

The philosopher who has most consistently repeated the plea that moralists should study thick concepts is Bernard Williams (1985). He is extremely knowledgeable about the history of moral ideas. He has brilliantly informed us, for example, about ancient concepts of honor and guilt (Williams 1993). But he clearly does not think there is much of a case for understanding thick moral concepts as historical entities whose form and force has been determined by their past. And by reading Homer in a straightforward way he has done a brilliant hatchet job on those who have argued that the Greek concepts of the archaic period—ideas such as causation—do not mesh with ours. "So much for historicism, be it old or new!" (one can imagine him exclaiming).

"Moral" inquiries not far removed from what I have in mind have, however, been undertaken in all sorts of piecemeal and goal-directed ways. No one commonly recognizes them as either philosophy or history. There is, for example, the "Social Problems" school responsible for Labeling Theory. Its adepts are interested in, among other things, how the invention of a classification for people (and its application) does several things. It affects how we think of, treat, and try to control people so classified. It affects how they see themselves. It has strongly to do with evaluation, with the creating of values, and in some cases (homosexuality, juvenile delinquency) with manufacturing a social problem about the kind of person, who must then be subjected to reform, isolation, or discipline. An almost entirely independent type of work is done by the Agenda-Setting school, pioneered by Gusfield's study of how "drunken driving" became firmly fixed on the political agenda. Note the title: *The Culture of Public Problems: Drinking-Driving and the Social Order* (Gusfield 1980). Often, I believe, public or social problems are closely linked with what are called problems of philosophy.

These sociologists provide quasi-historical studies of kinds of behavior—not natural kinds but social kinds, and I would say moral kinds. For a mature adult to drive under the influence of drink is immoral. If impaired judgment is an excuse, then to begin to drink, knowing that one will drink more and then drive, is immoral. Everyone knows that, but not, perhaps, how it *became* immoral. That leads to a question both historicist and philosophical: how do the conditions of formation of this conception determine its logical relations and moral connotations? Here we arrive at philosophical analysis, conducted in terms of the origins of the concept. That leads me to my final section. I have been discussing uses of history to philosophical students of science. Now I wish to be more general, considering, for example, not science but ethics, and at the same time more specific, considering not just philosophy but what I call philosophical analysis, and considering not just history but what Foucault called history of the present.

Philosophical Analysis and History of the Present

Philosophical analysis is the analysis of concepts. Concepts are words in their sites. Sites include sentences, uttered or transcribed, always in a larger site of neighborhood, institution, authority, language. If one took seriously the project of philosophical analysis, one would require a history of the words in their sites in order to comprehend what the concept was. But isn't "analysis" a breaking down, a decomposition into smaller parts, atoms? Not entirely; for example, "analysis" in mathematics denotes the differential and integral calculus, among other things. Atomism is one kind of analysis, to be sure, and in philosophy it is exemplified by Bertrand Russell's Theory of Definite Descriptions. (Even that did not analyze the definite article, "the," but it did analyze sentences in which the article occurs.) J. L. Austin did not analyze sentences in the sense of exhibiting their elements, but in the sense of providing an analysis of what we do with them and of what their uses are. Similarly, to invoke the history of a concept is not to uncover its elements, but to investigate the principles that cause it to be useful—or problematic.

If one embraced more specific conjectures about the ways in which the condition for emergence and changes of use of a word also determined the space in which it could be used, one would be well on the way to a complex methodology. In the third of my "Five Parables" in chapter 2, I have half-seriously described one of my own attempts at that. But whatever the methodology, one thing is clear. Such an attitude invites one to take a look. It is prompted by the Lockean imperative. Because of the post-Kuhnian events mentioned above, it was natural to take such looks at scientific concepts and their sites. Hence I have tried to display the network of possibilities and constraints that have been built into our present conceptions of chance, determinism, information, and control (Hacking 1975a, 1990).

But what about ethical concepts, following the transition just suggested? The example of this sort on which I have myself done most work is child abuse (e.g. Hacking 1988c, 1991a). Child abuse is not just immoral. It is at present an absolute wrong. I told a young man I was going to interview a lawyer who defends child abusers. He replied, "How could someone do *that?* Murderers have to be defended in court, but child abusers?" I believe I can show that our category "child abuse" began around 1960, and has been molded into its present shape. And if someone says, "Very interesting, but what has that got to do with philosophy and in particular ethics?" One reply: here is a living example of how an "absolute value," a prima facie absolute wrong, gets constructed before our very eyes. What if this is of the very nature of what we experience as absolute value? Discussions about ethical relativity come to life when substance such as this is breathed into them. Child abuse is used as an example for metaethics. A second reply: here is a thick moral concept demanding analysis and understanding both in its own right and because its structure is probably similar to a lot of other moral concepts being constructed this very day. (There are lots of other replies.)

Child abuse both describes a kind of human behavior and evaluates it, messily mixing fact and value. It is easier to argue that it has been constructed in a macrosociological set of exchanges than that Pickering's quarks and Latour's thyrotropin-releasing factor have been constructed in the microsociology of the laboratory. But just because it is evaluative it has an effect upon the investigator quite different from that of quarks. One becomes involved in the subject itself. I began looking at it merely as an example of the ways in which we make up kinds of people. No longer. Child abuse involves pressing moral (not to mention social, political, and when one gets down to cases, personal) issues in itself. It is an *intrinsically moral* topic.

It is also *extrinsically meta-moral.* By this I mean that it can be used to reflect on evaluation itself. The reflection can be done only by taking a look into the origin of our idea. That is fulfilling the Lockean imperative. But the look must be into the social rather than the personal formation of the concept. It involves history. The application is to our present pressing problems. The history is history of the present, how our present conceptions were made, how the conditions for their formation constrain our present ways of thinking. The whole is the analysis of concepts. For me that means philosophical analysis.

I know of only one sustained philosophical model for this sort of enquiry, namely some of the work of Michel Foucault. *Discipline and Punish* (1977) is numerous things: an account of a transformation in the nature of the prison and in the treatment of criminals; a study of our very concepts of criminality, recidivism, punishment, "correction" (as in California Department of Corrections), and prison reform. In my terminology it is an extrinsically metamoral book about the intrinsically moral. As proof that the author found the topic intrinsically moral one sees his inevitable engagement as a leading figure of a collective dedicated to the reform of the French penal system. Some people blame his book *Madness and Civilization* (1965) for the discharge onto the streets of thousands of helpless people who would otherwise be in the care of lunatic asylums. But his topics are also extrinsically meta-moral. As Foucault said in a 1977 interview, "When I think back now, I ask myself what else it was that I was talking about, in *Madness and Civilization* or *The Birth of the Clinic,* but power?" (Foucault 1980, 115). People who accuse Foucault of nihilism fail to see that one can be extrinsically meta-moral and intrinsically moral at the same time, or at least in the same person.

Foucault has become a cult figure, but there are plenty of analytic philosophers who have great trouble with what he is doing. I have never had this trouble, and so seem to be anomalous. My work has been seriously influenced by Foucault (or by successive Foucaults) for many years. Books I have written and books I am writing reek of his effect on me. Yet I was trained as a purebred analytical philosopher with primary emphasis on philosophical logic. I still regard myself as such, as one whose mind was formed by Frege, Moore, and Russell. It is perhaps significant that despite my respect for many logical positivists, they had little effect on the way I think. This is perhaps the fundamental way in which I differ from Rorty. He was fighting people to whom I never paid much attention. At any rate I feel no inconsistency between my analytic instincts and my ability to use some aspects of Foucault. I regard my investigations of chance or of child abuse as pursuing the Lockean imperative. My work is also, manifestly, the history of the present in the sense intended by Foucault. One conducts the analysis of the words in their sites in order to understand how we think and why we seem obliged to think in certain ways.

Philosophers are more than metaphysicians. Those whose roots lie in the tradition of philosophical analysis are concerned with concepts less grand than James's metaphysical twenty-one. Plenty of philosophical problems surround concepts such as "normal" (said of human behavior, characteristics, or customs) or "chance." Or, to pursue the Foucauldian chain: "Mad," "criminal," "diseased," "perverse." I believe that specific details of the origin and transformation of these concepts is important to understanding them and for understanding what makes them "problematic."

Thus I conclude by returning to one of the mandated queries: "How is the new historicism, or philosophy as conversation, connected with philosophy as problem-solving?" What I have been describing is not *the* new historicism, but in philosophy it is rather new. I mention Kuhn and Foucault as mentors with decisive impacts on the subject. It is historicist. It is not philosophy as conversation. It is philosophy as hard work. Or to use understatement, it s less talking than taking a look. How is this activity connected with problem solving?

There is a wonderful idea, rightly called Hegelian, that if you understand the source of a problem, you thereby make it go away. We find this conception in Freud and Wittgenstein alike. There is more than a whiff of it in *Madness and Civilization* and other early work of Foucault's. I think that is just a mistake. I do not see, for example, my investigations of chance or abuse as solving the problem of free will or of the respective rights of state, parents, and children. I certainly do not have the ludicrous self-indulgent conception that the problems go away when I am through. But I can show why these matters are problematic, whereas before we knew only that they were problematic. Sometimes one can hope to make a concept more problematic than before, for example, "information and control." And of course to use history in this way for the understanding of philosophical problems is not to resign one's right to use it in other ways. I may have been slightly ironic in naming the *Pen Pal* approach, but I continue to take pleasure in my "What Is Logic?" (1980c), a long paper that takes the early logicians, such as the younger Bertrand Russell and Ludwig Wittgenstein of the *Tractatus*, as my instructors in matters of importance to the philosophy of logic. And *of course* one does not give up one's birthright to engage in *Present-Timeless* philosophy, as in a paper written just before the present one, that examines a new fallacy in probable reasoning and its application to cosmology (1987).

To return to morals, when the concept—the words in their sites—at which one takes a look is a moral one or one that bears on action, the investigation will be what I have, with heavy hand, been calling extrinsically meta-moral. One may also have aspirations toward influencing the ethical decisions in which that concept is clothed. That is a step not toward problem solving but toward intrinsically moral action. That is a matter of deeds, not analysis. This distinction between deeds and analysis I owe to Moritz Schlick.

4

The Archaeology of
Michel Foucault

This essay was a review of *Power/Knowledge,* which is primarily a collection of interviews with Michel Foucault (1980). It appeared in 1981 in *The New York Review of Books.* Two books that I published in 1975, *The Emergence of Probability* and *Why Does Language Matter to Philosophy?,* were deeply influenced by reading Michel Foucault, but this was almost the first occasion on which I felt able to write about him. Page references in the text are to *Power/Knowledge.*

Power/Knowledge is a collection of nine interviews, an essay, and a pair of lectures in which Michel Foucault tried to work out new ways to talk about power. It was one more stage in a remarkable adventure of ideas that began in the late fifties. Key words in Foucault's work would be, for example: Labor, Language, Life, Madness, Masturbation, Medicine, Military, Nietzsche, Prison, Psychiatry, Quixote, Sade, and Sex. Be neither attracted nor repelled by this adolescent list of topics. Foucault had an original analytical mind with a fascination for facts. He was adept at reorganizing past events in order to rethink the present. He engagingly turned familiar truisms into doubt or chaos. These thoughts about power and knowledge were plainly part of a fermentation worth learning about.

What are the relationships between power and knowledge? There are two bad short answers: (1) knowledge provides an instrument that those in power can wield for their own ends; (2) a new body of knowledge brings into being a new class of people or institutions that can exercise a new kind of power. These two assertions parallel two opposed theses about ideology: (1) a ruling class generates an ideology that suits its own interests; and (2) a new ideology, with new values, creates a niche for a new ruling class. Virtually nobody likes either side of these simple dichotomies. Foucault is one of many who want a new conception of how power and knowledge interact. But he is not looking for a relation between two givens, power and knowledge. As always, he is trying to rethink the entire subject matter, and his knowledge and power are to be something else. Nobody knows this knowledge; no one wields this power. Yes, there are people who know this and that. Yes, there are individuals and organizations that rule other people. Yes, there are suppressions and repressions that come from authority. Yes, the forms of knowledge and of power since the nineteenth century have served the bourgeoisie above all others, and served a comparable class in the Soviet Union. But those ruling classes don't know how they do it, nor could they do it without the other terms in the power relation—the functionaries, the governed, the repressed, the exiled—each willingly or unwillingly doing its bit. One ought to begin an analysis of power from the ground up, at the level of tiny local events where battles are unwittingly enacted by players who don't know what they are doing.

Now this sort of project is not novel. Foucault's genius is to go down to the little dramas, dress them in facts hardly anyone else had noticed, and turn these stage settings into clues to a hitherto unthought series of confrontations out of which, he contends, the orderly structure of society is composed. For all the abstract schemes for which Foucault has become famous, he is also the most concrete of writers. He is a fact-lover. One of the interviews ends on a typical note. He was asked when bottle-feeding of infants was invented or at least introduced into France. He did not know and was delighted when his interlocutors could tell him, and at the same time cursed himself for being so dumb not to have asked the question himself.

Foucault is, then, no spinner of verbal fantasies. I enjoy his long books rather than these short interviews just because the books are denser with facts. The editor of *Power/Knowledge* was right, however, to say that the interviews can help us to understand the books. The interview is a French art form used to present work in progress which is destined, at first, for limited circulation, and which is couched in terms suitable for discussion among one specific audience. Hence there is a directness here that is often missing from the long and elaborately constructed books. But Foucault's notions of power and knowledge are so divorced from common speech that I need to recall how he arrived at them. His sequence of books is, despite its ups and downs, an intellectual progress, and I shall try to describe it by way of explaining the interviews.

Madness and Civilization (Foucault 1961) was a somewhat romantic work. It seems to have started with the hesitant belief, never stated, that there is a pure thing, madness, perhaps a good in itself, which is not something that we can capture in concepts. It is certainly not what the sciences of the insane call madness. We classify and treat and put away the mad by systems of our own creation. Our institutions create the phenomena in terms of which we see insanity. This first major book by Foucault hints at an almost Kantian story in which our experience of the mad is a mere phenomenon conditioned by our thought and our history, but there is also a thing-in-itself which can be called madness and which is uncorruptible. Moreover, reason is also only a phenomenon whose very existence requires its opposite to define itself against. In English the book is ironically subtitled, *A History of Madness in the Age of Reason.*

By the time that the book had been written it was clear that this romantic conception of a pure and prior madness was a mistake. There could be no such thing as this preconceptual way of being. The book had become a book about something else. What? That was not so clear, at first. "When I think back now", Foucault said in a 1977 interview, "I ask myself what else it was that I was talking about, in *Madness and Civilization* or *The Birth of the Clinic,* but power?" (p. 115).

The plot of the madness book, which is repeated in several of its successors, is plain enough. There are two notable events. First comes "the great exclusion" in mid-seventeenth century: a frantic locking up of deviants and a building of lunatic asylums. Much later, at the time of the French Revolution, there was a spurious liberation, when a new body of psychiatric knowledge invented new ways to deal with the insane. At least in the old asylums, Foucault suggests, the mad were left to themselves in all the horror that implied. Yet the horror was not worse than the solemn destruction of the mad by committees of experts with their constantly changing manuals of nostrums.

Foucault's stories are dramatic. He presents a reordering of events that we had not perceived before. The effect is heightened by brilliant before-and-after snapshots taken on either side of the great divide during which one tradition is transformed into another. We are given one snippet of description of a brain around 1780 and another twenty-five years later. The very "same" organ on the marble slab plays a role in the later physiology that corresponds to nothing in 1780.

Scholars remind us that the facts are vastly more complex than what

Foucault describes. His predilection for French examples projected on to European history leads to mistakes. Midelfort (1980) makes this point in general. But this is not an "anti-French" point. The *Revue d'histoire des sciences et leurs applications* devoted an entire issue to vigorous challenges to Foucault's emphasis on the role of Cuvier in inaugurating the study of "life" (vol. 23, 1970). Nevertheless, I think one can find balance between detailed criticism and overall admiration. Chapter 9 below is a very small example of how to make petty criticisms while respecting the larger picture.

There are two extremes of French historiography. The *Annales* school went in for long-term continuities or slow transitions—"the great silent motionless bases that traditional history has covered with a thick layer of events" (to quote from the first page of Foucault's 1969 *Archaeology of Knowledge*). Foucault takes the opposite tack, inherited from Gaston Bachelard, Georges Canguilhem, and Louis Althusser. He posits sharp discontinuities in the history of knowledge. In one interview he grants that this obsession with breaks creates an account of knowledge that fits some facts, but is not a general model (p. 112). "It is always at once a point of departure and a very relative thing" (p. 211). Now not only do we find that the facts are sometimes not quite right, that they are overgeneralized, and that they are squeezed into a model of brusque transformations; we also find that many of Foucault's dramas have already been told in calmer terms, by other people.

No matter. His histories stick in the mind. We can add our own corrective footnotes at leisure. These histories matter because they are in part political statements. They are also what I call philosophy: a way of analyzing and coming to understand the conditions of possibility for ideas—not only ideas of disease or insanity or imprisonment, but also the traditional concept of epistemology, namely knowledge, and of ethics, namely power.

An exclusion is an exercise of power. It is a putting away. Despite all the fireworks, *Madness and Civilization* follows the romantic convention that sees the exercise of power as repression, which is wicked. The dramatic and fundamental feature of Foucault's recent work is the rejection of this idea. But do not turn at once to his writings on power, for it is in his reflections on knowledge that this conversion occurs.

The psychiatrists, hygienists, forensic scientists, theorists of the prison, of education, or of population that emerge in the nineteenth century form a new band of experts. They had lots of hypotheses and prejudices and tidy theories that were constantly being revised, but which were embedded in an underlying conception of disease or crime or whatnot. Foucault used the French word *connaissance* to stand for such items of surface knowledge, while *savoir* meant more than science; it was a frame, postulated by Foucault, within which surface hypotheses got their sense. *Savoir* is not knowledge in the sense of a bunch of solid propositions. This "depth" knowledge is more like a postulated set of rules that determine what kinds of sentences are going to count as true or false in some domain. The kinds of things to be said about the brain in 1780 are not the kinds of things to be said a quarter-century later. That is not because we have different beliefs about brains, but because "brain" denotes a new kind of object in the later discourse, and occurs in different sorts of sentences.

The knowledge of *Power/Knowledge* is the *savoir* I'm calling depth knowledge. Maybe no one is conscious of this knowledge. We should expect that Foucault's power will turn out to be some sort of depth power that no one wittingly exercises. Foucault's worries about knowledge and power will not, then, be the important but trite questions about how geneticists or nuclear physicists are to use their new-won surface knowledge for the good or ill of our species.

A new knowledge is involved in the liberation of the insane as they are brought under the care of the medical man. New things are to be said and thought about the mad. Foucault's book on medicine has a connected story. *La clinique* denotes both an institution, the teaching hospital, and the clinical lecture, a way of talking. *The Birth of the Clinic* (1963) is another book about exclusion and about new candidates for truth-or-falsehood. It is also about the creation of a self-constituting class of experts located within a new knowledge. What makes this development possible? A familiar history of science would tell us a tale of heroes. We would learn of their problems, their goals, their luck, their experiments, their mistakes, their visible and invisible colleges, and their funding. Foucault does not aim at such a history of who said what and why, but a story about the web of specific sentences that were uttered, and a theory, called archaeology, of what made it possible for those sentences to be uttered (largely regardless of who uttered them). This impossible task will produce a bizarre account of what we might call pure knowledge. The first and probably last masterpiece in this genre is *The Order of Things* (1966).

The Order of Things tells of four epochs. The periodization is already familiar. There is the age of reason, from Descartes to the Revolution. There is a historicist nineteenth century that leads on to the present. There is the predecessor era that we call the Renaissance. Finally there is a future, starting now.

Life, labor, and language are concepts formed, so goes the argument, in the nineteenth century as the material of biology, economics, and linguistics. These sciences have objects that don't correspond with or map onto their predecessors of natural history, the theory of wealth, or general grammar. Those fields of inquiry have, in turn, no parallel in the Renaissance, says Foucault. Such nonmappings result not so much from new discoveries as from the coming into being of new objects of thought for which new truths and falsehoods are to be uttered. *The Order of Things* is about how one depth knowledge can mutate into another, and with what consequences.

The book is not only a new sort of historical performance. It is also a tract against the human sciences. The American reader should not identify these with the social sciences, for the French classification will include some admixture of psychoanalysis and ethnography, certain kinds of literary analysis, and various reflections of a Marxist origin. Foucault's book is about *Man,* a figure of less interest for our anglophone culture. "Man" is two-faced, knower and object of knowledge. He was formally announced when Kant one year (about 1775) put a new question into his annual Logic lectures: "What Is Man?" (Kant 1974, 29).

After "Man" came the study of man, or anthropology. Kant himself published an *Anthropology from a Pragmatic Point of View* in 1798 (Kant 1978). Foucault's dissertation, 1961, was precisely an *Introduction à l'"Anthropologie" de Kant* in some 465 pages. He then published the first French translation of the book (Kant 1964). He argued that philosophical anthropology generates an illicit way to talk that pretends to look like biology or linguistics. This is not the familiar criticism that says the method of the social sciences is inept. The method is all too well modeled on legitimate science. Foucault is denying that the human sciences have a genuine object to talk about. Luckily, he informs us, Man is on the way out. Discourse is coming in, pure discourse without the knowing subject who utters the words.

Some of this antagonism to the knowing subject is merely typical of Parisian discussions of the 1970s. Phenomenology was detested and despised by figures such as Lévi-Strauss. Foucault's own literary criticism—some of which can be read in a collection of his essays translated as *Language,*

Counter-Memory, Practice (1977)—argues that the concepts of "author" and *"oeuvre"* must be exchanged for less personal ways of grouping sentences. He also urges that literature is extinct. So much was the high fashion of the day. But in addition, Foucault had, if not a theory, at least a body of speculations that gave sense to it. He held that the class of sentences that can be uttered in a specified time and place is not determined by the conscious wishes of the speakers. The possibility of being true-or-false does not reside in a person's desire to communicate. Hence the author himself is irrelevant to the analysis of such "conditions of possibility."

Discourse is, then, to be analyzed not in terms of who says what but in terms of the conditions under which those sentences will have a definite truth value, and hence are capable of being uttered. Such conditions will lie in the "depth" knowledge of the time. This vision leads us far from material conditions of the production of sentences. Inevitably, *The Order of Things* looks like an idealist book, reminiscent once again of Kant. Perhaps in self-mockery Foucault briefly accepted the label of "the historical *a priori*" bestowed upon his work by Georges Canquilhem (1967). Where Kant had found the conditions of possible experience in the structure of the human mind, Foucault does it with historical, and hence transient, conditions for possible discourse.

This obsession with words was too fragile to stand. Foucault had to return to the material conditions under which the words were spoken. Not wanting to go back to individual speakers or authors, he at least had to consider the interests which spoken and written words would serve. The illegitimate sciences of Man were not just a lot of talk. They included legal medicine, which in the nineteenth century was busy reclassifying deviants (inventing even the concepts of norm and of pathology) and then allotting them to treatment. This legal reformism devised new architectures of prisons, schools, and hospitals, which are described in *Discipline and Punish: The Birth of the Prison* (1975). There are overt forms of power such as the judicial machinery with its new crowd of experts to testify on the mental health of the prisoner. Everywhere discipline is to the fore. It is revealed in the factory as well as in buildings avowedly erected for disciplining. Even the working man's cottage shall have its rooms divided and allotted to ensure the strictest morality.

Knowledge became power, all right. A new conception of human beings as disciplinary objects means one is to do something new with people. Not that anyone "knew" much that we would now call sound belief. If you read through the volumes of the *Annales d'hygiène publique et de médecine légale,* which commence in 1829, you will give credence to very little except the statistics, but you will be able to dine out for a year on horror stories, especially if you photocopy some of the engravings.

Foucault lifted from these *Annales* an event of 1835 now published as *I, Pierre Rivière, having slaughtered my mother, my sister and my brother . . .* (1973). For almost the first time, a horde of experts stood about in court theorizing about the supposedly crazed killer. The categories into which they slot him will determine what is to be done with him. That is one small way in which knowledge is power. It is less the facts about Pierre than the possibility of thinking of him in these ways that fixes his fate.

In his interviews, Foucault subscribed to the common wisdom that the failed Parisian revolts of May 1968 jolted him out of a one-sided fascination with discourse and also created a new audience that could discuss knowledge and power. There are also good internal reasons for at the very least expanding the project undertaken in *The Order of Things.* If you hold that a discourse consists in the totality of what is said in some domain, then you go beyond reading the intellectual highs of the heroes of science and you sample what is being said everywhere—including not only the annals of public hygiene but also the broadsheets of the day. You inevitably have to consider who is doing what to whom.

At that point Foucault made his fundamental break with tradition. Out with the who and the whom. He was primed by the denial of the knowing subject that I have just described. The old model of repression says there is a who: some identifiable party is organizing the lives of other people; as a result, we are not allowed to do certain things. Volume 1 of *The History of Sexuality* (1976) is a polemic against that model.

This book is, as Foucault remarked in one interview, not about sex but about power (p. 187). "Sexuality" denotes (in one dictionary definition) recognition of, or preoccupation with, sex. The book is partly about this preoccupation. The French title of volume 1 is *La Volonté de savoir,* the will to knowledge, depth knowledge. The will in question is nobody in particular's will; indeed the title is also an allusion to Schopenhauer. There is a will to create the possibility of saying truths and falsehoods about sex. Unlike the other figures of Foucault's histories, this will to sexual knowledge turns out to have been around for a long time.

Like the prison, sexuality has its own immediate interest, but Foucault's abiding concerns also call his attention to a certain positive knowledge of populations and what he calls biopolitics. Great webs of bureaucracy evolve endless ways to count and classify people. Birth, death, sickness, suicide, fertility: these inaugurate the modern era, the era of statistical data. There is an avalanche of printed numbers early in the nineteenth century (Hacking 1982a). It occurs not because people can count better but because new kinds of facts about populations are taken to be the things to find out.

Sexuality for Foucault is not only a preoccupation with sex. It intersects with a larger circle of ideas, of consciousness of the body, of bodies. It has to do with "political technologies of life." Two axes of sexuality are offered: "disciplines of the body, of harnessing, intensification and distribution of force, the adjustment and economy of energies. On the other hand [sexuality] was applied to the regulation of populations." Both "an entire micropower concerned with the body," and "comprehensive measures, statistical assessments and interventions" aimed at the entire social body: "Sex was a means of access both to the life of the body and the life of the species."

We once had a sovereign who exercised power upon subjects. Around the beginning of the nineteenth century there arises what Foucault described in an interview as "a new type of power, which can no longer be formulated in terms of sovereignty." It is one of the great inventions of bourgeois society. In one dimension this power is to be called "disciplinary," but discipline is only one aspect of it. New kinds of truth and falsehood are another. "Truth," Foucault tells us, "is to be understood as a system of ordered procedures for the production, regulation, distribution and operation of statements. 'Truth' is linked in a circular relation with systems of power which produce and sustain it" (p. 133). This truth is at one step removed from what we normally understand by truth. It is an abstract underlying element that takes its place with the depth knowledge and power. We are specifically enjoined not to think of all this in terms of ideology and Marxian superstructure, i.e., self-conceptions used after the fact to legitimate an economic arrangement. The truth, knowledge, and power are, on the contrary, the conditions of possibility for the bourgeois mode.

Most readers have already had a hard time making sense of Foucault's anonymous knowledge, discourse with a life of its own. Unowned power is even more mysterious. "All the same," one interviewer interjects with a touch of exasperation, "does someone initiate the whole business or not?" (p. 159). Prisons were under discussion. Foucault's answer goes like this.

The new technology of power does not originate with any identifiable person or group. We do indeed get individual tactics invented for particular needs. Prison architecture is modified to make it harder for prisoners to hang themselves—but always with a certain model of how a prison is to be built. The tactics take shape in piecemeal fashion without anyone's wittingly knowing what they add up to. If we turn to the practice of collecting information about populations, each new classification, and each new counting within that classification, is devised by a person or a committee with a straightforward, limited goal in mind. Then the population itself is increasingly classified, rearranged, and administered by principles, each one of which is innocently put forward by this or that technocrat. We obtain "a complex play of supports in mutual engagement, different mechanisms of power."

> Let us not, therefore, ask why certain people want to dominate, what they seek, what is their overall strategy. Let us ask, instead, how things work at the level of on-going subjugation, at the level of those continuous and uninterrupted processes which subject our bodies, govern our gestures, dictate our behaviours etc. In other words, rather than ask ourselves how the sovereign appears to us in his lofty isolation, we should try to discover how it is that subjects are gradually, progressively, really and materially constituted through a multiplicity of organisms, forces, energies, materials, desires, thoughts etc. We should try to grasp subjection in its material instance as a constitution of subjects. This would be an exact opposite of Hobbes' project in *Leviathan* . . . (p. 97)

The *exact* opposite: Foucault is not concerned with how the subjects shall form a constitution determining who or what is sovereign. He wants to know how the subjects themselves are constituted. Just as there was no pure madness, no thing-in-itself, so there is no pure subject, no "I" or "me" prior to the forms of description and action appropriate to a person. Literary historians have long noted that a person did not conceive of himself as a poet—as *that* kind of person—before the Romantic era. One just wrote poems. Some liberationists urge that the category of homosexual (and hence heterosexual) did not exist until the doctors of deviancy invented it. There were acts, but not a homosexual *kind* of person. It is a Foucauldian thesis that every way in which I can think of myself as a person and an agent is something that has been constituted within a web of historical events. Here is one more step in the destruction of Kant: the noumenal self is nothing.

I have just quoted Foucault saying, "Let us not, therefore, ask why certain people want to dominate . . ." Out of context you might wonder if he is telling us never to ask why Roosevelt, Stalin, or de Gaulle wanted to dominate. Are we not to ask why these very persons had vices and virtues, and how they left their marks upon hundreds of millions of subjects? Foucault implies no such thing. Compare his earlier work. At the height of his enthusiasm for abrupt changes in knowledge, he never denied the importance of the *Annales* methodology with its search for underlying stability. When he lashed out at the concept of author as critical tool, he never lost his affection for his favorite authors and their best books. In short, his own investigations do not preclude others. In context his quotation says, for *my* immediate purposes, don't ask why certain people want to dominate.

There are two distinct points here. One is that he is embarking on new inquiries about the constitution of the subject. The other is that the old inquiries, about the power of a particular despot, say, are distorted by the blind conception of the power always stemming from above. We may indeed, in a particular story, have a complete causal chain from a directive signed "Stalin" down to a particular victim in a Gulag. But that there should have been a Gulag-type institution is not, according to Foucault, personal or historical caprice. It looks as if this type of evil is inextricably connected with Eastern European socialist states, and its explanation will require an archaeology of communism. I have no idea how Foucault would have written one, but there are hints in these interviews. Moreover, to give an archaeological account is in no way to excuse or to fail to make distinctions. Don't, he urged, fall prey to the rhetoric that says we all have our own Gulags here at our own door, in our cities. That is false, but it is not power exercised from the top that has made it false.

Foucault propounds an extreme nominalism: nothing, not even the ways I can describe myself, is either this or that but history made it so. We may have been led along this route by reflections on knowledge and language, but we should drop the metaphors that they suggest. Instead turn to power, "war and battle. The history which bears and determines us has the form of a war rather than that of a language: relations of power, not relations of meaning" (p. 114). Every new way in which to think of a person—and hence a way in which people can think of themselves, find their roles, and choose their actions—"is the pursuit of war by other means." But he intends a reversal of Clausewitz's maxim, as he paradoxically explains (pp. 90f).

The Order of Things ends by prophesying a new era in which self-conscious discourse is not about Man or the thinking subject but about discourse alone. A good deal of this project remains in what Foucault calls genealogy (p. 83): "a form of history which can account for the constitution of knowledges, discourses, domains of objects, and so on, without having to make reference to a subject which is either transcendental in relation to the field of events or runs in its empty sameness throughout the course of history." But *The Order of Things* spoke as if there would be no reflective talk except talk about talk. Perhaps we should not see this book as bringing in a new era of such pure talk, but rather as the final instalment in a century or so of philosophical writing obsessed with language. Foucault's new concern with relations of power, rather than relations of meaning, should lead us away from the escapist metaphors about conversation that flow from a fixation on language.

It is not that language shall be deemed unimportant. He continued with the project of understanding how certain classes of sentences come up for grabs as true or false, at definite locations in history. Such investigations were, however, to be embedded in an account of the possibilities of action and the springs of power. The murmuring at the confessional is an "irrigation" (his word) of power. The word has not only its familiar agricultural sense but also refers to medical hygiene. Perhaps both senses are intended here. Confessions keep the power relation hygienic, and also run channels of water from one area to another so the whole can flourish. Without the performance of the individual acts of irrigation, the power would rot or dry up.

Even such events of pure philosophical inquiry as the introduction of the Cartesian *ego* into discourse may be seen in this light. The *ego* collects together a lot of fairly unrelated activities: hoping and hurting and proving theorems and seeing trees. Why should there be one thing—a substance, as Descartes had it—that is the subject of all these predicates? Suppose we guess that the confessional for novitiate monks is the place where people were first made to talk not only about what they have done, but also about what they have felt and thought and seen and above all dreamed. The *Rules* of Descartes for the direction of the mind, seemingly so purely concerned with the search for, and foundations of knowledge, may then appear to be one more item in a sequence of monastic *regulae,* rules in which a very specific type of talking integrates a system of bodily discipline.

Let power and knowledge be something like what Foucault has glimpsed. What then shall we do? We seem led to an immensely pessimistic body of doctrine. The politics of the left is usually founded upon a Romantic conception of getting back to the origin, as in Rousseau, or on to the end, as with Marx. Foucault makes plain that he has been discussing (and detesting) not only the discipline of bourgeois society. There will be an archaeology of Gulags too. In any particular context we can go some way without the Romantic illusions of the left, for there remains *praxis*, Marxist and somewhat Spinozan. We can distinguish the Gulag institution, which like the prison is to be studied and understood by a Foucault-like history, from the Gulag question, that is, what is to be done about these monsters, at this very moment? The Gulag, as well as being a historical object, was also, at the time of these interviews, "a positive present."

Prisons continue to be a positive present. One may well understand that prison reform is almost coeval with the penitentiary, as if it were an auxiliary to the institution, and still try to make prisons less intolerable right now. But although prison reform might be a popular front on which many of us can agree, Foucault clearly found more radical transformations attractive. But if the Romantic revolutionary illusion of liberation is in principle abandoned, how is it to be replaced? "It's not a matter of emancipating truth from every system of power . . . but of detaching the power of truth from the forms of hegemony, social, economic, and cultural, within which it operates at the present time." Liberation is the wrong concept for Foucault, but "detachment" might be possible. Now what is to "detach" truth from present hegemony?

There is a published joint interview with Foucault and Noam Chomsky (Chomsky and Foucault 1974). The linguist comes across as a marvellously sane reformist liberal: let's get justice working right. Foucault sounds more like an anarchist: destroy the judicial system. Is that a way to "detach" a power of truth from forms of hegemony? Maybe. *Power/Knowledge* begins with a 1972 interview with French Maoists. At the start of a revolution don't create people's courts, he urges. Don't reinstitute precisely the institutions of hegemony used to separate and control the masses. In 1980, when this collection of interviews was published, the courtroom ironically reopened in China for the Gang of Four, television rights for $40,000. Foucault was no anarchist, partly because anarchy is impossible. To have a regime for saying true and false things about ourselves is to enter a regime of power, and it is unclear that any detaching from that power can succeed.

We might have been content with the thought of replacing our "forms of hegemony" by others so long as we had the Romantic illusion of a true humankind, a true me, or even a true madness. But whatever Foucault means by detaching truth from forms of hegemony, he does not want the comfort of the romantic illusions. Minute radical acts of protest and reform are not to make sense against a backdrop of progress toward the hopes of the traditional left. That way leads to desolation. Foucault, let's say, has been completing a dialogue with Kant. Each question of Kant's is deliberately inverted or destroyed. "What Is man?" asked Kant. Nothing, says Foucault. "For what then may we hope?" asked Kant. Does Foucault give the same *nothing* in reply?

To think so is to misunderstand Foucault's hypothetical reply to the question about Man. Foucault said that the concept Man is a fraud, not that you and I are as nothing. Likewise the concept Hope is all wrong. The hopes attributed to Marx or Rousseau are perhaps part of that very concept Man, and they are a sorry basis for optimism. Optimism, pessimism, nihilism, and the like are all concepts that make sense only within the idea of a transcendental or enduring subject. Foucault is not in the least incoherent about all this. If we are not satisfied, it should not be because he is pessimistic. It is because he has given no surrogate for whatever it is that springs eternal in the human breast.

5

Michel Foucault's Immature Science

A talk prepared for a symposium of the Western Division meeting of the American Philosophical Association, 1979. The other symposiasts were Richard Rorty and Hans Sluga; all three papers were printed in *Noûs,* 13. Rorty's contribution is also to be found in *Foucault, a Critical Reader,* edited by David Cozzens Hoy (Oxford: Blackwell, 1986), which also includes chapter 4 above.

Most philosophers who write about systematic knowledge have come to restrict themselves to what they call "mature science," although they display a certain uneasiness. Thus Hilary Putnam says, "*physics* surely counts as a 'mature science' if any science does" (1978, 21). What if nothing counts as mature? I suspect that the distinction between mature and immature is, although not ill-founded, at least ill-understood. Putnam needs it because he wants the more established sciences to be about something, to *refer.* He sensibly thinks that most early speculation got things wrong. Similarly, in *The Structure of Scientific Revolutions,* T. S. Kuhn's many-faceted word "paradigm" almost implied "maturity," because an individual or group achievement (one sense of the term "paradigm") had to set the standards to which a "normal science" would conform. He owned that he could not tell whether sociology, economics, or psychology had paradigms. Likewise, Putnam counts some and perhaps all of these among the immature sciences. Neither Putnam nor Kuhn has much to tell us about immaturity.

Putnam has, and Kuhn had, an enormous range of interests, yet the objects on which they focused tended to be nonobservable and theoretical—electrons, or black bodies and quantum discontinuity, for example. Alongside their analyses of systematic knowledge we have a quite different enterprise: epistemology. It is a theory of our knowledge about familiar facts and events; it includes the theory of sense perception, of grounds for belief, and the analysis of "I know that *p*." An ethnographer studying British analytic philosophers fifty years ago would have to conclude that its practitioners were mostly acquainted with tables and chairs, although long before that there was one of G. E. Moore's hands. In the late 1970s (when the present paper was written), the action had moved to the United States, and the most salient object seemed to be Jones's Ford.

In this chapter I shall consider whether there may be anything of a theoretical sort to be said about the vast domain of speculative and common knowledge that falls between electrons and genes, on the one hand, and furniture and Fords on the other. Our doctors treat us, our bankers use mortgages to house the middle classes, our magistrates judge us, and our bureaucrats arrange us according to such systems of knowledge; even on the side of pure speculation far more of these everyday systems of knowledge resemble sociobiology than quantum mechanics.

Michel Foucault's *The Order of Things* (1970) is all about some immature sciences—chiefly those whose foci are "life, labor, and language." He writes of the biology, economics, and philosophy of one era, and of the natural history, analysis of wealth, or general grammar that preceded them. He has a new critique of our contemporary human sciences. The book is important at all sorts of levels. There is a radically challenging reorganization of the way we think about these disciplines. There is a dazzling but instructive plethora of newly chosen facts that give content to this reorganization. (He also cheats, or at least cuts corners on some of the facts.) The book is philosophical because life, labor, language, and "Man" are among the topics of philosophy. It is also philosophical because it exemplifies a theory of knowledge, in both theoretical and practical terms. His archaeology, as he calls it, is a way of investigating the groundwork of bodies of knowledge. The book is also a polemic about the kinds of inquiry that are appropriate for our time.

The Order of Things is incredibly rich both in historical detail and speculative suggestion. There is nothing like it in English. But that is no reason not to bring it down to (our) earth. I shall imagine that I am answering an examination question: "Compare and contrast Foucault's archaeology to current American theory of knowledge." This forces me to proceed in a manner that is both pedestrian and abstract. I shall set out certain hypotheses with which Foucault starts his enterprise. These range in status from proposals which he would be willing to modify to assumptions that he would never give up. They are starting points for inquiry. The first hypothesis is simply this: systems of thought in the immature sciences exhibit quite definite laws and regularities. Where Kuhn (1962, 16) had been inclined to throw up his hands and call Bacon's natural histories a disorderly "morass," Foucault finds an organization, although one different in kind from anything that Kuhn was looking for. General grammar of the seventeenth century, or nineteenth-century labor theory of value provide examples, but so do altogether inchoate domains such as what we now call iatrochemistry (which has been succeeded by real knowledge) or phrenology (which hasn't).

Such examples are misleading because they make us think of some specific theory and then model that on mature science with well-articulated postulates that lead, almost deductively, to a rich display of testable hypotheses. On the contrary, it is Foucault's second conjecture that we are concerned not with a corpus of theses but with systems of possibility. Certain questions arise in general grammar, and are met by a batch of competing answers. These questions and answers appear to have been quite inconceivable in Renaissance thought, nor do they occur in subsequent philology. It is Foucault's hypothesis that what it is possible to say in a body of discourse such as general grammar is vastly more rule-governed than we have commonly imagined.

By "what it is possible to say" I do not just mean actual doctrines, such as propositions about the copula or about labor. It is part of this second hypothesis that what counts as reason, argument, or evidence may itself be part of a system of thought, so that modes of "rationality" are topical and dated. That offends our sensibilities, which have been firmly fixed by Aristotle, Descartes, and Kant, who took as their models the mature or maturing sciences of their day. It is wise to ease the pain of the idea that "what counts as a reason" may be temporal and not timeless, by attributing it to "immaturity." Current philosophy makes the hypothetico-deductive style of reasoning the essence of science, adulterated at most by some admixture of induction. Not all the historicizing of Kuhn and Lakatos has dislodged this opinion one whit. Despite occasional programmatic remarks that one reads from time to time, the early chapters of my own *Emergence of Probability* (1975a) were the first detailed study in English of a changing style of reasoning. Those chapters learned much from *The Order of Things*.

Allow me to re-emphasize that the systems of thought to which Foucault addresses himself are not constituted by a unified set of beliefs advanced by a person or a school. Indeed, he has a teasing device that I call Foucault's fork, which surprises us by stating that competing bodies of belief have the same underlying rules of formation. Once there was a memorable contrast between the taxonomic *System* of Linnaeus and the *Method* of Adanson. We now have little difficulty in supposing that these antagonistic enterprises are part of the same web of possible alternatives, but some of us are more startled to read that positivism and phenomenology are equally constituted by a common underlying organization (Foucault 1973, 199; for an example drawn from economics, see 1970, 190). Evidently, neither hypotheses nor deductions are critical to the systems of thought that Foucault proposes to analyze.

The examples of Linnaean taxonomy or Comtean positivism are misleading in another way: they focus on proper names and famous philosophies. Foucault's third hypothesis is that systems of thought are both anonymous and autonomous. They are not to be studied by reading the final reports of the heroes of science, but rather by surveying a vast terrain of discourse that includes tentative starts, wordy prologomena, brief flysheets, and occasional journalism. We should think about institutional ordinances and the plans of zoological gardens, astrolabes, or penitentiaries; we must read referees' reports and examine the botanical display cases of the dilettanti. Many of these examples of things to read and examine are quite literally anonymous. Foucault believes that even the great positive achievements within a system of thought characteristically merely fill or elaborate certain preestablished uniformities. A typical phrase will convey how he uses historical personalities, "The figure whom we call Hume." The familiar proper name serves as a ready reference to a text, but we are not trying to analyze his *oeuvre.* Foucault suspects all concepts that focus on the consciousness and intent of an individual. Much literary criticism, especially in France, shared this theme in the 1970s. Foucault himself has done his best to obviate even the concept of "literature" and "author."

A fourth hypothesis is that the regularities that determine a system of thought are not a conscious part of that thought and perhaps cannot even be articulated in that thought. Foucault has variously used words such as *episteme, savoir* and *archive* in this connection. I once translated *savoir* as "depth knowledge" and *connaissance* as "surface knowledge," with an obvious allusion to Chomsky (Hacking 1972). In the *Archaeology,* Foucault uses *connaissance* to refer to particular bits of belief wittingly accepted. *Savoir* denotes his conjectured unconscious underlying structure that sets out the possibilities through which connaissance may run its course. The allusion to Chomsky is to be taken lightly, for grammar obviously is rule-governed and a hypothesis of depth grammar is immediately plausible. The immature sciences are not manifestly regular, and the supposition of "rules" is mere conjecture. Yet, after many years of eager research, we are not more in possession of a universally applicable "depth grammar" than of clearly stated *episteme*. Lévi-Strauss's structure of kinship relations is perhaps the only proposal of this sort that has come near to delivering the goods. Further detailed comparisons of Foucault and structuralists are empty; they would lump us with "those mimes and tumblers who debate whether I am structuralist."

A more insightful comparison is made by Georges Canguilhem, the distinguished historian of science. In an essay that is better than anything else written about *The Order of Things*, he concludes with well-documented allusions to Kant (Canguilhem 1967). Foucault has half-jokingly accepted that he has a notion of a "historical *a priori*." While Kant had taught that there is a fixed body of synthetic *a priori* knowledge that determines the bounds of possibility of coherent thought, Foucault has instead a "historical *a priori*." The *savoir* of a time, a place, a subject matter, and a community of speakers determines what may be said, there and then.

What is the "surface" of which the *archive* is the "depth"? Foucault's fifth hypothesis is that the surface is all that is actually said, and (with qualifications) nothing else. It is not what is meant, intended, or even thought, but what is said. Systems of thought have a surface that is discourse. He gropes about for a definition of *énoncé* that is not quite sentence nor statement nor speech act nor inscription nor proposition. It is not an atomistic idea, for enunciations are not isolated sentences that add up to a whole, but entities whose role is understood holistically by a set of interrelations with other bits of discourse. The same "sentence" about the bone structure of human hands and birds' talons is not the same enunciation in a Renaissance text as it is in a post-Darwinian comparative anatomy. Nor is the *énoncé* restricted to sentences: it will include tables, maps, and diagrams. It includes even more than inscriptions, not just because Foucault is often more concerned with specific types rather than concrete tokens, but also because it takes in some tableaux, displays, carvings, and decorated windows. But, having made such qualifications, the word "sentence" remains the best one to denote the elements of discourse that Foucault called *énoncés*. It reminds us that Foucault's discourse is constituted by fairly tangible or audible or legible human productions, and not by what these artifacts mean.

Much French writing of the 1970s shared and indeed antedated W. V. Quine's hostility to meanings. The objects of a *reading* are *texts:* both "reading" and "text" are code words that show one is ideologically pure, and writes only of relations between inscriptions and never of a meaning beneath the words. With such an audience, and with no French word that means "meaning" anyway, Foucault has no need to argue that sentences are the object of study. His notion of discourse and Quine's "fabric of sentences" are cognate ideas. But the resemblance soon falters. One reason is that Quine is ahistorical. His image of revising a conceptual scheme is Neurath's: it is like rebuilding a ship at sea, plank by plank. Foucault's intricate histories provide one more lesson that change is not like that. It is not just that Kuhnian revolutions intervene, but also that in the most normal of sciences the free-wheeling formulation of models and conjectures has none of the character of a tidy ship's carpenter.

A more fundamental difference is that Quine's fabric of sentences is different in kind from Foucault's discourse. Quine's is a body of beliefs, a "lore," partly theoretical, partly practical, but such as could be entertained as a pretty consistent whole by a single informant. Foucault's discourses are what is said by a lot of people talking, writing, and arguing; it includes the pro and the con and a great many incompatible *connaissances*.

Moreover, Quine's "conceptual scheme" is thoroughly impregnated by the hypothetico-deductive model. There is a "core" and a "periphery." The logical consequences of the "core" pervade the peripheral "fabric" which is more localized in its ramifications. A "recalcitrant experience" is one that is reported by a sentence inconsistent with the total "corpus." Recalcitrance demands revision. Revision, we are told, must conform to logic, but revisions are chosen not by the demand of logic but a desire for simplicity. Now if we examine the immature sciences we shall find nothing like this at all. One is led to an image quite different from Neurath's: it is as if these bodies of discourse existed in a conceptual space of possibilities, and as if the discourse were a play upon these possibilities.

Since the word "hermeneutics" is showing signs, in some quarters, of having an attraction for analytical philosophy, let me say that despite the concern with "reading" and "texts," Foucault's archaeology is the very opposite of hermeneutics. To recall an etymology, Hermes, the winged messenger of the gods, was thereby the deity of speech, writing, and traffic. Hermeneutics is the art of interpreting what Hermes brought. Hermeneutics tries to find what meaning lives beneath the sentences that have been written, if not by God, at least by the past. We are to relive that past to see what can have been meant. Archaeology is quite the opposite; it wants not to interpret the texts but to display the relationships between sentences that explain why just these were uttered and others were not. "What counts in the things said by men is not so much what they may have thought or the extent to which these things represent their thoughts, as that which systematizes them from the outset" (Foucault 1973, xix). Doubtless the able hermeneuticist will, thanks to his sensibility and learning, teach us much, but his mode and motivation are entirely different from those of either Quine or Foucault.

To return to American points of reference, Foucault's sixth hypothesis is like Kuhn's: an expectation of discontinuity. In France this is a commonplace, thanks partly to the Marxist background but also due to the historiography of science. The work which Alexandre Koyré did in the 1930s in Kuhn's acknowledged predecessor: it aimed at showing, *contra* Pierre Duhem, that Galileo effected a radical break with the past. In the twenties, Gaston Bachelard had already begun to elaborate a theory of "epistemological blocks" and ensuing "ruptures." (Bachelard 1928, through nine other books concluding with Bachelard 1953.) Bachelard has, in recent years, been far more widely read in France than Koyré, while, in a more scholarly way, Georges Canguilhem has systematically elaborated the details of scientific revolutions over the whole panoply of science. So Kuhn was a sensation for us, but rather old hat in France.

When we turn from a belief in revolutions to an attempt to analyze their structure, there is little agreement between Kuhn and Foucault, but possibly this is because Kuhn is less concerned with immature science. Kuhn's revolutions start with crises (that are by no means easy to document) and proceed through climax to an achievement. They are followed by normal science in which certain examplars are codified in textbooks and used as the norms of successful research. Moreover, by showing how to solve particular problems, they serve as the bridge between abstract theory and practical technique. This is an eminently accurate description of some science, but the whole emphasis on achievement as setting the rules of the game is the opposite of Foucault's quest for unarticulated structures that regulate immature science. Kuhn made us expect a kind of history using much of the methodology of current American social science. Few historians of science do what he seemed to suggest, and even the sociologists of knowledge profess kinship at a distance rather than actually operate from this point of view.

Kuhn's account of "achievements" and of research groups of one hundred individuals seems well fitted to many of the lesser triumphs that occur within the special sciences, but seems a far cry from events such as "the" scientific revolution of the seventeenth century, even if that event is in part composed of Kuhnian revolutions in optics, dynamics, iatrochemistry, and so forth. Foucault has no such modesty of focus. Although he writes of discontinuities in psychology, psychiatry, economics, linguistic theory, and biology, the ruptures conveniently coincide with the two nodes of history emphasized for French schoolboys, Descartes and 1789. More recent work on the prison, sex, and a French equivalent of Lizzie Borden (Foucault 1975; the case serves to illustrate a transformation in medical jurisprudence) does give us other dates, other themes. Foucault's "revolutions" (he does not use the word) are, on the surface, spontaneous events that are so widespread, and so lacking in individual models, that we come to fear that his inquiries will degenerate into vague and unexplanatory waffle about the spirit of the times.

This fear leads to my next contrast with Kuhn, who made us fix our attention on revolution. Who but the most pedestrian scholar could trouble himself with "normal science"? Such disdain for the normal is neither Kuhn's view nor his practice, but it is what philosophers seemed for a while to have learned from him. *The Order of Things* is, in contrast, a study of several overlapping and successive "normal" immature sciences. That a break intervenes, suddenly, is illustrated by one of the most powerful of Foucault's stylistic devices, the before-and-after-picture whose quotations or descriptions permanently fix in the mind of the reader the fact that some upheaval in thought has occurred. Crisis is not offered as the explanation of change (no loss: real crises are harder to find in Kuhn's own examples than he implies). Foucault's explanations of change are complex and programmatic, but for two reasons I am not troubled by this.

First, the events of *The Order of Things* are simultaneous with more familiar revolutions that historians will never fully explain, although each generation will lay on further discoveries that all add up to something like understanding. There can never be a finished story of *why* the scientific revolution occurred. When we turn to more specific and chronologically isolated mutations, like that in French medical jurisprudence mentioned above, then Foucault's implied explanations are more pointed, and each is linked to strongly external factors of the time as well as to events internal to the knowledge itself.

Secondly, for all his talk of "irruptions" and so forth, Foucault, unlike Bachelard, is preoccupied with normal science. This is not due to any conservatism: his heroes are the conventional heroes of French intellectuals (Nietzsche, Bataille, Artaud) who break up the organization of normal discourse, if only through a seeming madness (Quixote, Sade). But he is fascinated by the fact that normal discourse does get a grip on us, and he finds that, in all but the most exceptionally troubled of times, this group is a more potent tool of repression than force of arms. Such a conception is already implicit in his first well-known book, *Madness and Civilization*, and is at the forefront of his current preoccupations with knowledge and power. *The Order of Things* is a much less overtly political work. It is directed at the forms that underlie the content of sciences that followed a discontinuity in knowledge. His "before and after" pictures are such *tours de force* that it is too easy for us to read his books as being about Kuhnian revolution. If we are to use Kuhn's categories, these books are instead about normal science.

It is now time to list these six hypotheses. (1) In the immature sciences there are definite regularities for which the hypothetico-deductive model is irrelevant. (2) These regularities determine systems of possibility, of what is conceived of as true-or-false, and they determine what count as grounds for assent or dissent, what arguments and data are relevant. (3) The immature sciences are not pre-eminently modeled on definite achievements and are to be studied through the anonymous mass of material they have left behind, rather than through a few spectacular successes. (4) The regularities that determine such a system of possibilities are not articulated within a system of thought but constitute a sort of "depth knowledge." (5) The surface of a system of thought is what is actually said. Neither meanings nor intentions are to play any central role in the analysis. (6) There are sharp discontinuities in systems of thought, followed by smooth periods of stability. The "revolutions" are of interest because they are beginnings, and we can see right at the start the regularities that set out the normal science. But it is the "normality" that is of interest if we are to try to understand how systems of possibility can get a grip on how we think.

Now what are the consequences of entertaining such hypotheses? There are of course the detailed analyses of knowledge such as one finds in *The Order of Things*. The preceding paragraphs are *my* account of what Foucault is doing and not an example of what he does. On the basis of *Structure*, some readers forget that Kuhn is also a distinguished historian whose theories are the consequence of real encounters with old science. It would be a far worse mistake to infer Foucault's style from his *Archaeology*—a book about his previous work. Like my exposition here, it quite fails to convey the intensity and originality of Foucault's major works.

Aside from his own applications in detail, Foucault's hypotheses seem to me to bear on a good many questions that have exercised American philosophy. I have space only for two, "incommensurability" and "natural kinds," the former a rather exhausted philosophical notion, the latter a perennial one.

Kuhn makes much less use of the word "incommensurable" than is commonly thought, and indeed the first edition of *Structure* does not display the views on meaning commonly attributed to him. (Probably we owe the dust-up over incommensurability to the co-inventor of this use of the word, Paul Feyerabend.) Kuhn says subsequently that he wanted to use "incommensurable" with a minimum of metaphor, meaning "having no common measure." Discussion of the idea has become so divorced from familiar experiences that I shall begin by recalling two common-sense bits of data.

First, the Newtonian celestial mechanics, when written up by Laplace around 1800, is perfectly intelligible to the modern student of applied mathematics. (This is true even when, in Book V, it treats of caloric in fascinating detail. There is no such thing as caloric! The intelligibility is not to be attributed, as some would have it, to an agreement on the reference of key terms.) When I worked at Stanford, the most frequent borrowers from the Stanford Library were marked by the librarian's code as in the "Aero and Astro" department. Of course the linear accelerator people don't borrow Laplace because his theory is not even roughly true of small fast objects. But it is a plain fact that no one feels any incommensurability here, and not all the philosophical sophistry in the world will make a working physicist feel it.

Secondly, turn to the many volumes of Paracelsus. Today's physician, if she has imagination, can perhaps empathize with those bizarre writings which were, in their day, so much more influential than those of Copernicus. The historian who seeks origins has found in Paracelsus anticipations of all sorts of more recent chemistry and medicine. The herbalist can still comb this work for plant lore that we have forgotten. But the tone of Paracelsus is better suggested by interminable passages that go like this: "Nature works through other things, as pictures, stones, herbs, words, or when she makes comets, similitudes, haloes and other unnatural products of the heavens" (Paracelsus 1922, 460). We can come to understand this world of similitudes better, but there is, in a fairly straightforward way, no common measure between these writings and ours. One cannot but *feel* the incommensurability.

Foucault's hypotheses help one understand these extreme phenomena exhibited by the texts of Laplace and Paracelsus. It is not theories that are incommensurable, but bodies of discourse, systems of possibility. One recent but by now discredited philosophical idea was that theoretical terms get their meaning from conceptual relations expressed in the laws of the theory: if new theory, then new laws, so new concepts and new meanings, hence, no translation. Since there are hardly any laws of the hypothetico-deductive sort in Paracelsus, it is hardly surprising that such a model does not speak to the real incommensurability one finds in immature science. The incommensurability between Paracelsus and modern medicine has another root. Paracelsus's system of possibility is quite different from ours. What he had up for grabs as true-or-false does not enter into our grid of possibilities, and vice-versa. This is not due to different articulated theories or systems of conscious belief, but because the underlying depth knowledge is incommensurable. This idea lessens the metaphor in the very word: we cannot lay some number of Paracelsus's possibilities alongside ours and have two sets that match at the end. This is not to say we cannot understand him. One has to read a lot. The opening chapters of *The Order of Things* set out, for me, a structure which helped me understand much Renaissance writing. One can even go some way towards talking Paracelsan in English, once one has articulated concepts that Paracelsus was perhaps unable to. Translation is largely irrelevant. "Charity" and maximizing truth are worse than useless (I don't believe a word in all seventeen volumes of Paracelsus). "Benefit of the doubt" about what Paracelsus was "referring to" seldom helps. What counts is making a new canvass of possibilities, or rather, restoring one that is now entirely defunct.

Now I shall conclude with a few words on a more lively topic than incommensurability: this is the much discussed notion of natural kinds.

We may suppose that the natural kinds in the mature sciences usually match kinds of things found in nature, but even Putnam rejects such optimism in immature science. What indeed are the objects of immature science, when we later find that the objects once proposed "do not exist"? Two philosophical tendencies have appeared. There is straw realism, which holds that natural kind terms either pick out essential properties or else refer to nothing (almost "mean nothing"). Then there is a straw idealism-cum-nominalism holding that *all* natural kind terms are features of our "conceptual scheme," human artifacts that float freely on the surface of the world. Not enough good sense has yet been inserted between these straw extremes, and I find Foucault's archaeology points in directions that we would do well to explore.

In scholastic times, "realism" contrasted with nominalism, while Kant made it contrast with Berkeley's idealism. In either sense we must be, to abuse Kant's words, empirical realists. There is of course a rich plethora of things around us, really existing anterior to any thought. Moreover, we cannot help but sort many things as we do: we are, it seems, made to sort things much as we do. Not only translation and mutual understanding but also our sheer existence seem to depend upon this fact. But something else happens when we engage in reflective discourse. One of Foucault's projects is to understand how "objects constitute themselves in discourse." All our experience with immature science suggests that any chosen body of thought will define for us only some sorts of "objects" entering into only some sorts of "laws," falling under only some kinds of "kinds." About these we cannot fail to be "nominalists," but the "ism" is not what matters. Since most, if not all, knowledge is "immature" in this way, attempting to understand how objects constitute themselves in discourse must be a central topic, not exactly of the theory of knowledge, but of what I would now call historical ontology.

6

Making Up People

This paper was written for a wonderfully diverse gathering, "Reconstructing Individualism," held at Stanford in the fall of 1983. How do new ways to classify open up, or close down, possibilities for human action? How do classifications of people affect the people classified, how do we change in virtue of being classified, and how do the ways in which we change have a sort of feedback effect on our systems of classifications themselves? An incomplete look at the feedback issue is to be found in "The Looping Effects of Human Kinds" (1995).

I used one set of examples to illustrate Michel Foucault's "bio-politics": the influence of statistics upon the ways in which people are understood, governed, see themselves. The ample surroundings of that phenomenon were described in *The Taming of Chance* (1990). The other set bears on Foucault's "anatomo-politics." I referred to a topic whose study has been much influenced by Foucault himself, namely homosexuality. Homosexuality history is now an autonomous discipline in its own right, with its own journals, conferences, and a whole library of books. So I moved to another of my examples: multiple personality. Subsequent research produced *Rewriting the Soul: Multiple Personality and the Sciences of Memory* (1995). That book has a sequel, *Mad Travelers: Reflections on the Reality of Transient Mental Illnesses* (1998), which contains an astonishing story that tells itself.

Were there any perverts before the late nineteenth century? According to Arnold Davidson, "The answer is NO. . . . Perversion was not a disease that lurked about in nature, waiting for a psychiatrist with especially acute powers of observation to discover it hiding everywhere. It was a disease created by a new (functional) understanding of disease" (Davidson 2001, 24). Davidson is not denying that there have been odd people at all times.

99

He is asserting that perversion, as a disease, and the pervert, as a diseased person, were created in the late nineteenth century. Davidson's claim, one of many now in circulation, illustrates what I call making up people.

I have three aims: I want a better understanding of claims as curious as Davidson's; I would like to know if there could be a general theory of making up people, or whether each example is so peculiar that it demands its own nongeneralizable story; and I want to know how this idea of "making up people" affects our very idea of what it is to be an individual. I should warn that my concern is philosophical and abstract; I look more at what people might be than at what we are. I imagine a philosophical notion I call dynamic nominalism, and reflect too little on the ordinary dynamics of human interaction.

First we need more examples. I study the dullest of subjects, the official statistics of the nineteenth century. They range, of course, over agriculture, education, trade, births, and military might, but there is one especially striking feature of the avalanche of numbers that begins around 1820. It is obsessed with *analyse morale,* namely, the statistics of deviance. It is the numerical analysis of suicide, prostitution, drunkenness, vagrancy, madness, crime, *les misérables.* Counting generated its own subdivisions and re-arrangements. We find classifications of over 4,000 different crisscrossing motives for murder and requests that the police classify each individual suicide in twenty-one different ways. I do not believe that motives of these sorts or suicides of these kinds existed until the practice of counting them came into being (Hacking 1982a).

New slots were created in which to fit and enumerate people. Even national and provincial censuses amazingly show that the categories into which people fall change every ten years. Social change creates new categories of people, but the counting is no mere report of developments. It elaborately, often philanthropically, creates new ways for people to be.

People spontaneously come to fit their categories. When factory inspectors in England and Wales went to the mills, they found various kinds of people there, loosely sorted according to tasks and wages. But when they had finished their reports, millhands had precise ways in which to work, and the owner had a clear set of concepts about how to employ workers according to the ways in which he was obliged to classify them.

I am more familiar with the creation of kinds among the masses than with interventions that act upon individuals, though I did look into one rare kind of insanity. I claim that multiple personality as an idea and as a clinical phenomenon was invented around 1875: only one or two possible cases per generation had been recorded before that time, but a whole flock of them came after. I also found that the clinical history of split personality parodies itself—the one clear case of classic symptoms was long recorded as two, quite distinct, human beings, each of which was multiple. There was "the lady of MacNish," so called after a report in *The Philosophy of Sleep,* written by the Edinburgh physician Robert MacNish in 1832, and there was one Mary R. The two would be reported in successive paragraphs as two different cases, although in fact Mary Reynolds was the very split-personality lady reported by MacNish (Hacking 1986).

Mary Reynolds died long before 1875, but she was not taken up as a case of multiple personality until then. Not she but one Félida X got the split-personality industry under way. As the great French psychiatrist Pierre Janet remarked at Harvard in 1906, Félida's history "was the great argument of which the positivist psychologists made use at the time of the heroic struggles against the dogmatism of Cousin's school. But for Félida, it is not certain that there would be a professorship of psychology at the Collège de France" (Janet 1907, 78). Janet held precisely that chair. The "heroic struggles" were important for our passing conceptions of the self, and for individuality, because the split Félida was held to refute the dogmatic transcendental unity of apperception that made the self prior to all knowledge.

After Félida came a rush of multiples. The syndrome bloomed in France and later flourished in America, which is still its home. Do I mean that there were no multiples before Félida? Yes. Except for a very few earlier examples, which after 1875 were reinterpreted as classic multiples, there was no such syndrome for a disturbed person to display or to adopt.

I do not deny that there are other behaviors in other cultures that resemble multiple personality. Possession is our most familiar example—a common form of Renaissance behavior that died long ago, though it was curiously hardy in isolated German villages even late in the nineteenth century. Possession was not split personality, but if you balk at my implication that a few people (in committee with their medical or moral advisers) almost choose to become splits, recall that tormented souls in the past have often been said to have in some way chosen to be possessed, to have been seeking attention, exorcism, and tranquility.

I should give one all-too-tidy example of how a new person can be made up. Once again I quote from Janet, whom I find the most open and honorable of the psychiatrists. He is speaking to Lucie, who had the once-fashionable but now-forgotten habit of automatic writing. Lucie replies to Janet in writing without her normal self's awareness:

Janet. Do you understand me?
Lucie (writes). No.
J. But to reply you must understand me!
L. Oh yes, absolutely.
J. Then what are you doing?
L. Don't know.
J. It is certain that someone is understanding me.
L. Yes.
J. Who is that?
L. Somebody besides Lucie.
J. Aha! Another person. Would you like to give her a name?
L. No.
J. Yes. It would be far easier that way.
L. Oh well. If you want: Adrienne.
J. Then, Adrienne, do you understand me?
L. Yes. (Janet 1886, 581)

If you think this is what people used to do in the bad old days, consider poor Charles (or Eric, or Mark—a multiple), who was featured on a whole page of *Time* magazine on October 25, 1982 (p. 70). He was picked up wandering aimlessly and was placed in the care of Dr. Malcolm Graham of Daytona Beach, who in turn consulted with Dr. William Rothstein, a notable student of multiple personality at the University Hospital in Columbia, South Carolina. Here is what is said to have happened:

After listening to a tape recording made in June of the character Mark, Graham became convinced he was dealing with a multiple personality. Graham began consulting with Rothstein, who recommended hypnosis. Under the spell, Eric began calling his characters. Most of the personalities have been purged, although there are three or four being treated, officials say. It was the real personality that signed a consent form that allowed Graham to comment on the case. (*The State,* Columbia, S.C., 4 October 1982, p. 3A.)

Hypnosis elicited Charles, Eric, Mark, and some 24 other personalities. When I read of such present-day manipulations of character, I pine a little for Mollie Fancher, who gloried in the personalities of Sunbeam, Idol, Rosebud, Pearl, and Ruby. She became somewhat split after being dragged a mile by a horse car. She was not regarded as especially deranged, nor in much need of "cure." She was much loved by her friends, who memorialized her in 1894 in a book with the title *Mollie Fancher, The Brooklyn Enigma: An Authentic Statement of Facts in the Life of Mollie J. Fancher, The Psychological Marvel of the Nineteenth Century* (Dailey 1894). The idea of making up people has, I said, become quite widespread. *The Making of the Modern Homosexual* (Plummer 1981) is a good example; "Making" in this title is close to my "making up." The contributors by and large accept that the homosexual and the heterosexual as kinds of persons (as ways to be persons, or as conditions of personhood) came into being only toward the end of the nineteenth century. There has been plenty of same-sex activity in all ages, but not, it is argued, same-sex people and different-sex people. I do not wish to enter the complexities of that idea, but will quote a typical passage from this anthology to show what is intended: "One difficulty in transcending the theme of gender inversion as the basis of the specialized homosexual identity was the rather late historical development of more precise conceptions of components of sexual identity" (Marshall 1981, 150). And in a footnote to this passage: "It is not suggested that these components are 'real' entities, which awaited scientific 'discovery.' However once the distinctions were made, new realities effectively came into being" (249, n. 6).

Note how the language here resembles my opening quotation: "not a disease . . . in nature, waiting for . . . observation to discover it" versus "not . . . 'real' entities, which awaited scientific 'discovery.'" Moreover, this author too suggests that "once the distinctions were made, new realities effectively came into being."

This theme, the emergence of the homosexual as a kind of person, is often traced to a paper by Mary MacIntosh, "The Homosexual Role," which she published in 1968 in *Social Problems* (MacIntosh 1968). That journal was much devoted to "labeling theory," which asserts that social reality is conditioned, stabilized, or even created by the labels we apply to people, actions, and communities. Already in 1963, "A Note on the Uses of Official Statistics" in the same journal anticipated my own inferences about counting and kinds of people (Kituse and Cewrel 1963). But there is a currently more fashionable source of the idea of making up people, namely, Michel Foucault, to whom both Arnold Davidson and I are indebted. A quotation from Foucault provides the epigraph—following one from Nietzsche—for *The Making of the Modern Homosexual;* and although its authors cite some 450 sources, they refer to Foucault more than anyone else. Since I shall be so concerned with names, let me state at once that for all his famous fascination with discourse, naming is only one element in what Foucault calls the "constitution of subjects" (in context a pun, but in one sense the making up of the subject): "We should try to discover how it is that subjects are gradually, progressively, really, and materially constituted through a multiplicity of organisms, forces, energies, materials, desires, thoughts etc." (Foucault 1980, 97).

For those of us influenced by Foucault, the choice of topic and time may be biased. My examples dwell in the nineteenth century and are obsessed with deviation and control. Thus among the questions on a complete agenda, we should include these two: is making up people intimately linked to control? Is making up people itself of recent origin? The answer to both questions might conceivably be yes. We may be observing a particular medico-forensic-political language of individual and social control. Likewise, the sheer proliferation of labels that began in the nineteenth century may have engendered vastly more kinds of people than the world had ever known before.

Partly in order to distance myself for a moment from issues of repression, and partly for intrinsic interest, I would like to abstract from my examples. If there were some truth in the descriptions I and others have furnished, then making up people would bear on one of the great traditional questions of philosophy, namely, the debate between nominalists and realists. John Boswell (1982–3) has already pointed out how this intersects with questions about homosexuality.

A traditional nominalist says that stars (or algae, or justice) have nothing in common with others of their kind except our names for them ("stars," "algae," "justice"). The traditional realist in contrast finds it amazing that the world could so kindly sort itself into our categories. He protests that there are definite sorts of objects in it, at least stars and algae, which we have painstakingly come to recognize and classify correctly. The robust realist does not have to argue very hard that people also come sorted. Some are thick, some thin, some dead, some alive. It may be a fact about human beings that we notice who is fat and who is dead, but the fact itself that some of our fellows are fat and others are dead has nothing to do with our schemes of classification.

The realist continues: consumption was not only a sickness but also a moral failing, caused by defects of character. That is an important nineteenth-century social fact about TB. We discovered in due course, however, that the disease is transmitted by bacilli that divide very slowly and that we can kill. It is a fact about us that we were first moralistic and later made this discovery, but it is a brute fact about tuberculosis that it is a specific disease transmitted by microbes. The nominalist is left rather weakly admitting that even though a particular kind of person, the consumptive, may have been an artifact of the nineteenth century, the disease itself is an entity in its own right, independently of how we classify.

It would be foolhardy to have an opinion about one of the more stable human dichotomies, male and female. But very roughly, the robust realist will agree that there may be certain physiological borderline cases once called "hermaphrodites." The existence of vague boundaries is normal: most of us are neither tall nor short, fat nor thin. Sexual physiology is unusually abrupt in its divisions. The realist will take the occasional compulsive fascination with transvestitism, or horror about hermaphrodites as human (nominalist) resistance to nature's putative aberrations (Greenblatt 1986). Likewise, the realist will assert that even though our attitudes to gender are almost entirely nonobjective and culturally ordained, gender itself is a real distinction.

I do not know if there were thoroughgoing, consistent, hard-line nominalists who held that every classification is of our own making. I might pick that great British nominalist Hobbes out of context. Near the beginning of his *Elements of Philosophy* (II.4) he said, "How can any man imagine that the names of things were imposed by their natures?"

Equally, one could pick Nelson Goodman as the heir of Hobbes. Trendy nominalists might refer to his *Ways of Worldmaking* (1978), whose very title is a paean to what he calls his irrealism, but the hard line was drawn much earlier in his *Fact, Fiction, and Forecast* (1954)—a line so hard that few philosophers who write about the "new riddle of induction" presented in that book appear even to see (what I think is) the point. Goodman was saying that the only reason to project the hypothesis that all emeralds are green rather than grue—the latter hypothesis using a made-up word that implies that those emeralds which are in the future examined for the first time, will prove to be blue rather than green—is the that word "green" is entrenched. That is, it is a word and a classification that we have been using. Where the inductive skeptic Hume allowed that there is a real quality, greenness, which we project out of habit, for Goodman there is only our habit of using the word "green." Douglas Stalker's (1994) anthology of papers about Goodman's riddle confirms, I think, that most philosophers who write about the topic do not take it very seriously. I do: see my piece in that anthology (1994), and my discussion of Kripke and Goodman (1993b). Following Goodman, one usually thinks of his riddle arising after Hume has been disposed of. I argue that in a certain sense the difficulty is "pre-Humian" (Hacking 1993c).

The nominalism that one can extract from Hobbes, Goodman, and their vibrant scholastic predecessors such as Ockham and Duns Scotus still pales before a perhaps nonexistent kind of nominalist, who thinks that (a) all categories, classes and taxonomies are created and fixed by human beings rather than found in nature, and that (b) classifications may grow or be revised, but once in place they are basically fixed and do not interact with what is classified. I believe that this sort of static nominalism is doubly wrong: I think that many categories come from nature, not from the human mind, and I think our categories are not static. A different kind of nominalism—I call it dynamic nominalism—attracts my realist self, spurred on by theories about the making of the homosexual and the heterosexual as kinds of persons or by my observations about official statistics. The claim of dynamic nominalism is not that there was a kind of person who came increasingly to be recognized by bureaucrats or by students of human nature, but rather that a kind of person came into being at the same time as the kind itself was being invented. In some cases, that is, our classifications and our classes conspire to emerge hand in hand, each egging the other on.

Take four categories: horse, planet, glove, and multiple personality. It would be preposterous to suggest that the only thing horses have in common is that we call them horses. We may draw the boundaries to admit or to exclude Shetland ponies, but the similarities and differences are real enough. The planets furnish one of T. S. Kuhn's examples of conceptual change (Kuhn 1962, 115). Arguably, the heavens looked different after we grouped Earth with the other planets and excluded Moon and Sun, but I am sure that acute thinkers had discovered a real difference. I hold (most of the time) that strict nominalism is unintelligible for horses and the planets. How could horses and planets be so obedient to our minds? Gloves are something else: we manufacture them. I know not which came first, the thought or the mitten, but they have evolved hand in hand. That the concept "glove" fits gloves so well is no surprise; we made them that way. My claim about making up people is that in a few interesting respects multiple personalities (and much else) are more like gloves than like horses. The category and the people in it emerged hand in hand.

How might a dynamic nominalism affect the concept of the individual person? One answer has to do with possibility. Who we are is not only what we did, do, and will do, but also what we might have done and may do. Making up people changes the space of possibilities for personhood. Even the dead are more than their deeds, for we make sense of a finished life only within its sphere of former possibilities. But our possibilities, although inexhaustible, are also bounded. If the nominalist thesis about sexuality were correct, it simply wasn't possible to be a heterosexual kind of person before the nineteenth century, for that kind of person was not there to choose. What could that mean? What could it mean in general to say that possible ways to be a person can from time to time come into being or disappear? Such queries force us to be careful about the idea of possibility itself.

We have a naive picture of the gradations of possibility. Some things, for example, are easy to do, some hard, and some plain impossible. What is impossible for one person is possible for another. At the limit we have the statement: "With men it is impossible, but not with God: for with God, all things are possible" (Mark 10:27). (Christ had been saying that it is easier for a camel to pass through the eye of a needle than for a rich man to enter the kingdom of heaven.) Degrees of possibility are degrees in the ability of some agent to do or make something. The more ability, the more possibility, and omnipotence makes anything possible. At that point, logicians have stumbled, worrying about what were once called "the eternal truths" and are now called "logical necessities." Even God cannot make a five-sided square, or so mathematicians say, except for a few such eminent dissenters as Descartes. Often this limitation on omnipotence is explained linguistically, being said to reflect our unwillingness to call anything a five-sided square.

There is something more interesting that God can't do. Suppose that Arnold Davidson, in my opening quotation about perversion, is literally correct. Then it was not possible for God to make George Washington a pervert. God could have delayed Washington's birth by over a century, but would that have been the same man? God could have moved the medical discourse back 100-odd years. But God could not have simply made him a pervert, the way He could have made him freckled or had him captured and hung for treachery. This may seem all the more surprising since Washington was but eight years older than the Marquis de Sade—and Krafft-Ebing has sadomasochism among the four chief categories of perversion. But it follows from Davidson's doctrine that de Sade was not afflicted by the disease of perversion, nor even the disease of sadomasochism either.

Such strange claims are more trivial than they seem; they result from a contrast between people and things. Except when we interfere, what things are doing, and indeed what camels are doing, does not depend on how we describe them. But some of the things that we ourselves do are intimately connected to our descriptions. Many philosophers follow Elizabeth Anscombe and say that intentional human actions must be "actions under a description" (Anscombe 1957). This is not mere lingualism, for descriptions are embedded in our practices and lives. But if a description is not there, then intentional actions under that description cannot be there either: that, apparently, is a fact of logic.

Elaborating on this difference between people and things: what camels, mountains, and microbes are doing does not depend on our words. What happens to tuberculosis bacilli depends on whether or not we poison them with BCG vaccine, but it does not depend upon how we describe them. Of course we poison them with a certain vaccine in part because we describe them in certain ways, but it is the vaccine that kills, not our words. Human action is more closely linked to human description than bacterial action is. A century ago I would have said that consumption is caused by bad air and sent the patient to the Alps. Today, I may say that TB is caused by microbes and prescribe a two-year course of injections. But what is happening to the microbes and the patient is entirely independent of my correct or incorrect description, even though it is not independent of the medication prescribed. The microbes' possibilities are delimited by nature, not by words. What is curious about human action is that by and large what I am deliberately doing depends on the possibilities of description. To repeat, this is a tautological inference from what is now a philosopher's commonplace, that all intentional acts are acts under a description. Hence if new modes of description come into being, new possibilities for action come into being in consequence.

Let us now add an example to our repertoire; let it have nothing to do with deviancy, let it be rich in connotations of human practices, and let it help furnish the end of a spectrum of making up people opposite from the multiple personality. I take it from Jean-Paul Sartre, partly for the well-deserved fame of his description, partly for its excellence as description, partly because Sartre is our premium philosopher who writes about choice, and partly because recalling Sartre will recall an example that returns me to my origin. Let us first look at Sartre's magnificent humdrum example. Many among us might have chosen to be a waiter or waitress and several have been one for a time. A few men might have chosen to be something more specific, a Parisian *garçon de café,* about whom Sartre writes in his immortal discussion of bad faith: "His movement is quick and forward, a little too precise, a little too rapid. He comes toward the patrons with a step a little too quick. He bends forward a little too eagerly, his eyes express an interest too solicitous for the order of the customer" (Sartre 1956, 59). Psychiatrists and medical people in general try to be extremely specific in describing, but no description of the several classical kinds of split personality is as precise (or as recognizable) as this. Imagine for a moment that we are reading not the words of a philosopher who writes his books in cafés but those of a doctor who writes them in a clinic. Has the *garçon de café* a chance of escaping treatment by experts? Was Sartre knowing or merely anticipating when he concluded this very paragraph with the words: "There are indeed many precautions to imprison a man in what he is, as if we lived in perpetual fear that he might escape from it, that he might break away and suddenly elude his condition." That is a good reminder of Sartre's teaching: possibility, project, and prison are one of a piece.

Sartre's antihero chose to be a waiter. Evidently that was not a possible choice in other places, other times. There are servile people in most societies, and servants in many, but a waiter is something specific, and a *garçon de café* more specific. Sartre remarks that the waiter is doing something different when he pretends to play at being a sailor or a diplomat than when he plays at being a waiter in order to be a waiter. I think that in most parts of, let us say, Alberta (or in a McDonald's anywhere), a waiter playing at being a *garçon de café* would miss the mark as surely as if he were playing at being a diplomat while passing over the french fries. As with almost every way in which it is possible to be a person, it is possible to be a *garçon de café* only at a certain time, in a certain place, in a certain social setting. The feudal serf putting food on my lady's table can no more choose to be a *garçon de café* than he can choose to be lord of the manor. But the impossibility is evidently different in kind.

It is not a technical impossibility. Serfs may once have dreamed of travel to the moon; certainly their lettered betters wrote or read adventures of moon travel. But moon travel was impossible for them, whereas it is not quite impossible for today's young waiter. One young waiter will, in a few years, be serving steaks in a satellite. Sartre is at pains to say that even technical limitations do not mean that you have fewer possibilities. For every person, in every era, the world is a plenitude of possibilities. "Of course," Sartre writes, "a contemporary of Duns Scotus is ignorant of the use of the automobile or the aeroplane. . . . For the one who has no relation of any kind to these objects and the techniques that refer to them, there is a kind of absolute, unthinkable, and undecipherable nothingness. Such a nothing can in no way limit the For-itself that is choosing itself; it cannot be apprehended as a lack, no matter how we consider it" (Sartre 1956, 522). Passing to a different example, he continues, "The feudal world offered to the vassal lord of Raymond VI infinite possibilities of choice; we do not possess more."

"Absolute, unthinkable, and undecipherable nothingness" is a great phrase. That is exactly what being a multiple personality, or being a *garçon de café*, was to Raymond's vassal. Many of you could, in truth, be neither a Parisian waiter nor a split personality, but both are thinkable, decipherable somethingnesses. It would be possible for God to have made you one or the other or both, leaving the rest of the world more or less intact. That means, to me, that the outer reaches of your space as an individual are essentially different from what they would have been had these possibilities not come into being.

Thus the idea of making up people is enriched; it applies not to the unfortunate elect but to all of us. It is not just the making up of people of a kind that did not exist before: not only are the split person and the waiter made up, but each of us is made up. We are not only what we are but what we might have been, and the possibilities for what we might have been are transformed.

Hence anyone who thinks about the individual, the person, must reflect on this strange idea of making up people. Do my stories tell a uniform tale? Manifestly not. The multiple personality, the homosexual or heterosexual person, and the waiter form one spectrum among many that may color our perception here.

Suppose there is some truth in the labeling theory of the modern homosexual. It cannot be the whole truth, and this for several reasons, including one that is future-directed and one that is past-directed. The future-directed fact is that after the institutionalization of the homosexual person in law and official morality, the people involved had a life of their own, individually and collectively. As gay liberation has amply proved, that life was no simple product of the labeling.

The past-directed fact is that the labeling did not occur in a social vacuum, in which those identified as homosexual people passively accepted the format. There was a complex social life that is only now revealing itself in the annals of academic social history. It is quite clear that the internal life of innumerable clubs and associations interacted with the medico-forensic-journalistic labeling. Whatever the medico-forensic experts tried to do with their categories, the homosexual person became autonomous of the labeling.

The *garçon de café* is at the opposite extreme. There is of course a social history of waiters in Paris. Some of this will be as anecdotal as the fact that croissants originated in the cafés of Vienna after the Turkish siege was lifted in 1683: the pastries in the shape of a crescent were a mockery of Islam. Other parts of the story will be structurally connected with numerous French institutions. But the class of waiters is autonomous of any act of labeling. At most, the name *garçon de café* can continue to ensure both the inferior position of the waiter and the fact that he is male. Sartre's precise description does not fit the *fille de salle;* that is a different role.

I do not believe there is a general story to be told about making up people. Each category has its own history. If we wish to present a partial framework in which to describe such events, we might think of two vectors. One is the vector of labeling from above, from a community of experts who create a "reality" that some people make their own. Different from this is the vector of the autonomous behavior of the person so labeled, which presses from below, creating a reality every expert must face. The second vector is negligible for the split but powerful for the homosexual person. People who write about the history of homosexuality seem to disagree about the relative importance of the two vectors. My scheme at best highlights what the dispute is about. It provides no answers.

The scheme is also too narrow. I began by mentioning my own studies in official statistics and asserted that these also, in a less melodramatic way, contribute to making up people. There is a story to tell here, even about Parisian waiters, who surface in the official statistics of Paris surprisingly late, in 1881. However, I shall conclude with yet another way of making up people and human acts, one of notorious interest to the existentialist culture of a couple of generations past. I mean suicide, the option that Sartre always left open to the For-itself. Suicide sounds like a timeless option. It is not. Indeed it might be better described as a French obsession.

There have been cultures, including some in recent European history, that knew no suicide. It is said that there were no suicides in Venice when it was the noblest city of Europe. But can I seriously propose that suicide is a concept that has been made up? Oddly, that is exactly what is said by the deeply influential Esquirol in his 1823 medical-encyclopedia article on suicide (Esquirol 1823, 53, 213). He mistakenly asserts that the very word was devised by his predecessor Sauvages. What is true is this: suicide was made the property of medics only at the beginning of the nineteenth century, and a major fight it was (Hacking 1982b). It was generally allowed that there was the noble suicide, the suicide of honor or of state, but all the rest had to be regarded as part of the new medicine of insanity. By mid-century it would be contended that there was no case of suicide that was not preceded by symptoms of insanity (Bourdin 1845, 19).

This literature concerns the doctors and their patients. It exactly parallels a statistical story. Foucault suggests we think in terms of "two poles of development linked together by a whole cluster of intermediary relations" (Foucault 1978, 139). One pole centers on the individual as a speaking, working, procreating entity he calls the "anatomo-politics of the human body." The second pole, "focused on the species body," serves as the "basis of the biological processes: propagation, births, and mortality, the level of health, life expectancy and longevity." He calls this polarity "biopolitics of the population." Suicide aptly illustrates patterns of connection between both poles. The medical men comment on the bodies and their past, which led to self-destruction; the statisticians count and classify the bodies. Every fact about the suicide becomes fascinating. The statisticians compose forms to be completed by doctors and police, recording everything from the time of death to the objects found in the pockets of the corpse. The various ways of killing oneself are abruptly characterized and become symbols of national character. The French favor carbon monoxide and drowning; the English hang or shoot themselves.

By the end of the nineteenth century there was so much information about French suicides that Durkheim could use suicide to measure social pathology. Earlier, a rapid increase in the rate of suicide in all European countries had caused great concern. Some authors have suggested that the growth may have been largely apparent, a consequence of improved systems of reporting (Douglas 1967, chap. 3). It was thought that there were more suicides because more care was taken to report them. But such a remark is unwittingly ambiguous: reporting brought about more suicides. I do not refer to suicide epidemics that follow a sensational case, like that of Heinrich von Kleist, who shot his lover and then himself on the Wannsee in 1811—an event vigorously reported in every European capital. I mean instead that the systems of reporting positively created an entire ethos of suicide, right down to the suicide note, an art form that previously was virtually unknown apart from the rare noble suicide of state. Suicide has of course attracted attention in all times and has invited such distinguished essayists as Cicero and Hume. But the distinctively European and American pattern of suicide is a historical artifact. Even the unmaking of people has been made up.

Naturally, my kinds of making up people are far from exhaustive. Individuals serve as role models and sometimes thereby create new roles. We have only to think of James Clifford's study of the two most famous Anglo-Poles, Joseph Conrad and Bronislaw Malinowski (Clifford 1986). Malinowski's work largely created the participant-observer cultural-relativist ethnographer, even if Malinowski himself did not truly conform to that role in the field. He did something more important—he made up a kind of scholar. The advertising industry relies on our susceptibilities to role models and is largely engaged in trying to make up people. But here nominalism, even of a dynamic kind, is not the key. Often we have no name for the very role a model entices us to adopt.

Dynamic nominalism remains an intriguing doctrine, arguing that numerous kinds of human beings and human acts come into being hand in hand with our invention of the ways to name them. It is for me the only intelligible species of nominalism, the only one that can even gesture at an account of how common names and the named could so tidily fit together. It is of more human interest than the arid and scholastic forms of nominalism, because it contends that our spheres of possibility, and hence our selves, are to some extent made up by our naming and what that entails. But let us not be overly optimistic about the future of dynamic nominalism. It has the merit of bypassing abstract hand-waving and inviting us to do serious philosophy, namely, to take a look: to examine the intricate origin of our ideas of multiple personality or of suicide. It is, we might say, putting some flesh on that wizened figure, John Locke, who wrote about the origin of ideas while introspecting at his desk. But just because dynamic nominalism invites us to examine the intricacies of real life, it has little chance of being a general philosophical theory. Although we may find it useful to arrange influences according to Foucault's poles and my vectors, such metaphors are mere suggestions of what to look for next. I see no reason to suppose that we shall ever tell two identical stories of two different instances of making up people.

Self-Improvement

This piece was written overnight in Berkeley during the summer of 1984, when Alan Graubard, then editing *University Publishing,* told me that someone had let them down and they had to fill a few pages immediately. In 1982 Herbert Dreyfus and Paul Rabinow created a (Paris-style) interview with Michel Foucault, "On the Genealogy of Ethics," which they printed in the second edition of their book about Foucault. All page references here are to Dreyfus and Rabinow, *Michel Foucault: Beyond Structuralism and Hermeneutics* (Chicago: University of Chicago Press, 2nd ed., 1983).

In an exhilarating interview, Michel Foucault described some of his work in progress. He agreed to the interview title "On the Genealogy of Ethics." Indeed, many of his new ideas were captured in an only slightly unusual sense of the word "ethics." Perhaps Foucault had written enough about what we say and do to other people. He had now become preoccupied with what we say and do to ourselves. Official or prevalent or private moral codes would be part of that story, but there is

> another side to the moral prescriptions, which most of the time is not isolated as such but is, I think, very important: the kind of relationship you ought to have with yourself, *rapport à soi,* which I call ethics, and which determines how the individual is supposed to constitute himself as a moral subject of his own action. (pp. 237–8).

Where previous nominalists thought of the self as making up its own categories, Foucault did not imagine that there is any self, any ego, any I, writing to do that. Each human subject—you, me—is an artifact. Because of Foucault's almost doctrinaire loathing of most forms of repression, and his radical shake-up of standard accounts of it, many readers would still think of him as believing that the human subject is created by forces of repression. That is too limited an outlook. In this interview, he says "we constitute ourselves as subjects acting on others"—as agents, that is, not as victims.

One domain of his projected genealogy of ethics was certainly the "power" we exercise. Another was an account "of ourselves in relation to truth through which we constitute ourselves as subjects of knowledge." Again, it is *we* who are doing it, not having it done to us. The knowledge/power story has been elaborately illustrated in Foucault's books, but those are outer-directed narratives—what we say about others, say to others, have said to ourselves by others, do to others, or have done to ourselves. They leave out the inner monologue, what I say to myself. They leave out self-discipline, what I do to myself. Thus they omit the permanent heartland of subjectivity. It is seldom force that keeps us on the straight and narrow; it is conscience. It is less knowledge produced in the human sciences that we use as our guide in life, than self-knowledge. To say this is not to return to subjectivity. There is nothing private about this use of acquired words and practical techniques. The cunning of conscience and self-knowledge is to make it *feel* private.

We have long been barraged by manuals giving techniques for self-improvement. A genealogy of ethics would be a study of what these techniques really are and how we use them upon ourselves. In the most superficial respect such work would be radically different from Foucault's early work, for it would not involve abrupt transformations. He thought that many types of knowledge commonly undergo sharp breaks, as do the forms of power. Much of his early writing is about discontinuities, which for Foucault usually coincided with the arrival of Descartes and the bourgeois economy or with the French Revolution and Kant.

But moral codes change very slowly. It is not just that we swear on, and often swear by, books written millennia ago. By "codes," Foucault meant quite specific general instructions. The Ten Commandments form a model code. They are brief and quite easy to obey. In America today some version of most of them is still inculcated into infants, and the rules are honored about as well as they were in the time of Isaiah, say. Christ's injunctions are something else. To live by them is to aspire to sanctity. They do not form a code but describe one way of working upon ourselves, of setting impossible ideals, or creating guilt. It is worth recalling that most techniques of the self—meditation, confession, exercise, diet, exemplary role models—are as old as the old codes, but how they are employed may differ from generation to generation.

Foucault had been writing a good deal about early Christian patristic practices, and those of the Greeks. He claimed that classical Greek texts are first of all concerned with health, and then with food. At a famous banquet described by Plato—an occasion of much eating and drinking—abstinence was commended as the healthiest regime in both food and sex. There is a specific problem in such texts having to do with boys. It is not the case, claimed Foucault, that Greeks were untroubled by love for boys. On the contrary, that they write about it so much betrays malaise. The difficulty was that the boy was supposed to be passive, pleasureless, and this was inconsistent with the fact that the same boy was supposed to grow up to be an active citizen. Greek sex, however, had to do with the active pleasures of adults, pleasures that supposedly interfered with health. The early Christian evolution, which often adapted pagan practices and conceptions, made pleasure passive. Foucault had a complex story to tell here: of dreams, retreats, confessions, penance, and disciplines to control both mind and its physical outlets in the body.

Foucault was gifted at imposing new organization on old material. "Ethical substance" was his name for the sheer stuff that you worry about if you are a moral agent. It is the part of ourselves and of our behavior that is relevant for ethical judgement. The definition of this can differ substantially. For us, said Foucault, it is feelings. For Kant it was intentions. Foucault's own example in the interview is the contrast between an Athenian philosopher and Saint Augustine. The Athenian in love with a boy worries whether he should touch him or not. Not touching is valued; the emphasis is on the act linking pleasure and desire. Augustine, recalling a relationship with a young friend when he was eighteen, is worried about the nature of the desire itself. "So you see that the ethical substance has changed."

A second element in ethics is the "mode of subjection:" whatever it is that you use to internalize these concerns, and what you take as being the relevant Truth about them—Holy Writ, the voice of a drug, the sanction of reason, political conviction, personal obsession, anything from the outside that we take as authority.

A third element of ethics is how we get it to work. "What are we to do, either to moderate our acts, or to decipher what we are, or to eradicate our desires, or to use our sexual desire in order to obtain certain aims like having children, and so on?" Foucault calls that "asceticism in a very broad sense." He also calls it "the self-forming activity:" "in order to be faithful to your wife you can do different things to the self" (p. 239). This is asceticism, because it is cutting off some possible ways to be or to behave in order to serve some immediate end. Behind such an end we may present to ourselves the fourth element of ethics, a teleology, "the kind of being to which we aspire when we behave in a moral way. For instance, whether we shall become pure, or immortal, or free, or masters of ourselves, and so on."

What we more commonly call ethics has, in its nobler forms, tended to address the questions, what shall we do? What is of value? Foucault was in the terrible predicament of being rich in values and able in action, yet at the same time asking what makes the ethical question possible at all. It is common for intellectuals, be they self-styled pragmatists or Critical Theorists or academic social democrats, to harass Foucault about this supposed predicament, and imagine debates like this:

"And what, then, shall we do?"

"Well, if you want to do something, why don't you start trying to make San Quentin less horrendous?"

"No, that doesn't answer the question. If you're in the tradition of unmasking the origins of moral codes and our ethical practices, then where do you stand? How can you have any values at all? How can you have any grounds for action, even for joining a league for prison reform?"

Even his generous interviewers, Dreyfus and Rabinow, have a sense that Foucault "owes us a criterion of what makes one kind of danger more dangerous than another" (1983, 264).

I am a little reminded of the tale of David Hume's death. It is said that the rabble of Edinburgh congregated around his house demanding to know when the atheist would recant. I suspect it won't be long before the solemn clamor of the intellectuals about Foucault sounds as quaint as the baying of the Edinburgh mob. That expectation does not, however, help remove the present tension. For that purpose, it may be more useful to think of Kant than of Hume.

Foucault was a remarkably able Kantian. It is seldom remembered that his longest and perhaps most important book, *The Order of Things,* arose from an attempt to write an introduction to a book Foucault had translated into French, Kant's *Anthropologie.* Kant had been the first to ask, as a professorial question, "What Is Man"? Foucault's book is a prehistory of that question, ending with a probably misguided prediction that the question in its present forms will soon be erased. His actual and projected work on ethics could also use some Kantian spectacles, for a moment. I don't know what weight to put on the interview title "Genealogy of Ethics." There are overtones of Nietzsche's *Toward a Genealogy of Morals,* of course. Should we take the morals/ethics contrast seriously? Nietzsche used the German word *Moral.* Kant's titles use the word *Sitte,* which we translate as "ethics." The contrast does fit Foucault's concerns. He was writing about *Sitten,* not *Moral.* The German word *Sitte* refers to customs and practices, not exclusively moral. They were precisely what preoccupied Foucault.

But let us go further. What did Kant do? One thing was to make something quite new out of ethics. In ancient Greece, the topic of ethics had been the good life. Values were out there in the world, and the good life could be perceived and, with diligence, lived. After that, after divine ethics, after Humean naturalized ethics, and after much else, Kant made ethics utterly internal, the private duty of reason. In that respect Foucault explicitly reverses Kant. "Couldn't everyone's life become a work of art?" This was not some vapid plea for aestheticism, but a suggestion for separating our ethics, our lives, from our science, our knowledge. At present, rhetoric about the good life is almost always based on some claim to know the truth about desire, about vitamins, about humanity, or about society. But there are no such truths to know.

That takes me to the Kantian side of Foucault's ethics. Among the radical novelties of Kant was the notion that we *construct* our ethical position. Kant said we do this by recourse to reason, but the innovation is not reason but construction. Kant taught that the only way the moral law can be moral as if we make it. Foucault's historicism combined with that notion of constructing morality leads one away from the letter and the law of Kant, but curiously preserves Kant's spirit. Kant founded his metaphysics of ethics on the idea of freedom. That was another radical departure: what on earth do ethics and freedom have to do with each other? Foucault was always skeptical of liberation movements, whether political or sexual, except as means, for they always assumed a knowledge of how the liberation would create the true and objectively desirable natural state of people. Kant made freedom something that is necessarily outside the province of knowledge. Only in the inherently unknowable could there be a Kantian

Foundations for a Metaphysics of Ethics. "Unknowable" is meant literally; it pertains not just to the knowledge of the physicist or the gnosis of the hermit, the mysticism of the visionary or the high of the jogger. It means that there is nothing to be said about freedom, except that within its space we construct our ethics and our lives. Those who criticize Foucault for not giving us a place to stand might start their critique with Kant.

8

How, Why, When, and Where
Did Language Go Public?

This essay was written for the first year of issue of the ambitious new quarterly, *Common Knowledge,* founded by Jeffrey Perl. The aim was to join in common discussion many different aspects and styles of writing and research in the humanities that had too often been put asunder. It is deeply in debt to Isaiah Berlin's *Vico and Herder.* I like to think that our correspondence may have reawakened Berlin's fascination with Hamann, and contributed to his digging up and publishing his old manuscript, *The Magus of the North: J. G. Hamann and the Origins of Modern Irrationalism* (1993).

Some time ago I published a small primer about philosophy and language (Hacking 1975b). It blithely skipped along in three parts: a heyday of ideas, a heyday of meanings, and a heyday of sentences. To get a sense of how an analytic philosopher could see things, call that Locke, Frege, and Now. There is a howling gap in there. The hole in time is disgraceful, given that my story was told against Michel Foucault's larger archaeological canvas, but I don't mind that. What's missing is any account of the passage from language as private to language as public. That transition cannot be structured in terms of heydays or for that matter of Foucault's *epistemes.*

What do I mean by private and public? Hobbes spoke for the era of ideas when he wrote that language is mental discourse. At the beginning of *Elements of Philosophy,* which he published in 1656, he said that language has two distinct values. First, words, being signs of ideas, serve as memory aids that help us to recall previous thoughts. Secondly, but only secondly, words are wonderfully adapted to communication, so that they enable me to transfer ideas in my mind to yours. Language is essentially private and only accidentally public. Descartes and Hume, Locke and Leibniz, even Kant, were much of the same mind.

Long after ideas had yielded to meanings, some philosophers, such as Bertrand Russell (1956, 195), also thought that meanings are as private as Hobbesian ideas. "When one person uses a word, he does not mean by it the same thing as another person means by it" (1956, 195). And in our latter-day world of sentences, many theorists, especially the cognitive scientists, continue in that vein. Marvin Minsky (1987, 270) writes (in italics) that *"a word can only serve to indicate that someone else may have a valuable idea—that is, some useful structure to be built inside the mind."*

Hobbes, then, lives, but since his day there has arisen an entirely different conception of language, as essentially public. Analytic philosophers are the least likely of our contemporaries to break with old ways. Most of their discussions and problems are recreations of Enlightenment models. That was one conclusion of my primer: structurally identical problems are rephrased, over three centuries, in the successive idioms of ideas, meanings, and sentences. In at least one respect that won't do at all. Even the analytically minded now believe, or write as if they believed, that language is essentially public. They take for granted that, aside from codes and other derivative kinds of record keeping, a strictly private language is impossible. That is hardly their discovery: thinkers in other traditions are astonished at the notion of an essentially private language. Bertrand Russell and cognitive science notwithstanding, language went public. How, why, when, and where did that happen?

A full response to the question of my title would be a prolix analysis of many times and places. A brisk answer whose merit is brevity results from adding a "who?" to my roster of queries. Who was the first unequivocal public linguist? J. G. Hamann (1730–88). I learned that by reading Isaiah Berlin. As he wrote in a letter dated 14 November 1985, "Poor Hamann—he really was original—tangled, dark, absurd, but first-hand, he got on to something; but I do not believe that anyone in the English-speaking world, except eccentric truffle-hunters like me, will ever read him."

Not Wittgenstein

What's wrong with the more straightforward answer that language went public in the 1930s as Wittgenstein's philosophy evolved? Because the event happened long before. Wittgenstein's readers did want a short name for a long stretch of *Philosophical Investigations,* and they called it the private language argument (Wittgenstein 1953, sec. 243–315). The passages in which the argument or arguments are presented are original and profound. Nevertheless, the conception of language as essentially public long precedes those thoughts, and runs along quite different lines.

I shall soon turn to Hegel as a public linguist of long ago, but we need not move beyond philosophers favored in the analytic tradition to show that the idea precedes our century. Two of the three nineteenth-century philosophers most respected by analytic philosophers were public linguists. I mean C. S. Peirce and Gottlob Frege, as opposed to J. S. Mill (an inveterate private linguist). In an essay published in 1868, Peirce astoundingly found it hard to answer the question, "What distinguishes a man from a word?" He held that "the word or sign which man uses *is* the man itself." The fact "that every thought is an *external* sign, proves that man is an external sign. That is to say, that the man and the external sign are identical . . . my language is the sum total of myself; for the man is the thought" (Peirce 1984, 240). Peirce is uncommonly hard to understand, but whatever he meant, he was in a publicizing mood, making consciousness, the self, language, inference, and words not only external but also communal. A couple of pages earlier, he had been insisting on COMMUNITY, printed in capital letters.

Frege was equally a public linguist. His core theory about language consists of sense, reference, and associated idea. The third item is mentioned by Frege deliberately to exclude it from his theory of meaning. To hold that language is essentially public you don't have to deny that words conjure up various thoughts in various minds. You say only, with Frege, that these thoughts are "associated ideas" that are not the sense of what is said. Associated ideas may be private, but in Frege's theory the sense of a word "is not a part or a mode of the individual mind." Frege found this obvious even from the fact that "mankind has a common store of thoughts which is transmitted from one generation to another" (Frege 1952, 59).

Hegel

Frege and Peirce did not invent publicity. One might guess that Hegel did, in 1807, perhaps, with *The Phenomenology of Spirit*. Time and time again the man will say something like, "Language is self-consciousness existing *for others*" (Hegel 1977, 395, 308). He spoke of language as an "outer reality that is immediately self-conscious existence." There are problems about Hegel. He was a bit of a backslider, apparently espousing a more private view of language later in life. For example, in 1830 he said that language, in one of its aspects, "is a product of intelligence for manifesting its ideas in an external medium" (Hegel 1971, 214). Those are not the words of a convinced public linguist. But let us ask whether this date of 1807, which is not quite arbitrary, makes sense. Is this a reasonable time to think of language going public?

Yes. Should one not expect a change in conceptions of language, given the many changes in the place of Europe in the world, which inevitably affected the way its citizens thought about language? They had access to a large number of new texts in languages that they had never known or had forgotten: Sanskrit, Persian, Celtic, Norse. There were many newly met nonliterate peoples in Polynesia, the Amazon region, aboriginal Australia, the American Midwest. Travel and conquest gave Europe ancient texts of the Indian subcontinent and new speech in the South Pacific. It is inviting to imagine that these two kinds of imperial discovery directly suggested the idea of language as public. Almost the only item that you cannot wrest from another people by barter or victory is language. Language cannot be private property, or one could take it. So it is not private. That would seem like a bad pun, were it not that bourgeois individualism is (or is often argued to be) an admixture of the self-as-owner-of-its-thoughts and the self-as-owner-of-its-goods.

Yet that won't quite do. European contact with foreigners had always been going on. The founding of colonies was as much an enterprise of earlier years as it was of Hegel's time. Jesuit missionaries had learned the Algonquin languages from Newfoundland to Manitoba, and their adventures were eagerly followed in France, where examples of "Huron" activities, languages, and even games were bandied about. Leibniz was fascinated by Chinese language and writing. New linguistic discoveries and encounters are not sufficient for revolutionary thoughts about language. They did surprisingly little for Locke. He knew of voyages as well as anyone, but he made only wan observations about differences among languages. It is true that Hans Aarsleff, a great admirer of Locke, claims to find in Locke and his French *idéologue* successors the source of "linguistic relativism" (Aarsleff 1982, 22, 27, 30f, 181, 185f, 189f, 301, 306f, 345–7, 376). Despite the depth of his scholarship, I have argued elsewhere that Aarsleff's interpretation goes awry (Hacking 1988a).

If we wish to find in Enlightenment philosophy the beginning of a historical, culture-laden vision of language and its study, a true linguistic relativism, to repeat Aarsleff's phrase, then we must turn to Leibniz. His most extended discussion of language is in Book 3 of his *Nouveaux Essais,* which were an analysis of and attack on much of Locke's *Essay.* The *New Essays* were not published until 1765, half a century after Leibniz had quite finished them. So the people who read them were from a new generation. A long review was published in the *Göttingische Anzeigen* (10 January 1765). One of the early advocates of the publicity of language was Herder, who was then in Riga. Hamann, however, was in Königsberg, and he wrote Herder a detailed but unenthusiastic account of the book on 21 January (*Briefwechsel;* henceforth B 2:296–303). Before thinking about these two individuals, however, let us examine more closely the period of language study leading up to Hegel.

There are three widely read accounts of a radical transition in the conception of language around that time: by Michel Foucault, Noam Chomsky, and Isaiah Berlin. All three attribute something, in different degrees, to newly circulated ancient texts and encounters with nonliterate peoples. Each has cast his own stamp on reports of the transition. I shall also call in an expert witness, Hans Aarsleff, for yet another version of events. None of these four men was addressing my question—of when language went public. Yet the going public of language may be the core event that links their otherwise conflicting analyses.

Michel Foucault

During the Cartesian or "classical" era, so goes *The Order of Things,* students of language were preoccupied by General Grammar. Words are signs of ideas. General Grammar aimed at understanding how thoughts can be represented by articulated strings of words. Actual languages were studied but with no sense of their particularity. The questions asked were truly general: how do signs work? That exactly parallels the philosophical debate: how do our ideas correspond to the world? Toward the end of the eighteenth century, as colonial advance provided ancient texts and new languages, the study of abstract grammar was replaced by a fascination with the varieties of syntax within linguistic families. Languages became historical entities, fit for empirical investigation. Foucault famously claimed that the emergence of life, labor, and language as objects of study was part of a widespread transformation from representation to history.

Foucault's account *is,* in its large features, correct, at least for the case of grammar—although in chapter 9 below I observe that in many points of detail it is not quite right. His is not an unusual version, for it parallels the official history of the emergence of philology in Germany. The philological seminar in Göttingen was founded in 1761. When Prussia restored itself in 1810, after humiliating defeat, Alexander von Humboldt recreated the educational system with philology at its core. His brother, Wilhelm, played a remarkable part in bringing home from the South Pacific new languages to study and new thoughts about how to do it. Philology became the premier academic subject in Germany. Nietzsche may be its most remembered professor, but Foucault's lesson is about Franz Bopp.

Bopp's first major publication was in 1816. General Grammar was dead and philology had replaced it, but Bopp does not help us much with public and private language. He had little to say about meaning, for he wrote of syntax and the historical development of the verb form in comparative grammars of Sanskrit, Persian, Greek, Latin, Lithuanian, Old Church Slavonic, Gothic, and German (I recite from one of his titles). He also wrote on aspects of Malay and Polynesian. Bopp's primarily syntactic concerns are perfectly consistent with a private view of meaning. So none of this explains why language went public, which was, of course, never Foucault's intention. He aimed only at establishing a point at which certain kinds of knowledge became historical. He fixed on Cuvier, palaeontologist, Ricardo, economist, and Bopp, philologist. Bopp was twenty years younger than the other two men, and I want to begin Foucault's philological story long before Bopp.

Noam Chomsky

Cartesian Linguistics is Chomsky's brilliant, brief exposition of his rationalist forbears. He published it soon after he had decisively established transformational grammar as the wave of the future. He was, he implied, restoring to prominence the attitude to knowledge that underlay projects of General Grammar. A single text serves as focal point for both Chomsky and Foucault, namely Port Royal's *Grammaire générale et raisonnée* of 1660. Where Foucault had seen a theory about how to represent continuous reality in disjointed words, Chomsky found systematic attention to the creative aspect of language use—our ability to say endlessly many things. The transition from the good, Universal Grammar, to the bad, descriptive philology, was hardly the main point of the book, but Chomsky did find it important to say that Humboldt's *Linguistic Diversity* was the last work in the great tradition of Cartesian linguistics. Humboldt's study of Polynesian languages, combined with much theoretical reflection, published posthumously in 1836, was fully aware of the "creative aspect" so emphasized by Chomsky: the idea that language must "make infinite employment of finite means" (Humboldt 1988, 91). It also had attractions for an innatist: "Language could not be invented or come upon if its archetype were not already present in the human soul."

Chomsky observes that Bloomfield (1933, 18), the villain of Chomsky's essay, "refers to Humboldt's treatise 'as the first great book on general linguistics.'" "Considered against the background that we are surveying here," Chomsky continues (1966, 86, n. 36), "it seems to mark the terminal piece of Cartesian linguistics rather than the beginning of a new era of linguistic thought." It may seem a fine point, to discuss whether a posthumously published book was the last work of the old regime or the first of the new. Chomsky himself knew well that Humboldt held that historical languages serve to define a people, a vision of the world, and serve to constitute an individual within a community. In that respect, Chomsky admitted, Humboldt "departs radically from the framework of Cartesian linguistics" (Chomsky 1966, 21).

In Chomsky's version, Humboldt retained old truths but promulgated new errors. In Bloomfield's version, Humboldt advanced a new vision while cleaving to old mistakes. Humboldt impresses the less dogmatic reader by emphasizing the duality in language as arising partly from the very nature of human beings (Chomsky), but also as being formed as part of the historical individuality of a community or nation. Humboldt can well serve to represent the battlefront between cognitive science and cultural anthropology in our day.

Bopp's ideas reached maturity just when Humboldt's life work came to an end. Hegel's *Phenomenology* reminds us that the idea of language as public had been around for some time, and so must precede whatever claim could be made for Bopp or Humboldt. Indeed, if Humboldt were understood only as an innatist and the last practitioner of General Grammar, we would expect to file him among the private linguists. Hans Aarsleff does exactly that. He argues that Humboldt's philosophy is in part driven by "the radical impossibility that others can have direct access to what goes on in our minds . . . it involves what had long been recognized as the privacy of language" (Aarsleff 1988, xxii). Those are not my perceptions.

Humboldt must be understood as part of a different lineage, in the sequence of Isaiah Berlin's favored trio of Hamann, Herder, and Humboldt. If we push back to Hamann we come to a very public conception of language—within which, I venture, the subsequent transformations in the study of language take place.

Isaiah Berlin

Philology is one of the strands in German romanticism to which an immense literature has been devoted. It is the very literature that Foucault ostentatiously ignored by directing us to the dusty Bopp. I choose to mention only one elegant and rather loving version of a more standard account. Isaiah Berlin much admired Herder, who taught that there can be no thought without language, that a language characterizes a culture, and that language is the medium in which a human being becomes a person. Berlin distinguishes three doctrines distinctive of Herder's thought. *Pluralism*, as Berlin calls it, is "the belief not merely in the multiplicity, but in the incommensurability, of the values of different cultures and societies" (Berlin 1977, 153). *Populism* has to do with the necessity of being part of a group or culture in order to be an individual person. *Expressionism* is the holistic doctrine that human activity expresses the entire personality of the individual or group, and is intelligible only to the degree that it does so.

Guiding all three is the way in which, according to Herder, a language defines or even constitutes a culture, and thereby its people. I have mentioned travel to past times and foreign climes as bringing a new awareness of languages as repositories of a group or civilization. We must not forget the inverse, that in those days, following the lead of Leibniz, German thinkers were trying to forge their own identity by creating and writing in their own tongue. This was a political act. Herder's king, Frederick the Great, read only books in French and spoke German "like a coachman." The Academy in Berlin was filled with Frenchmen of brilliance (Maupertuis was its president), Frenchmen of promise, and plain Frenchmen— even Frederick's head tax collectors (Hamann's bosses) were expected to write memoranda in French. Frederick's contempt for religion was that of the *philosophes*. His "French" sexual preferences were veridical gossip. The new idea that language defines a culture was part of an attempt to define a German culture, something anti-Frederician, un-French, in both manners and speech.

Let us call this family of ideas—Isaiah Berlin's trio of pluralism, populism, and expressionism, plus the emphasis on the language of a people defining that people as a political entity—the "culture-concept." In variant forms, it is characteristic of romanticism, and, notoriously, it can be exploited by master racism. Many agree that Herder was one of the earlier exponents of a generous culture concept. Berlin has a less widely shared affection for Herder's friend Hamann, by fourteen years the senior of the two men:

> Herder had derived from Hamann his notion that words and ideas are one. Men do not think, as it were, in thoughts and ideas and then look for words in which to "clothe" them, as one looks for a glove to fit a fully formed hand. Hamann taught that to think was to use symbols, and that to deny this was not so much false as unintelligible. (Berlin 1977, 165f.)

We are on the verge of the essential publicity of language when we add Hamann's insistence that the symbols are part of a historical and public language. On the one hand, language characterizes a culture and helps define a people as a collectivity: the culture concept. On the other, all thoughts are in symbols located within a culture, so there is no autonomous "private object" for words to denote.

Hans Aarsleff

Things are never so simple. Hans Aarsleff has been a vociferous opponent of Berlin's version of events. (See Aarsleff 1981 and Berlin's astonished rejoinder 1981.) He rightly insists that Berlin's favored German writers learned much from French ones. But he goes further. He gives us the impression that, aside from wrong turnings, the German writers were unoriginal. There is a certain piquancy to this. Aarsleff himself appears to be a private linguist. Hence, he does not want to acknowledge the very concepts that the likes of Herder brought into being.

Just as one of Berlin's more obscure heroes is Hamann, so Condillac (1715–80) is one of Aarsleff's. The French philosopher nicely serves to clarify a difference between public and private language. Aarsleff thinks that you can find in Condillac, for example, the radical thoughts supposedly invented by the Germans. That is because Aarsleff won't acknowledge the existence of the really radical thoughts. Condillac was an *idéologue*, a Lockean, and a private linguist if ever there was one. We have ideas. Words signify ideas, which are private objects. He did go so far as to say that "it appears that every language expresses the character of the people that speak it" (Condillac 1971, 285). Is that not Herder's culture-concept? No. Condillac was noticing a merely empirical fact, on a par with the influence on a people of climate and prosperity. It never occurred to him that a language and a people are co-constitutive.

Condillac agreed to the ancient truism that none of the characteristic features of the mental life of humans is possible without language. We need language in order to sharpen and classify ideas, and to make them determinate and distinct. Those private linguists of today, the cognitive scientists, would agree. The word is the sign of the idea. A private object, an idea, might not have been formed had humans lacked the power of speech, but it is private all the same. Words signify ideas, their private referents. Condillac did not imagine the lesson that (according to Berlin) Herder learned from Hamann, namely that words and ideas are one.

Having separated Herder from the private linguist Condillac, can we say that Herder inaugurated the publicity of language? He is commonly regarded as a progenitor of the great German philological tradition. May he not also have loosed the bonds of the Lockean idea-ology and its private references of words? Yes, but he was not the first nor did he do it thoroughly. Aarsleff (quoting in part from another scholar) writes of "Herder's principle that each human being 'in the true metaphysical sense' speaks his own language" (Aarsleff 1982, 344). Herder may not have learned quite as much from Hamann as Berlin would have wished. Hamann had qualms on this very point. His own published animadversions on Herder's famous prize essay on the origins of language can certainly be read as worries about, among many other things, publicity. Hamann, at any rate, was sure that in the true metaphysical sense no person speaks his or her own language.

Role Models

Around 1800, give or take a few years, something fundamental happened to the way in which we think about language. Chomsky thinks it was a bad thing. Berlin thinks it was a good thing. Foucault thought it was a remarkable thing. Aarsleff, the professional, thinks that it did not happen. The history of thinking about language was an enthusiasm of Berlin, Chomsky, and Foucault, but it was incidental to their grander themes and greater enterprises. All three are passionate about a big transition, but are totally at odds about its nature. Worse, when we call in an expert, he polemically denies that there was a significant change at all. What is going on?

Aarsleff is partly defending his territory against the incursions of amateurs such as Chomsky and Berlin. The title of his 1970 attack, "The History of Linguistics and Professor Chomsky," does not belie its tone (Aarslett 1982). Chomsky, we are in effect told, made a big mistake. There is no such thing as Cartesian linguistics: there is only a great Lockean tradition adopted in France. And much later Aarsleff (1981) savaged Berlin for failing to understand that the Germans had merely aped the French. Aarsleff's fierce rebuttals connect him with two of our authors. As for other pairings, I think that Chomsky and Foucault never discussed their opposed views about language, but there is one remarkable confrontation between the two men. The topic was not language, but justice and human nature. Each hammed up the role of himself—Foucault as manic post-Maoist, Chomsky as wrathful rationalist republican; Chomsky as *philosophe*, Foucault as terrorist (Chomsky and Foucault 1974). Although the debate had nothing to do with anything so recondite as the history of language study, it displays the politics that underwrites our authors' analyses of language. For we are not talking here only about language, but about high politics, about the person and the state, about individual rights, about the self, and much else.

Chomsky's role as spokesman for egalitarian rationalism is too well known to need elaboration here. The creative aspect of language use, together with the innate species-specific powers of the human mind have, for him, a deep political significance. To think that something so constitutive of humanity as language is merely embedded in cultures is to encourage illiberalism and perhaps to invite despotism. Because Foucault, at the time of *Les mots et les choses* and his later debate with Chomsky, had despaired of liberalism, only he, among our four authors, is indifferent to the connotations of theories of language for liberal values.

Aarsleff and Berlin, both émigrés, see deep connections between the theories and the values. Each, in his view of language, is, like Chomsky, expressing his own profoundly held liberalism. For the Danish-born expert, the virtues are those of English tolerance, and Locke is the man. For the assimilated German Jew, the virtues are those of reform during the early days of German liberal culture. The golden age of Germany, lost so long ago, was none other than the period when Hamann, Herder, and Humboldt could flourish. Berlin's Herder is the man who "protests, not without a certain malicious satisfaction (as Hamann also did, with equally ironical pleasure), that the great liberal Kant in his *Anthropologie* emphasized race and color too much" (Berlin 1977, 163). It is not literally correct to say that Hamann too was commenting on the *Anthropologie*—it was published some time after Hamann's death—but what Berlin meant is right. More specifically, Berlin read Herder's comments on Jews in an optimistic way (pp. 159f.), and never gave up his confidence in Herder's good sense to the end of his life (cf. Berlin 1991). Singing the praises of Herder, Berlin is honoring a larger set of values. Aarsleff, finding in Locke the fount of linguistic wisdom, knows that Locke helped frame the legal basis within which toleration can prosper, compared to which Berlin's nostalgia for Herder seems idle sentiment. So the curious theme underlying these diverse stories is less language than a celebration of liberalism, perceived from different quarters. Each of our protagonists, save Foucault, no liberal, implies, "I am more liberal than you, and my guys are more liberal than your guys."

Hamann

A standard account of the study of language tells of the Romantic attitude starting with an almost invisible Hamann profoundly influencing the highly visible Herder. This attitude was, in turn, cast into institutional form through the work of the Humboldts. Aarsleff has rightly insisted that this version of history is manifestly impoverished, if only because of the immense amount that both Herder and Humboldt took from their French predecessors and contemporaries. Hamann is not too promising a figure for those of us who favor unequivocal statements over visions, clouds of erudition, and abrupt aphorisms. If you become captured by his more flamboyant prose, your own becomes tinctured with it. Yet he had many of the tastes of the rationalist that favor elegance of style and clarity of exposition. After he had read Kant's first *Critique*, he wrote Herder: "Hume is always my man" (*B*, 6:187). He translated Hume's *Dialogues Concerning Natural Religion*. His great admirer, Søren Kierkegaard, understated the number of Hamann's preserved words, but the spirit of this note in one of his journals is exactly right: "Just as Socrates left no books, Hamann left only as much as the modern period's rage for writing made relatively necessary, and furthermore only occasional pieces" (Kierkegaard 1989, 435).

The only systematic view of Hamann's work, by a first-class mind, was written by Hegel in 1828 (Hegel 1956). It accompanied the publication during that decade of Hamann's works, many of which had not been printed earlier. By Hegel's lights, Hamann was too dark, too obscure, despite flashes of brilliance. One can also sense that Hegel felt somewhat threatened by Hamann's words. Those less scared have been, in their own ways, more receptive: not just Berlin but Kierkegaard or Gershom Scholem, commending Hamann and his tradition to Walter Benjamin (Benjamin 1966, 2, 526).

Hamann was a born-again Christian whose practices make little sense in our age, which is so simplistic with regard to religion. Here was a young man who—after low life in London, where he had been sent on a confidential commercial mission by his prospective father-in-law, a powerful Baltic merchant, and where he had taken up with a lute player, found himself betrayed, survived a breakdown by studying the Bible, and had experienced an intense conversion to a personal and fundamentalist Lutheranism—proceeded to write his fiancée and her father in quite vivid detail about all that had happened: end of engagement. Shocked by his emotional and religious state and his indifference to the values of reasonable analysis, his best friend Berens (brother of the former fiancée) arranged with Kant to try to restore him to sound principles. The result was a disastrous weekend *à trois* that left Hamann unmoved. He was involved with God throughout his life. But he would on occasion deny the immortality of the soul. He lived in domestic harmony with his common-law wife whom he declined to marry and who bore him four children. Ever Lutheran, he spent his last couple of years in the intellectual company of Catholics, and was buried in the Roman churchyard of Münster. He was explicit about physical sex, which he identified with mystical union. Vastly franker in print than his peers, he would yet win no admirers from most sexual revolutionaries of recent times and much contempt from many feminists. It is easy to read him as even more anti-Semitic than most of his contemporaries: that is, profoundly absorbed in Hebrew history as revealed in the Bible, well aware of cabalistic and talmudic writing, but contemptuous of most European Jews in his own time.

Kant

What can we learn from Hamann, the self-styled "Magus of the North," about conceptions of language? It is useful to begin by playing him off against Kant. The two men form a paradoxical contrast of public and private. Kant was a very public personality, but founded his philosophy on privacy. Hamann was a very private man whose world view was founded upon community. Kant was the elder by six years and outlived Hamann by fifteen. They knew each other well, although toward the end Kant distanced himself. Hamann edited a good number of Kant's occasional pieces and read the first *Critique* in proof, probably before Kant himself. His short essay about the great book was scathing, yet Hamann retained much respect and affection for Kant, whom he long called the "Prussian Hume." "My poor head is a broken pot compared to Kant's—earthenware against iron" (*B*, 5:108). No one will disagree.

Kant was Enlightenment, Hamann its opposite, but it is not the tag that counts. However much we tend to think of Kant as dry, withered, obsessive, Kant was a truly public man. He attracted large audiences and, in the *Anthropologie* and elsewhere, wrote meticulously about how to arrange the best dinner parties, where all the news of the world would be exchanged before moving to the later stages of frivolity. But Kant's philosophy is founded upon privacy, quite as much as that of Descartes or Locke or Leibniz. A person is an ego with a buzzing sequence of sense impressions and thoughts. Hence arises the challenge of discovering a basis for objectivity. Throughout Kant's final work, we find the same solution for the natural and the moral sciences: one's judgment must be the judgment of every rational man, when placed in the same circumstances. In our knowledge of the world, we obtain objectivity because of certain preconditions for experience in space, time, and causality, substance, and the like; in the moral realm, we attain objectivity by willing (as noumenal private agents) to will only what we would wish any other like being to will. The voice of reason is the voice of standardization and of public norms. These are required by a self whose essence is private, an essence whose objectivity is assured only by "the transcendental unity of apperception" according to which every thought is accompanied by the thought, "I think this."

Kant's attempts to solve the problem of public objectivity gave him a metaphysics, an epistemology, an ethics, and a theory of the state. Hamann did not have Kant's problems. He thought that there is no such thing as a person except what is constituted in a social setting, characterized by a unique historical language. Language is essentially public and shared; it is prior to the individuation of one's self. For Kant, the "I think" had to accompany every thought in order for there to exist an objective and continuous "I": for Hamann, there is an "I" only in linguistic communities, where, as a child becomes formed publicly within a language, the objective and continuous "I," such as it is, comes into being.

One's self is constituted within a society and a language. Hamann did not infer that there is an unchanging and irrevocable linguistic framework. On the contrary, it is Kant who requires the standardized language, for without that, the world dissolves into solipsism.

His whole philosophy was founded upon the classical notion of the private ego, so he had to construct a theory of shared judgments in order to assure any objectivity for the person at all. Hamann, taking for granted a self that is constituted in the public world of language and social intercourse, was empowered to become a thoroughly private figure. For Kant, the objectivity of the self was always in principle threatened and so required a metaphysical foundation. For Hamann, there was no threat and no foundation. He was a person from the very fact that he spoke. He did not need to be obeisant to public guarantees of objectivity because there was no need of guarantee. He could afford to make fun of the public. In 1759 he stated on the title page of his *Socratic Memorabilia* that they are "Compiled for the Boredom of the Public by a Lover of Boredom, with a Double Dedication to Nobody and to Two." The two are Hamann's lifelong friends Berens and Kant, who had tried to restore him to Enlightenment conventions. The work is dedicated as well to the public, that is, to nobody (*Werke*; henceforth *W* 2:59, cf. O'Flaherty 1967).

Flashforward

There is much in common between today's analytic philosophy and the projects of enlightened Europe from the time of Hobbes to that of Kant. I've taken as premise that there is one radical difference. Aside from those influenced by cognitive science, few think that there could be a private language. There may be as many versions of this idea as there are widely read philosophers. That vogue owes nothing to Hamann, Herder, or Humboldt, nor even (despite "the private language argument") to a present enthusiasm for Wittgenstein. It is a common enough complaint "about many contemporary American philosophers that they appear never to have read Wittgenstein" (Dummett 1991, xi).

Language, I claim, went public at the time of Hamann, but the present analytical enthusiasm for the publicity of language may have quite different roots. As Victoria McGeer has pointed out to me, there may be various ways to go public, one of which stems from Kant. The theory of shared judgments was both essential to and novel in Kant's philosophy of objectivity. That leads to the conception that what is asserted must be public in order to be objective—an idea quite alien to Hamann. This, perhaps, is the kind of publicity that has been made a commonplace of the analytic philosophers. It follows that answers to the question, "what are the roots of a modern analytic enthusiasm for the publicity of language?" may be entirely different, and vastly more Kantian, than my answer to my title question.

If one were to pursue this thought, one might better understand why the modern analytic "Kantians" are so at odds about what "the private language argument" is. Wittgenstein's argument may lie within a vision of language and the soul that shares much with Hamann. It is preoccupied not with reason, not with objectivity, but, in the end, with what it is to be a person. That is not to deny that Wittgenstein has mattered to the analysts. One paradoxical effect of his work has been to depoliticize the idea of language as essentially public. Language becomes regarded as an abstract phenomenon. One need not become involved in practical consequences of the idea: hence (perhaps) its background appeal to analytic philosophy. Writing about language as some sort of abstract entity has made it possible to leave aside questions about what it is to be a person in a community. Hence questions about the soul, and personal identity, have continued to be discussed in very much the manner of the Enlightenment. Analytic philosophy found thereby a protective screening from other strands of contemporary philosophical thought. It is as if Wittgenstein vaccinated analytic philosophy against more radical transformations: by giving us the cow-pox of public language, he left the rest of our constitution intact.

Pure Reason and Its Critique

Hamann wrote several pieces on Kant's first *Critique*. One is a "Metacritique of the Purism of Reason," of 1784. This title is typically packed with allusions. The metacritique is not just "about a critique"—in it Hamann used the word "metaschematism" both with reference to Kant's schematism, and with reference to Paul's Epistle (1 Cor. 4:6), a pun that takes several pages to elucidate (Unger 1911, 501–505). The word "purism" in the title is of Hamann's invention *(Purismum)*. It has connotations of the purity of reason. But, as he wrote to his friend and Kant's critic Jacobi,

"With me it is not so much the question, What is reason? but rather, What is language"? (*B* 3:294, Smith 1960, 249).

It is significant that Hamann begins this piece with a paragraph about Berkeley and Hume. Not any Berkeley, not any Hume. He writes of Berkeley on abstract ideas, and of Hume saying that Berkeley's proof that there are no abstract ideas is one of the greatest and most valuable discoveries of the day. Assuredly, Berkeley and Hume were private linguists, but they abandoned one core tenet of Locke, the private reference of general words to abstract ideas in the mind. There are no abstract ideas to refer to. How then do general words succeed in referring to more than one entity? Well, we so use them. "The *third*, chief, and as it were *empirical* purism concerns language, the only, the first and the last organon and criterion of reason, with no other credentials but tradition and usage (*W* 3:284, Smith 260). That doctrine Hamann attributes, not to Berkeley or Hume, but to the poet Edward Young: "language, the organon and criterion of reason, as Young says. Here is to be found pure reason and its critique" (*B*, 5:360). Or, more bluntly with reference to pure reason: "All chatter about reason is pure wind: language is its organon and criterion, as Young says. Tradition is its second element" (*B*, 5:108).

Hamann can evidently be made to come out sounding like Wittgenstein, what with language having no credentials but tradition and usage, and with "the whole of philosophy is grammar." That way lies anachronism and would betray a complete incomprehension of what Wittgenstein did teach. One nevertheless recognizes a kindred spirit in the matter of writing. We would not be astonished to find in notes for the *Tractatus* Hamann's gentle saying, "the more one considers language the deeper and more inward is one's dumbness and loss of all desire to speak" (*W* 3:285, Smith 216).

Kant provided a critique of pure reason in order to vindicate reason by preserving it against its excesses. Hamann is dismissive of reason, not necessarily because he wants us to be unreasonable, but because all the certainty that is attributed to reason is to be found only in the language used to reason. This applies even to mathematics, which Kant took so seriously and to which Hamann was indifferent. Kant had a brilliant explanation for the mathematical rigor he so much admired. Arithmetic and geometry are not merely the glories of reason but, as the synthetic *a priori* laws of the pure concepts of space and time, are preconditions for possible knowledge of the world. Hamann? "If mathematics is noble, then it should give way to the *instinct* of insects" (*W*, 3:285). So much for the synthetic *a priori*. He was hardly one to be moved by mathematical argument, but he had a considered view of apodictic certainty and *a priori* knowledge, and of the experience of discovering geometrical proofs that has so impressed mathematical minds from Plato to the present. Hamann's view anticipates the opinion made popular by the Vienna Circle, largely acquired from Wittgenstein's *Tractatus:* "The whole certainty of mathematics depends upon the nature of its language" (*B*, 5:360).

Linguistic Idealism

Hamann called himself a philologue and also a verbalist. His philology was not that which was emerging at the famous philological seminar at Göttingen (Hoffman 1972). His was an older sense of the word, that of John the Evangelist. He was a lover of *logos*. Referring once again to the organon and criterion of reason he wrote, "Without words, no reason, no world. Here is the source of all creation and order!" (*B*, 5:95). This is a characteristic sentence that looks two ways. I shall try to indicate the directions.

One is what I would call backwards, although another sensibility would take Hamann's words differently. "Speech is translation—out of angel speech, that is thoughts into words—things into names—forms into signs" (*W*, 2:199). "This kind of translation is . . . analogous more than anything else to the reverse side of a tapestry ('and shows the stuff but not the workman's skill')? (*W*, 3:287). In the celebrated debates on the origin of language, and in particular in criticism of Herder's famous essay on the topic, he held that there is no such thing as a question about how language came into being. Much later, Humboldt would rather somberly state that the archetype of language had to be already present in the human soul. That's diluted Hamannism, not innate General Grammar. Hamann more dramatically thought, like the Evangelist, of language and the world as coming into being together. The backward-pointing Renaissance version of this is the idea that God created man and language when the world was created, or shortly thereafter, with the words being true signs both of the things and of Adam's ideas of the things, which are, in turn, true ideas of God's creation of the things.

The forward-looking version of Hamann (say I, with distorting hindsight) was altogether different. It was quite properly called "verbalism" by

Hamann himself. There is nothing, neither substance nor form, without language. That is a kind of linguistic idealism that has been common enough in our century. I introduced this phrase "linguistic idealism" as a name for the extraordinary idea that nothing exists unless it has been spoken about (Hacking 1975b, 182). To paraphrase Berkeley, "to be is to be mentioned." As I said at the time, the phrase "linguistic idealism" is a bit of a solecism, since "idealism" is the doctrine that nothing exists except ideas—ideas in the sense of Locke, that is, ideas in the sense of the *idéologues.* A correct and parallel formation, and better name than "linguistic idealism," would be "lingualism." The phrase "linguistic idealism" was soon used to good effect, but with a slightly different meaning, by Elizabeth Anscombe (1976), and has since been picked up by a number of writers, including Hilary Putnam. Perhaps Hamann was the first lingualist, or linguistic idealist.

According to Hamann, the fable of the first naming is misunderstood. There were not things, to which names were then attached by God or man. Individuated things are there only when there are words to describe them. Moreover, these words are not the private artifact of some Enlightenment Adam, discoursing within his soul. They are the words of what is to be the first human community. "In the language of every people we find the *history* of the same," not just because there are traces in the language of the history but because there is no people aside from historical language (*B*, 1:393).

In short, language for Hamann is profoundly nonrepresentative. It is the exact opposite to what was claimed by the linguistic theories of the Enlightenment. Language is creative; to it we owe the existences and structures that populate our world-versions. Thanks to language alone do we have the forms and logic that we call reasoning. Moreover, by an apparent circularity that Hamann found totally unproblematic, this language, which is creative, has its existence and regularity only within tradition and use. The human being who would be an original is not the one who has a great private thought within him that he then makes public. The original is the one who can change the very language that we share, in which we think, and which is our communal version of the world, both inner and outer.

9

Night Thoughts
on Philology

The title of this short piece alludes to Edward Young's long poem, *Night Thoughts* (1743–1745), and also to the circumstance that, like chapter 7, it was written overnight to fill a space in *History of the Present,* a short-lived quarterly newsletter for fans of Michel Foucault. Here I complained that Foucault, who was so keen on dating ruptures in thought, was not so reliable when it comes to easily checkable dates. Yet at least in this case, Foucault's grander thesis about the nature of the change from universal grammar to philology still seems to me sound. The original version of these "Thoughts" concluded with several pages on Hamann, the substance of which was later incorporated into chapter 8, and which have been deleted here. When first published, the paper had the dedication, "For Mr. I. B. Bopp of Columbia, S.C." The page references in the text are to *The Order of Things* (Foucault 1970).

The Order of Things is, among many other things, a story of abrupt transitions in what is said. One of these breaks, for whose description Foucault is rightly admired, is a matter of language. General Grammar became philology. Language ceased to be the double means of representation: double because words and sentences were thought of as representing ideas and mental discourse, and at the same time as able to represent things and facts. With the advent of philology, language was no longer studied primarily as a system of representation. Individual languages were treated as historical entities, and the focus of attention was grammar and word formation. Comparative, rather than general, grammar became the order of the day. This happened "early in the nineteenth century—at the time of [Friedrich] Schlegel's essay on the language and the philosophy of the Indians (1808),

[Jacob] Grimm's *Deutsche Grammatik* (1818) and [Franz] Bopp's book on the conjunction of Sanskrit (1816)" (p. 282).

As is well known, Foucault described this mutation as one member of a trio, in which life, labor, and language came into being as objects of thought. Yet it is language that stands out in Foucault's account. There are several plain reasons for this. One is that at the time the book was being written, language was the pre-eminent professed interest of Foucault and indeed of *tout Paris*. Another is that it is within a certain recent conception of language that Foucault frames the rest of *The Order of Things*. A third is that the events concerning language were and are still far less familiar than those connected with life and labor. We all knew that life and labor had been transformed conceptually, for we knew about Darwin and Marx, and even if Cuvier and Ricardo were not quite household names, they were hardly unknown to the general reader. But who was Grimm (1785–1863) except a maker of dictionaries and a brother who collected fairy tales? Who on earth was Bopp? The answer to the latter question, to be gleaned only from thorough reference books, is that Bopp (1781–1867) wrote, for example, *A Comparative Grammar of Sanskrit, Persian, Greek, Latin, Lithuanian, Old Church Slavonic, Gothic and German*, later turning his attention to Albanian, Celtic vowel systems, Malay, and Polynesian. That is not the stuff of which fashionable texts are made, or which resonates in the minds of the young.

It was all the more astonishing, then, that Foucault could make a tour de force out of his discussion of Grimm and Bopp, and tell us, for example, that the transition effected in their work made literature possible. It was they who marked the threshold between "our prehistory and what is still contemporary" (p. 304)—one of Foucault's reformulations of what he more commonly calls "classicism and modernity" and what is more widely thought of as a transition between the Enlightenment and the Romantics. It was of course part of Foucault's strategy to expel those clichéd labels from intellectual history, to make us think not about the celebrated Romantics, but the utterly unromantic-sounding Grimm and Bopp. Yet even he found it necessary to add that Wilhelm von Humboldt was "not merely Bopp's contemporary; he knew his work well, in detail" (p. 290). The point was that Humboldt might be taken (although by only the most casual of readers) to stand for the very opposite of what we think of as philology, because he exhibited "the tendency to attribute to language profound powers of expression." Foucault might, at this juncture, have been a trifle more explicit. It is stretching our modern use of the term to call Bopp the contemporary of Humboldt, 14 years his senior, which is relevant because Humboldt's support enabled Bopp to get the chair of Sanskrit in Berlin in 1821. Humboldt may, for some, be the paradigm of the Romantic expressionist, but his final, his most energetic, and in the opinion of many, his greatest work, is built around a study of certain Polynesian languages, using, among other tools, some principles of Bopp's (Humboldt 1988). The latter repaid the compliment, turning his attention to Malayan/Polynesian languages after Humboldt's death.

In what follows I want to emphasize the connection between grammar and romanticism, and to turn attention to, for a chief example, a man who died before Bopp was born. This is to call in question Foucault's implication of a sharp break between the old general grammar and the new philology, one that took place within the stated timespan of books by Friedrich Schlegel (1808) and Jacob Grimm (1818). At the time that he wrote *The Order of Things,* Foucault was rather keen on precisely dated discontinuities in thought and speech: a decade, in this case 1808–18, was just what he liked to find. Now this procedure has been amply criticized by historians of ideas, who tend to notice long spans of time and fairly uniform evolution. That is not a camp to which I wish to belong, or to which I can be accused of belonging, for nothing could be much more *coupure*-oriented that my own *Emergence of Probability* (Hacking 1975a), with its claim that our ideas of probability brusquely entered human life and practice about 1650. Here I shall urge only that now Foucault's picture of the philological revolution is firmly in place in the minds of his readers, it can be enriched by conjuring up a longer period of time. More importantly, what happens within that longer period is profoundly important to the very break in thought about which Foucault wrote, and helps to understand not only the proximate causes of the break, but also its longstanding effects that still act strongly, silently but blindingly, when we try to think about language.

My case in no way rests upon idiosyncrasies of dating to be found in *The Order of Things.* But I should remark them, in order to evade some straightforward rebuttal that would merely re-cite several pages of that book. Thus, for a moment Foucault nods in the direction of those who would argue that Bopp and Schlegel are less inaugurators than participants in an onflowing process of change. He writes of "what distinguishes the analyses of Schlegel and Bopp from those that may perhaps have seemed to anticipate them in the eighteenth century" (285, n34). The grounds of

Foucault's distinction are sound; it is a point about syllables and roots and the formation of sense. I want merely, for a moment, to call attention to the dating.

Schlegel's "date" for an essay on the language and philosophy of the Indians (from the subcontinent, not America, by the way) was given as 1808. Now the contrasting reference for eighteenth-century writers, from note 34 just cited, is 1798: a work published in London in that year by John Horne Tooke, with the title *On the Study of Language*. When the claim to "eighteenth-century writers" turns out to be 1798, one may admire the audacity of the claim to a break between 1798 and 1808 (Schlegel).

Unfortunately there is no such book of 1798. There is a famous book on the study of language by John Horne Tooke (1736–1812); the second edition, in two volumes, had its first volume published in 1798, under the title ΕΠΕΑ ΠΤΕΡΟΕΝΤΑ *or, the Diversions of Purley;* the second volume was published in 1805. The first volume is a minor revision of the first edition, of 1786; the second published in 1805 is new. Horne Tooke had not been idle in the years between the two volumes. He had to stand trial in 1796 for High Treason; the second volume is dedicated to the named twelve members of the jury that acquitted him and thereby made that volume possible. When one reflects that Schlegel's 1808 book on India was, on all accounts, largely composed in Paris in 1802, the sharp datings do not look so good. Nor do they when we find that Grimm's *Deutsche Grammatik,* given as 1818, appeared in 1819, and that virtually everything Foucault ascribes to Grimm is from the second and entirely rewritten edition of the work, whose first volume appeared in 1822, and whose four volumes took 15 years to complete. All of which is nit-picking at its worst, were it not for my incidental purpose of reminding ourselves that Foucault's picture of clean sharp dates and decades is rather tidier than the record reveals.

The preceding paragraph does not put in question Foucault's major theses, but makes one look more closely at his dates. Not only was Horne Tooke no writer who began in 1798: some work in his volume of 1786 had been published two decades earlier under the title of "A Letter to Mr. Dunning," and he assures us that "all that I have farther to communicate on the subject of Language, has been amongst the papers in my closet," when the man was thirty years of age—1766 (Tooke 1798, 74). Horne Tooke was eminently a writer of the eighteenth century, confirming Foucault's mention of eighteenth-century writers far better that the misleading footnote 34. Yet putting Horne Tooke's writings back to 1766 or so makes less compelling the talk of a mutation occurring precisely during the second decade of the nineteenth century! And Foucault does make something of just that periodization, stating that the break creating "the new philology" (285) occurred substantially later than that for biology and political economy.

If one finds the periodization to be less sharply defined, one creates a space for other texts which shift the way in which one should think of "the new philology." First a word on how Horne Tooke does contrast with Bopp or Grimm. The man is not uninteresting, quite aside from the vagaries of his public life. He aimed at rewriting Locke in terms of etymology. He accepted that we may begin by thinking that words are signs for things or signs for ideas. But it has been supposed that each word must have a grammar corresponding to the nature of the mental operation or event (idea), or to the thing to which it corresponds, or which it represents. The error was to fail to notice that most words are abbreviations for other words; most words are "the signs of other words" (Tooke 1798, 26). "The first aim of Language was to *communicate* our thoughts: the second to do it with *dispatch*" (ibid.). And each language effects its "abbreviations" differently. When the penny finally drops, the interlocutor says, "I thought we were talking of Universal Grammar" (46); to which it is replied that we are; certain features are necessary for all languages, but a study of how words get their signification cannot be conducted "unless you confine it to some particular language with which I am acquainted" (46–47). Our work is Universal, only in the sense that the principles with which we work on English, Gothic, or Greek "will apply universally." The principles concern the historical study of how words came, in the long past of ours and other languages, to stand for the longer sequences of words of which they are abbreviations. Note that in this methodology there is an implicit standard of linguistic appraisal, for the best language is one that communicates its abbreviations of other words with greatest "dispatch." "Words have been called *winged:* and they well deserve that name when their abbreviations are compared with the progress which speech would make without these inventions; but compared with the rapidity of thought, they have not the smallest claim to that title" (28). The metaphor of language and Hermes, the winged messenger, is an old one. Horne Tooke's title ΕΠΕΑ ΠΤΕΡΟΕΝΤΑ is even more the Greek of Augustine England than of Athens. It means "winged words." The frontispiece of volume I is an androgynous Hermes tying the wings on his heels.

There is a certain ambivalence in Horne Tooke, between the private and public nature of language. Language is to communicate thought, which runs far faster than speech. The study of thought, of what Hobbes called mental discourse, would then seem a fit and proper one, as for all other writers on language during the Enlightenment. Do we not demand a theory of the mind and its relation to language? No, we are told (51): "The business of the mind, as far as it concerns Language, appears to me to be very simple. It extends no further than to receive Impressions, that is, to have Sensations of Feelings. What are called its operations are merely the operations of Language." From the consideration of ideas, the mind, or things, we at most get some clues to the noun, nothing else. It appears, then, that language has been *externalized.* By this I mean the following. In the Classical theory of representation, language is first of all something internal, which can then be used to communicate with others, to transfer thoughts in my mind to yours. Horne Tooke still believes this is the primary purpose of language, but there is nothing peculiarly mental or private about language. Language appears to be public and historical, and the origin of ideas, à la Locke, is nothing more than the origin of words in the evolution of particular languages.

These many paragraphs of mine may make a little more plain the half paragraph of Foucault to which they refer, and which cites Horne Tooke. Why is it that the author of "Winged Words" may only "have seemed to anticipate" Bopp and Schlegel? Does he not anticipate, in that he is turning the theory of ideas into etymology? Does he not anticipate by beginning to shred the whole doctrine of inner representation, replacing it with the study of public language? The point, for Foucault, is now not the mere historicizing of language, but the study of historical languages as complex grammatical structures. Etymology, or what we might call comparative word-study, does not mark the decisive transition. Instead, it is comparative grammar. That is not part of a theory of signs at all, whereas Horne Tooke is propounding what is, in effect, a new variant on an old theory of signs. Comparative grammar is concerned with the way in which internal structures of the word and of the entire sentence are guided and modified by rules for language change—regardless of that for which the word or the sentence is a sign.

It is one among many consequences of this new perspective that no languages are better or worse than others. Hence the genuine lack of condescension in examining the languages of isolated, "primitive," or "uncivilized" peoples. Their languages are objects exactly in the way in which the languages of mainstream Europe or of the high ancient civilizations of the Orient are objects. Moreover, a certain relativity about the very aims of a conversation are implied. Horne Tooke could compare different languages in terms of the "dispatch" with which they could communicate. But that assumes that speakers of all languages want to communicate the same things. What is dispatch for one community may be tardiness for another.

Such contrasts between the new philology and the old confirm the exactness of Foucault's observations, aside from the trifling matter of dating. I drew attention to the dating only to make room for the possibility that the new philology has a longer and denser history than that implied by Foucault's proposed decade, 1808–1818.

A new philology implies an old one. What was that? Not necessarily one thing. *Philology,* the love of words, was a neologism or revival intended to contrast with *philosophy,* the love of wisdom. There must be as many ways to love words as to love wisdom. The word "philology" quickly acquired a number of fairly specialized senses. One of these, well suited to my purposes, may be illustrated by work of J. M. Chladenius (1710–1749). Hitherto obscure, he has attracted some attention by those looking for precursors or originators of the hermeneutic tradition. It is not, I think, an attention that he deserves, but here I attend only to the role that he ascribes to the philologian, the man he calls *Philologus.*

Chladenius's philologian is one of four partners who share the task of making intelligible a difficult text. A "text," it is to be understood, is the physical object or its transcription left behind by an ancient author; this is the traditional usage of "textual criticism" as opposed to that recently fashionable parlance in which almost anything comes out as a text. The first partner in making sense of a text is, indeed, called the *critic.* The task of the critic is to restore, as best he can, the text of the author, for we typically have only an object with gaps, corruptions, the erasures of time.

After the critic has done his job, we have the best available sequence of complete sentences. The next task is to construe the grammar of the best text. *This* is the task of the philologian. The implied picture is familiar to anyone who has found it necessary to read some material in a language whose words are dimly familiar (Norwegian, say); having looked up the words in a dictionary, one may well be unable to understand any of the interesting sentences for lack of following the grammar. *Philologus* is called for. After the philologian has done his job, two kinds of obscurity remain. There is the relatively uninteresting one, that some words may be ambiguous. Then there is the relatively interesting one, that somehow the text that we are now able to read, in the most elemental sense, we still do not understand. Chladenius' approach to this last problem has suggested to some that he is addressing the problem of modern hermeneutics.

I follow Robert Leventhal (1986) in the above exposition, and also in his argument that Chladenius was *not* a precursor of hermeneutics. For Chladenius had the standard Enlightenment view that words are the expression of inner discourse, and as he saw the problem, the concepts, in the mind of the writer, may be inadequately expressed in the words that he has used. So the task of the fourth and last partner of interpretation is to construct concepts that adequately reflect the mind of the writer. The writer, far from being the historical personage of the hermeneuticists, is a timeless mind, or ego, of the Enlightenment, one whose concepts may be inadequately expressed by his words. The words are defective signs of ideas: in short, we are in Foucault's "Classical" epoch, not the modern one where language is public and words get their sense in the public domain.

Chladenius is not definitive of "the old philology" (as if there were one such thing): he is merely illustrative. The love of words has become specific. The philologian is an applied grammarian. That is important, for the lover of words might have remained merely a lover of the ancient authors or of scripture. Instead, he became the grammarian of typically dead tongues, and made possible the characterization of Bopp and Grimm as philologians. But this was only the slightest and most terminological of steps towards the new philology. For Chladenius, the job of philology is to parse the text reconstructed by the textual critic. The parsing is not in itself an object of study. For Bopp and Grimm, the structures as objects of study are exactly those that make parsing possible, and whose history is the topic of philology.

I have been saying that the extending of Foucault's span of dates makes a space for more events in the creation of the new philology than he allows for. I have now explained at some length his briefly noted contrast worth calling a divide between an old and a new philology. It is now my turn to introduce some new class of events and distinctions, consistent with my (I hope) sympathetic expansion of Foucault, but also supplementary to it. Naturally, there are many events from which to choose. I will fix on some that connect with the previous chapter, and which center on that cranky eccentric whom I introduced there, J. G. Hamann. I do so with a view to restoring a connection between the so-called Romantic movement in literature, and the new philology. Foucault wanted to sever that connection and put all the action in philology, so that we would see the grammarians Bopp and Grimm as the progenitors of what we now call "literature" itself.

My choice of entry is old-fashioned. Standard accounts of the emergence of the Romantic theory of language and literature accent, among others, the 3 H's of the previous chapter, Hamann (1730–1788), Herder (1744–1803), and Humboldt (1767–1835). Even Foucault, we noticed, thought it prudent to mention that Humboldt was well acquainted with Bopp's work. One of his motives was to connect that Romantic student of far-flung languages, namely Humboldt, to the supposedly dry and pedantic scholar of comparative grammar, namely Bopp. It was as if he expected the general reader to take it for granted that Humboldt was a key player in the emergence of romanticism, while Bopp was the very opposite of all that we understand by "Romantic": a student of syntax.

What I take to be the standard view shows Hamann influencing Herder, who led on to Humboldt. This version of history is impoverished (as Hans Aarsleff has insisted), if only because of the immense amount of material that Herder and Humboldt took from their French predecessors and contemporaries. But I want again to draw attention to the first of the three. I certainly do not claim Hamann as a precursor of Bopp, or as someone who anticipated the new philology or hermeneutics. Volker Hoffman (1972) describes him as "between" what he calls encyclopedic micrology and hermeneutics. (He examines Hamman's intellectual relationship to Chladenius on pp. 154–160.) Hermeneutics, as Levanthal (1986) shows, has other roots. Here we should think of Hamann rather as a philosopher of language who is one of the progenitors of the Romantic movement.

For all the importance of theories imported from France for German reflections on language, Hamann's own lines of filiation are British, not French. Recall from chapter 8 that he actively hated French, because, as Frederick the Great's civil servant, he toiled in a bureaucracy that had to draw up its reports using that alien tongue. Hamann's anglophilia is no surprise. He had spent a remarkable year of his youth in London; he translated Hume's work on natural religion. His highest praise for Kant was to call him "the Prussian Hume." And he had another model, not Scots this time but English. Not philosophy but poetry. I mean Edward Young (1683–1765).

Young was a London dramatist whose fame was made by *Night Thoughts on Life, Death and Immortality in Nine Nights*—a poem in nine parts and some 6,900 lines of blank verse that were published between 1742 and 1745. The finest edition, of only the first four nights, appeared in 1797, with 537 small but superb illustrations by William Blake (Young 1975). Now, I suppose, the poem is never read though often quoted. ("Procrastination is the thief of time," and so on) But beware, author and reader, of what Young says in another poem, *Love of Fame:*

> Some for renown, on scraps of learning dote,
> And think they grow immortal as they quote.

Night Thoughts was inspired by the death of Young's stepdaughter in 1736, her husband in 1740, and the poet's wife in 1741. It began with *The Complaint* and ended with *The Consolation.* Mournful stuff, but it captured the imagination of many, including Hamann, who at the age of 22 was there in London to revel in it half a dozen years after its publication. Hamann was not the only German to be moved. The poem came to have a far larger readership in Germany than in England (Barnstorff 1895, Kind 1906). But Hamann himself was able to say that he knew not how much he had learned from Young, perhaps everything.

One of the things he learned from Young was the possibility and value of originality. Young's *Conjectures on Original Composition* (1759) came out when Hamann was still an impressionable 29 years of age. The *Conjectures* were written in the form of an epistle to Samuel Richardson, the epistolary novelist so admired by the British middle classes of his day and the French *philosophes* alike. The age of the two gentlemen should be remembered: we now think of the lust for originality and genius as most marked in youth, yet Young was 76 when he published his communication to his friend, aged 70. Yet it is this feuilleton that serves as a marker, if not the originator, of the Romantic idea of the genius who creates what is wholly new from within his own inimitable resources. Julia Kristeva (1999) has argued in her recent book on Hannah Arendt that the idea of genius is truly a notion of the Renaissance, but here let us stick to the time-honored cliché that it is a creature of the Romantic era.

Hamann certainly acted as if he felt free to be original, even to the point of reforming the language into which he was born, and which, he theorized, constituted him as a person. Some of his prose intended for publication is as rupturing as anything by Artaud or Joyce in *Finnegans Wake.* It was *original* language that he wanted. In recasting one's own language, one recast one's self. He had only contempt for rational and systematic linguistic reform, a characteristic demand of the German Enlightenment. For example, reformers were trying to get rid of the silent *h* of old German orthography. But that letter was rich in meaning, argued quirky Hamann. It indicated a silent breath, a ghostly sigh, almost a *Geist*. To rationalize spelling in this way was to strip the German language of its spirit, of its mind, of its soul.

Hamann called himself a philologue, and also a "verbalist." I ended the last chapter by comparing him to the linguistic idealists, or lingualists, of our day. Yet that is in one way misleading. His philology was not that of either Chladenius or Bopp, but an older love of words, of *logos*. "Without words, no reason, no world. Here is the source of all creation and order!" In Hamann's vision, the fable of Adam and the naming of things is false. God did not create things, and then assign them names, which He imparted to Adam. Hamann's verbalism is not the incoherent and rather trivial linguistic idealism of our times, even if it is its precursor. For it is a theory of creation, of how what is material comes from the word. Incoherent, perhaps, but not trivial. Moreover, it is a theory of continuous creation, for as we change our language, so we change ourselves, so we make up ourselves, each from his own genius.

How much of all this does Hamann really owe to Young? Precious little, of what I in turn learn from Hamann. The *Night Thoughts* are in good measure a dialogue with Reason. A dying man is considering the grounds for immortality: something prior to reason provides him with consolation. That prior is, among other things, "speech." Whatever inspiration Hamann found in his frequent readings of the long poem, together with Young's *Original Composition*, it was only a resource for rethinking the nature of language. Hamann happened to have loved Young's phrases—there are many more that are mimicked in his writings than he acknowledges—but the notion of language as prior to thinghood and to reason is Hamann's own.

Hamann's sentences, along with those of many subsequent writers, helped put in place those very features of modernity that Foucault attributes too specifically to the philological revolution. Hamann participated in a revolution broader in scope: the termination of a theory of language as something inner and representational. Language becomes outer and creative. It is not merely historical and evolving, as the philologists and comparative grammarians were to teach. It is mutable. It is both what makes us possible as selves, and what we can transform in order to change not only ourselves but our world. Nietzsche, the most famous person ever to hold a chair of philology, was necessarily the heir of Bopp and Grimm. But he was also the heir of Hamann. Without Hamann and the Romantic tradition, philology would have been a merely technical enterprise. The new philology did not by itself create a new space in which literature could exist. That space was the creation of more forces than Foucault wanted to acknowledge, and one that is essential is Hamann's excessive verbalism, *logos* as creator.

In Foucault's reading, the emergence of life, labor, and language as objects of study has to do with the matrix in which Man comes into being. Yes, there is Kant's question posed around 1775, "What is man?" But even before the question was uttered, Hamann was providing the rudiments of Humboldt's partial response to Kant: "Man is Man only through language" (Humboldt 1903, 4, 15). That could well be the epigraph to Foucault's chapter, "Man and His Doubles." There had to be philologists for the epigraph to be composed, but there also had to be that other tradition of philo-logy, of logos-loving, of "verbalism," of which Hamann is so satisfactory a representative.

10

Was There Ever a
Radical Mistranslation?

W. V. Quine's doctrines of the indeterminacy of translation and the inscrutability of reference have been immensely influential. The doctrines are about logical possibilities, and not about what happens in fact, but they have been bolstered by tales of fairly permanent mistranslations. This note argues that these amusing fables are false. Some readers will protest that this shows nothing about Quine's logical point. I am not so sure. If something is claimed as a logical possibility about translation, which is never known to be approximated for more than a few moments in real life, may we not begin to suspect that the conception of translation that is being taken for granted may be erroneous?

On their voyage of discovery to Australia, a group of Captain Cook's sailors captured a young kangaroo and brought the strange creature back on board their ship. No one knew what it was, so some men were sent ashore to ask the natives. When the sailors returned they told their mates, "It's a kangaroo." Many years later it was discovered that when the aborigines said "kangaroo" they were not in fact naming the animal, but replying to their questioners, "What did you say?"

That would be a radical mistranslation if the story were true. A radical mistranslation is defined as follows. (1) Speakers of two very different languages are trying to communicate. (2) A speaker of one language says *s*. Speakers of the other language take him to be saying *p*. (3) This translation is completely wrong. Yet (4) neither party realizes it, although they continue to converse. Moreover (5) the mistranslation persists until it is too late to correct.

Condition (1) restricts us to people who are talking to each other and excludes the decoding of ancient texts. Condition (3) rules out mere differences of nuance, moderate misunderstandings, and misclassifications that occur to all of us all the time. Since my story is about naming, I shall call this kind of radical mistranslation *malostension*. That occurs when (6) an expression of the first language is taken by speakers of the second language to name a natural kind. (7) It does nothing of the sort, but (8) the second language incorporates this expression as the name of the natural kind in question. (7) is intended as a strong condition. Malostensions are not just misclassifications, or the taking of the name of an individual as the name of a class.

I cannot prove that radical mistranslations never occur. But I shall show that some famous alleged malostensions are frauds, founded upon rumor and refuted by facts. This may matter, because of W. V. Quine's thesis of the indeterminacy of translation. His doctrine is *a priori,* but it gains credence partly from anecdotes. We tend to feel that indeterminacy is radical mistranslation carried to the limit, where no possible information can settle which of two incompatible translations is correct. I reject this plausibility argument by rebutting the anecdotes with which it begins. The remarkable thing about human interaction is that mistranslations are so readily cleared up.

My opening story about "kangaroo" has been repeated many times. Like many other people, I was gullible, and worse, I repeated it. I took the version in my first paragraph from a Sunday newspaper and quoted it as an example (Hacking 1975b, 150). That sturdy Australian matter-of-fact philosopher, Jack Smart, taught me that the story is just false, the sort of thing that is now called an urban myth, except that it is an aboriginal myth. Cook's team recorded many words of a language they encountered in the Endeavour River area of Australia. They were confident of the spelling and meaning of only 60 of these words. "Kangaroo" was among them. Later travellers did not in fact encounter the word. Hence the story with which I began—people made up an explanation of Cook's word. But the story is based only on the fact that few subsequent travellers spoke with the Australian community that Cook had met. This was apparently pointed out in a letter to an Australian newspaper in 1898, but did not become common knowledge until the work of the anthropologist John Havilland in 1972 (Dixon 1980, 8–9). He wrote up a vocabulary for a dialect called Guugu Yamidhirr, spoken by people in just the area that Cook landed. Their word for kangaroos is "ga*n*urru," where I use "*n*" for a phoneme which is a bit like "ng." Kangaroo, in short, was no malostension, although perhaps our spelling is the result of poor phonetics.

There is a printed conversation in which Quine and Putnam mention two other alleged malostensions:

> *Quine:* David Lewis pointed out a nice example to me [. . .] There was, in the nineteenth century, a French naturalist named Pierre Sonnerat, who was doing field work in Madagascar. A lemur went up a tree, and Sonnerat asked a native "Qu' est que c'est?" The native said "in dri," which in Malagasy means "There he goes." Sonnerat thought that the native understood his question and had given the answer, and the animal is known as the indri to this day.
>
> *Putnam:* That's like the word "vasistas."
>
> *Quine:* Right. The French word for transom is "Was ist das." (Quine et al. 1974, 500)

Putnam and Quine do not actually assert that *vasistas* is a malostension, but others have told me that it is. Yet it is hard to imagine the circumstances. Were some German tourists pointing at a French transom, asking "Was ist das?" Did some French people overhear that and think, "Hah, that little window must be called a *vasistas*"? One can hardly credit that. In fact, the French word was first written, in French, with German spelling. It is thus used by the French mining engineer J. F. C. Morand in a 1776 book chiefly describing foreign equipment for mines. He speaks of a *Wass ist das* and means a little grille, built into a door and which can be opened to see what is outside or pass small objects or messages in or out.

Thus the "What is that?" does not have the force of a question, namely, what is this funny little window or opening. Rather *vasistas* is a word intended to convey a function. The *vasistas* is the grille through which you look to find out "What is that?" that is, what is that thing outside, who is knocking, who is there?

In 1784 one finds *Wasistdas* as the name of a proposed small window in an enclosed platform attached to a Montgolfier balloon. The passengers could be completely protected, but could open the *Wasistas* from time to time to see the view (von Proschwitz 1964, 329). The spelling of the word soon became completely gallicized. The *vasistas* had been a grille to separate the house from outsiders, but by 1793 popular justice gave it the reverse role. The lunette in the guillotine was jocularly called the vasistas, as in *Passer la tête au vasistas!* No malostension here.

Indri is a little trickier. I suspect that we have exactly the same situation as with "kangaroo," namely a word used in a dialect encountered by Sonnerat, but not noticed by later travelers. Beware of thinking that such writers were careless. Cook was reporting back to Sir Joseph Banks, one of the most critical Newtonian inductivists of all time. Cook did not rely on casual reports of his sailors (as is suggested by the story with which I began). His team sifted all their data and settled on only 60 words, including "kangaroo," of which they were sure. Likewise, Pierre Sonnerat (1748–1814) was no tripper watching lemurs scoot up trees (as Quine's version tends to imply). He was one of the most detailed of reporters and it is on work like his that Cuvier was glad to rely.

The word "indri" refers not to lemurs in general but to an unusual species, the largest lemur in Madagascar, about 25 inches long. It has the characteristic pointed muzzle and tree-climbing habit of lemurs, but is otherwise quite distinctive. Unlike the familiar ring-tailed lemurs often seen in zoos, it has only a rudimentary tail. It is black with white splotches on the head, throat, arms and buttocks. It is gregarious, lives mostly at tree-top level, and eats fruit. It climbs in an upright position. The species, once plentiful in the forests of Madagascar, is now almost extinct, and survives only in remote forests of the northeast.

When it comes to "indri," we cannot fault our philosophers for carelessness. The OED said in its first printing and continues to say that the word is "An erroneous application of the Malagasy exclamation *indry!* 'lo! behold!', or *indri izy!* 'there he is,' mistaken by the French naturalist Sonnerat for the name of the animal, when first seen by him c 1780: the only Malagasy name is *babakoto*." Webster's *Third International* repeats the story, asserting that the word comes from the French, in turn from "Malagasy *indry,* look!: probably from an erroneous belief by the French naturalist Pierre Sonnerat, who observed the animal in its native habitat about 1780, that the natives were uttering its name when in fact they were only calling attention to its presence." *Le Petit Robert* confirms that the French word *indri* derives from the "exclamation malegache 'le voilà' prise à tort pour le nom du singe." Who would question these august authorities? Only someone who takes a look at *their* authority. The OED directs us to a remark made by a missionary from Madagascar writing, in 1893, in a magazine that he edited. Rev. J. Sibree says of the short-tailed lemur that

> their native name is *Bàbakòto*, literally "Father-child" (or boy), not *Indri*,
> as said by Sonnerat, who discovered the species. *Indri* (or *indry*) is a Malagasy word meaning "lo!" or "behold!" and was probably mistaken by

him for a name and other Europeans for a name, when the natives ex-
claimed: "Indry izy!" ("There he is!"). (Sibree 1893, 83)

Was this then the perfect malostension? First let us get our authorities
straight. This quotation from Sibree is an unacknowledged word-for-word
translation of the observation made by François Pollen (1868, 20), another
missionary and naturalist. Whether we owe the story to Rev. Sibree or Father Pollen, Quine has certainly captured its spirit. We imagine that Pierre
Sonnerat visits Madagascar in 1780 and asks what a certain lemur is called.
He gets *indri* or somesuch in reply, and the animal scoots up a tree. We get
the picture of Sonnerat never getting much closer to an indri—they are
forever getting away.

But in fact, as Sonnerat tells us, indri are very easily tamed, and in the
southern part of the island are used in hunting, much as we use dogs. Far
from just overhearing a cry of indri he asks what it means, and is told that
it means little man of the woods. (Sonnerat 1782, II 141–3; 1806a, IV 89,
92). So Sonnerat not only heard the word, but discussed it. He later printed
his engraving of a nice fat indri eating a . . . banana? (Sonnerat 1782 II,
plate 88; 1806b, plate 86). Might that be a fanciful reconstruction of a
glimpsed animal that he never got close to? No, he took one aboard ship
and later presented it to his king. For a while it played in the royal garden
and was later stuffed and put in the Paris natural history museum.

None of this proves conclusively that Sonnerat got the name right. You
will not find the word *indri* in dictionaries translating from Malagasy into
European tongues. But taking a hint from the kangaroo story, we may ask
if Sonnerat got the phonemes slightly wrong. Sure enough.

The first printed bilingual dictionary for Malagasy was compiled by
agents of the London Missionary Society, which had been rather temporarily welcomed when the British, acting out of Mauritius, supported a
Malagasy leader's drive to control the whole island. (When this king died
in 1828, his widow reversed the policy of Europeanization and Christian
evangelism. The island preserved its restored autonomy against French and
British assaults until 1895, although it was forced to concede more and
more in the preceding few years.) The English-Malagasy part of the dictionary (Freeman 1835) contains no entry for lemur, but in the reverse direction (Johns 1835) we find the word *endrina* translated as "monkey." (At
that time there were no true monkeys on the island except a few escaped
from passing ships.) The next printed English-Malagasy dictionary (Rich-

ardson 1885) translates "endrina" as "a kind of lemur." Sibree's own copy of Freeman's dictionary is now in the library of Yale University. The book was printed with alternating blank pages so that the user could enlarge the list of entries. Sibree made few additions, none having anything to do with natural history. It is Sibree, I venture, who got it wrong, not Sonnerat.

This evidence is not absolutely conclusive. Johns (1835) could have given *endrina* as a back-formation from the French usage of *indri*, rather than as something heard in the field by uncontaminated locals. But why would he add a syllable to a French noun? In all probability we can accept Sonnerat at his word. Just as with "kangaroo," it is eminently possible that Sonnerat encountered people who called large short-tailed lemurs *indri* or *endrina,* even if much later Europeans elsewhere on the island did not. To confirm this, let us look at the larger picture.

First of all, Madagascar is big. Texas prides itself on being larger than any country in Europe except Russia; Madagascar is in the same league. It is also long: a thousand miles in length, 200 miles longer than California. In 1780 the island was divided among many small "kingdoms." There was only one core language—of Malay-Polynesian origin—but there were many dialects, of which Merina was perhaps the most common. Merina did not become the "preferred" dialect until after 1820, after which the London Missionary Society—sponsor of the dictionaries I have cited—helped create the Latin alphabet form of Merina. Another dialect was used as the basis for the Arabic alphabetization of the language, which was established in 1620 (and quite possibly texts from that period would tell us more about the name given to lemurs). Sibree, writing in 1893, after Merina had been made the standard dialect for the island, and writing from the capital in the middle of Madagascar, which was anyway the Merina heartland, may well have found that *bàbakòto* was the only name for the short-tailed lemur. Sonnerat was primarily quartered in the south, 500 miles away, long before Merina, with English and missionary help, had taken over the island. We see no reason to take Sibree's possibly correct linguistic judgment of 1893 as applicable to somewhere else in 1780.

Quine's charming extrapolation from the dictionary account of *indri* makes one think it was one of the first ever encounters between a Frenchman, or even a European, and an isolated islander. But thanks to its geographical position, Madagascar was inevitably in the path of world travel. The Indonesian stock that came to constitute the entire permanent population arrived about 700. The island played a significant role in Afro-Arab shipping routes. The Portuguese navigator Diogo Diaz got there in 1500. The most southern coastal city, now named Tôlanaro (or Faradofay), was settled in 1528. In 1642, as Fort-Dauphin, it became one of the essential outposts of the French East India Company. It was a natural choice for a port for Europeans traveling to India or the spice islands, conveniently located between the Cape and Ceylon. Etienne de Flacourt (1607–1660) used it as his base when writing his big *Histoire de la grande Isle de Madagascar* (1658, 1661). Much of the book was an account of French activities out of Fort-Dauphin (1642–1655), with the last 42 pages explaining why the East India Company lost money in its operations there. But it also served as the basis for a minimal French-Malagasy dictionary, which unfortunately seems to provide no information about lemurs (Ferrand 1905). So Madagascar was not exactly unknown territory when Sonnerat arrived in 1780. Sonnerat, a notable naturalist, would already have known a good deal about the fauna and flora of the island—and its language. He wrote up Madagascar on his way home from China, the Philippines, and Ceylon, which has its own kinds of lemur. He had a great interest in language, including in the account of his voyage a long chapter on spoken and written Tamil (also published separately in 1806). Not exactly the man to ask casually "What's that?" in French and to expect the Malagasy response, "look at him go!", to mean the name of the animal. The French had been settled at the southern end of Madagascar for a century and a half, and the region was infested with indri, some of which been tamed long before the arrival of Europeans. I imagine the curious Sonnerat getting off the boat and saying, "Take me to your lemur."

Certainly there are errors of understanding that do persist, but they contrast with what I call radical mistranslation. Here are two examples. Among the Malagasy words that now apply to lemurs we find *gidro* and *rajako* (or *jako*). A gidro is a smallish grey lemur. The word is derived from the Swahili *ngedere*, which means monkey. There are no lemurs in most of Africa, nor were there any monkeys native to Madagascar. So it was some sort of mistake when traders speaking Swahili called a lemur by the name of *ngedere*, but it was an error of classification, not of translation. As for *jako*, it too, ought strictly to apply only to monkeys. Why? Because Richardson (1885) tells us that an English sea captain had a pet monkey that escaped, and the sailors ran after it, calling it by name. "Jack! Jack!" they cried, and the name stuck.

11

Language, Truth, and Reason

This essay was written for a collection of papers about rationality and relativism edited by Martin Hollis and Steven Lukes. Both were advocates of a sensible and sensitive rationalism and disliked the increasingly relativist tendencies of the time (1980). Edinburgh had recently become the most threatening well-argued English-language power base for relativism in epistemology. The Edinburgh School, led by Barry Barnes and David Bloor, had a "strong programme in the sociology of knowledge" that cheerfully avowed that it was relativist. Lukes and Hollis arranged their contributors from left to right, the most relativist at the beginning of the book, and the most rationalist at the end. A new paper by Bloor and Barnes came first. I was perhaps disingenuous to be surprised when I found that my own paper was placed as the second most relativist contribution.

This is the first piece in which I took up the idea of a "style of reasoning" that I first encountered in 1978, in Pisa, listening to a paper by the senior historian of science, Alistair Crombie. He himself did not bring out his gigantic three-volume study of "styles" until 1994, but I was able to read a good deal of it many years before. Chapter 12 is a more systematic development of these ideas.

I wish to pose a relativist question from within the heartland of rationality. It is not about the confrontation between science and alien cultures, for it comes out of our own scientific tradition. It does not rehearse the Kuhnian stories of revolution, replacement, and incommensurability, but speaks chiefly of evolution and accumulation. Its sources are not hermeneutics but the canonical writings of positivism. Far from invoking "the dogma of the dualism of scheme and reality" from which, according to Donald Davidson, "we get conceptual relativity," it may well learn a trick from Davidson himself (Davidson 1974).

159

I start from the fact that there have been different styles of scientific reasoning. The wisest of the Greeks admired Euclidean thought. The best minds of the seventeenth century held that the experimental method put knowledge on a new footing. At least part of every modern social science deploys some statistics. Such examples bring to mind different styles of reasoning with different domains. Each has surfaced and attained maturity in its own time, in its own way.

An inane subjectivism may say that whether p is a reason for q depends on whether people have got around to reasoning that way or not. I have the subtler worry that whether or not a proposition is as it were up for grabs, as a candidate for being true-or-false, depends on whether we have ways to reason about it. The style of thinking that befits the sentence helps fix its sense and determines the way in which it has a positive direction pointing to truth or to falsehood. If we continue in this vein, we may come to fear that the rationality of a style of reasoning is all too built-in. The propositions on which the reasoning bears mean what they do just because that way of reasoning can assign them a truth value. Is reason, in short, all too self-authenticating?

My worry is about truth-or-falsehood. Consider Hamlet's maxim, that nothing's either good or bad but thinking makes it so. If we transfer this to truth and falsehood, it is ambiguous between (*a*) nothing which is true is true, and nothing which is false is false, but thinking makes it so, and (*b*) nothing's either true-or-false but thinking makes it so. It is (*b*) that preoccupies me. My relativist worry is, to repeat, that the sense of a proposition p, the way in which it points to truth or falsehood, hinges on the style of reasoning appropriate to p. Hence we cannot criticize that style of reasoning as a way of getting to p or to not-p, because p simply is that proposition whose truth value is determined in this way.

The distinction between (*a*) and (*b*) furnishes a distinction between subjectivity and relativity. Let (*a*) be subjectivism: by thinking, we might make something true or make it false. Let (*b*) be the kind of relativity that I address in this paper: by thinking, new candidates for truth and falsehood may be brought into being. Many of the recent but already classical philosophical discussions of such topics as incommensurability, indeterminacy of translation, and conceptual schemes seem to me to discuss truth where they ought to be considering truth-or-falsehood. Hence bystanders, hoping to learn from philosophers, have tended to discuss subjectivity rather than relativity. For my part, I have no doubt that our discoveries are "objective," simply because the styles of reasoning that we employ determine what counts as objectivity. My worry is that the very candidates for truth or falsehood have no existence independent of the styles of reasoning that settle what it is to be true or false in their domain.

Styles of Reasoning

It is not the case that *nothing's* either true or false but thinking makes it so. Plenty of things that we say need no reasons. That is the core of the discredited philosophical doctrine of observation sentences, the boring utterances that crop up in almost any language, and which make radical translation relatively easy. Translation is hard when one gets to whole new ranges of possibility that make no sense for the favored styles of reasoning of another culture. It is there that ethnographers begin to have problems. Every people has generated its own peculiar styles. We are no different from others, except that we can see more clearly, from our own written record, the historical emergence of new styles of reasoning.

I take the word "style" from A. C. Crombie's title, *Styles of Scientific Thinking in the European Tradition* (1994). He concluded an anticipatory paper with the words:

> The active promotion and diversification of the scientific methods of late medieval and early modern Europe reflected the general growth of a research mentality in European society, a mentality conditioned and increasingly committed by its circumstances to expect and to look actively for problems to formulate and solve, rather than for an accepted consensus without argument. The varieties of scientific method so brought in to play may be distinguished as,
> (a) the simple postulation established in the mathematical sciences,
> (b) the experimental exploration and measurement of more complex observable relations,
> (c) the hypothetical construction of analogical models,
> (d) the ordering of variety by comparison and taxonomy,
> (e) the statistical analysis of regularities of populations and the calculus of probabilities, and
> (f) the historical derivation of genetic development.
>
> The first three of these methods concern essentially the science of individual regularities, and the second three the science of the regularities of populations ordered in space and time. (Crombie 1981, 284.)

Coincidentally, at the same conference to which Crombie read these words, Winifred Wisan (1981) presented a paper on "the emergence of a new scientific style." Both Crombie's and Wisan's papers were about Galileo, who has long been a favorite candidate for advancing a new style of thought. Sometimes words more dramatic than "style" are used, as when Althusser (1972, 185) wrote of Thales opening up a new continent, that of mathematics, Galileo opening up the continent of dynamics, and Marx that of history. But often the word "style" is chosen. It is to be found in Collingwood. Stephen Weinberg, the theoretical physicist, recalled Husserl speaking of a Galilean style for "making abstract models of the universe to which at least the physicists give a higher degree of reality than they accord the ordinary world of sensation" (Weinberg 1976, 28). Weinberg found it remarkable that this style should work, "for the universe does not seem to have been prepared with human beings in mind." The linguist Noam Chomsky picked up this remark, urging that "we have no present alternative to pursuing the 'Galilean style' in the natural sciences at least" (Chomsky 1980, 9).

Like T. S. Kuhn's "paradigm", the word "style" serves my four contemporary authors to point to something general in the history of knowledge. There are new modes of reasoning that have specific beginnings and trajectories of development. Even these four thinkers would surely not agree in carving up histories into styles. The historian will find many styles where Chomsky sees only one. Doubtless the very word "style" is suspect. It is cribbed from art critics and historians, who have not evolved a uniform connotation for the word. Nor would all their remarks about style tidily transfer to modes of reasoning. That is a problem that Wisan's paper begins to address. The success of the word "style," as an analytic term for the history of science, may depend on the reception of Crombie's immensely learned historical analysis. Use of a borrowed word needs detailed examples to flesh it out. Despite these reservations, I shall take the fact that these recent writers employ the word in similar ways as an excuse for not attempting my own exegesis here.

Arch-Rationalism

The existence of styles of reasoning does not immediately suggest relativism. Before elaborating the relativist worry sketched at the beginning of this chapter, I shall first state a rationalist position informed by a proper respect both for history and for the idiosyncrasies of ourselves and others. I shall call it arch-rationalism. (I, too, am an arch-rationalist most of the time.)

The arch-rationalist believes what right-thinking people have known all along. There are good and bad reasons. It has taken millennia to evolve systems of reasoning. By and large our Western tradition has contributed more to this progress than any other. We have often been narrow, blinkered, and insensitive to foreign insights. We have repressed our own deviant and original thinkers, condemning many to irretrievable oblivion. Some of our own once-favored styles of reasoning have turned out to be dead ends and others are probably on the way. However, new styles of reasoning will continue to evolve. So we shall not only find out more about nature, but we shall also learn new ways to reason about it. Maybe Paul Feyerabend's (1975) advocacy of anarchy, or at least dadaism, is right. To compel people to reason in approved ways is to limit us and our potentialities for novelty. Arch-rationalism is convinced that there are good and bad reasons, but since it does not commit us to any specific regimentation like that of formal logic or that of Karl Popper, it is fairly receptive to Feyeraband's imitation anarchy.

My arch-rationalist thinks that there is a fairly sharp distinction between reasons and the propositions they support. Reasons merely help us find out what is the case. The arch-rationalist wants to know how the world is. There are good and bad reasons for propositions about nature. They are not relative to anything. They do not depend on context. The arch-rationalist is not an imperialist about reason. Maybe there could be people who never reason nor deliberate at all. They tell jokes, make and break promises, feign insults and so forth, but they never reason. Just as statistical reasons had no force for the Greeks, so one imagines a people for whom none of our reasons for belief have force. On the other hand, the arch-rationalist is an optimist about human nature. We who value truth and reason do imagine that a truthless and unreasoning people would, if left alone, evolve truth and reason for themselves. They would in their own way acquire a taste for speculation about the diagonal of a square, for motion on the inclined plane, for the tracks of the planets, for the inner constitution of matter, the evolution of the species, the Oedipus complex, and amino acids.

The arch-rationalist not only grants that our kinds of truth and reason may not play as great a role in the life of other peoples as in our own culture; he may also be a romantic, hankering after a simpler, less reason-impregnated life. He will grant that our values are not inevitable, nor perhaps the noblest to which our species can aspire. But he cannot escape his own past. His admission of the historicity of our own styles of reasoning in no way makes it less objective. Styles of reasoning have histories, and some emerged sooner than others. Humankind has got better at reasoning. What ground for relativism could there be in all that?

Instead of challenging the assumptions of the arch-rationalist, I shall extract a hint of incoherence from his heartland, which is, in the end, positivism.

Positivism

Positivism is commonly taken to be a hard-headed antagonism to all forms of relativism. I shall create a question for the arch-rationalist from three aspects of positivism itself. I draw them from Auguste Comte, Moritz Schlick, and Michael Dummett, that is, the original positivist of the 1840s, the leader of the Vienna Circle in 1930, and the most gifted present exponent of one among that family of doctrines.

Comte. He was a historicist. His epistemology is a massive and almost unreadable account of human knowledge, a narrative of the human mind in which each intellectual innovation finds its own niche. One of his ideas is that a branch of knowledge acquires a "positivity" by the development of a new, positive, style of reasoning associated with it. He is none too clear what he means by "positive"; he sometimes says he chose the word chiefly because it had overtones of moral uplift in all European languages. A positive proposition is one that is by some means befitting the branch of knowledge to which it belongs. We may pun on his word: a positive proposition is one that has a direction, a truth value. It is no distortion to say that for Comte a class of positive propositions is a class of propositions that are up for grabs as true-or-false.

There are many aspects of Comte's thought from which one hastily withdraws—I refer both to questions of ideology and to issues of interest to analytic philosophers of science (his analysis of causation, for example). I draw attention only to the idea of a historical evolution of different styles of reasoning, each bringing in its train its own body of positive knowledge. Each finds its place in great tabular displays of the sciences that serve as pull-outs from his gigantic epistemological text, the *Cours de philosophie positive.* Comte did not think that the evolution of styles and of positive knowledges had come to an end. His life goal was the creation of a new positive science, sociology. This would require a new style of reasoning. He ill foresaw what this style would be, but his meta-conception of what he was doing was sound.

Schlick. One of the more memorable statements of logical positivism is Moritz Schlick's, "the meaning of a sentence is its method of verification" (1936, 361). Those words could not stand unmodified, because the Vienna Circle had succumbed to Gottlob Frege's dictum that meanings are definite, objective, and fixed. Schlick's maxim would imply that a change or advance in a method of verification would change the meanings of a sentence. Rather than give up the idea of meanings handed down from generation to generation, tranquil and unmodified, logical positivists revised Schlick's maxim again and again, although with no satisfactory outcome. (See Hacking 1975b, ch. 9, for an account of repeated failures.) But for Comte, or any other of those fortunate writers of 1840 not yet infected by Fregean theories of meaning, Schlick's statement would be just fine. It is precisely, for Comte, the methods of verification—the ways in which the positive truth values are to be established—that determine the content of a body of knowledge.

Dummett. In logic, a proposition that has a definite truth value, true or false, is called *bivalent.* Dummett's work has made philosophers think closely about bivalence (Dummett 1976). It was first inspired by a philosophical reconstruction of some of the thoughts behind intuitionist mathematics. In what is called a nonconstructive proof, one cannot exhibit the mathematical objects that are proved to exist. (So one might have a step in which one asserts that there is a prime number with a certain property, but be unable to say which prime number it is.) Nonconstructive proofs may also assume of a proposition that it is either true or false, without being able to show which truth value it has. Some philosophical mathematicians, including Dummett, have doubted whether such nonconstructive proofs are admissible.

Dummett is attracted to the following basis of his doubt. Whether or not a proposition is bivalent must depend upon its meaning. He wonders how we can confer meanings on statements in nonconstructive mathematics—meanings in virtue of which the statements are bivalent, although there is no known way to settle the truth values. It is we who, through our linguistic practices, are the sole source of the meanings of what we say.

How then can we confer a meaning on a statement, such that it is bivalent, when nothing we know how to do bears on the truth or the falsehood of the statement? Maybe statements of nonconstructive mathematics acquire bivalence only as we perfect means of determining their truth values or exhibiting the mathematical objects of which they speak?

Although this subtle question arose in sharp form in the intuitionist critique of classical mathematics, Dummett extends it to other forms of discourse. Many statements about the past cannot now be settled by any practicable means. Are they bivalent? Might bivalence recede into the past as historical data become irrevocably erased? Dummett does not claim that his worries are conclusive, nor does he expect parallel answers for every kind of discourse. One might, on reflection, come out for bivalence in the case of history, but reject it for nonconstructive mathematics.

Positive and bivalence. I have spoken of being true-or-false, and have used Comte's word "positive." Is this the same idea as bivalence? Not as I shall use the words. Being positive is a less strong characteristic than bivalence. Outside mathematics, I suspect that whether a statement is bivalent or not is an abstraction imposed by logicians to facilitate their analysis of deductive argument forms. It is a noble abstraction, but it is a consequence of art, not nature. In the speculative sciences that concern me in this paper, the interesting sentences are the ones that are up for grabs as true or false—ones for which we believe we have methods that will determine the truth values. The applications of these methods may require as yet unimagined technological innovation. Moreover, as we find out more about the world, we find out that many of our questions no longer make sense. Bivalence is not the right concept for science. Allow me a couple of examples to point to the distinction required.

At the time of Pierre-Simon de Laplace it was very sensible to think that there are particles of caloric, the substance of heat, that have repulsive forces that decay rapidly with distance. Relying on this hypothesis, Laplace solved many of the outstanding problems about sound. Propositions about the rate of extinction of the repulsive force of caloric were up for grabs as true or false, and one knew how to obtain information bearing on the question. Laplace had an excellent estimate of the rate of extinction of the repulsive force, yet it turns out that the whole idea is wrongheaded. I would say that Laplace's sentences once were "positive." They were never bivalent. Conversely, James Clerk Maxwell once said that some propositions about the relative velocity of light were intrinsically incapable of determination, yet a few years after he said that A. A. Michelson had invented the technology to give precise answers to Maxwell's questions. I would say that the sentences of interest to Maxwell had positivity when he uttered them, but were bivalent only after a transformation in technology—a transformation whose success depends on delicate experimental details about how the world works.

In short, Comte's "positive" is drawing attention to a less demanding concept than Dummett's "bivalent". Yet the two are connected, and so are the thoughts of both writers. Dummett says: not bivalent unless we have a proof of the truth value, or a known sure-fire method for generating the proof. Comte says: not positive, not in the running for being true-or-false, until there is some style of reasoning that will bear on the question.

Comte, Schlick, and Dummett are no more relativist than Crombie or Chomsky. Yet a positivist train of thought, combined with an emphasis on styles of reasoning, has the germ of relativism. If positivity is consequent upon a style of reasoning, then a range of possibilities depends upon that style. They would not be possibilities, candidates for truth or falsehood, unless that style were in existence. The existence of the style arises from historical events. Hence, although whichever propositions are true may depend on the data, the fact that they are candidates for being true is a consequence of a historical event. Conversely, the rationality of a style of reasoning as a way of bearing on the truth of a class of propositions does not seem open for independent criticism, because the very sense of what can be established by that style depends upon the style itself.

Is that a nasty circle?

I shall proceed as follows. First, I observe that by reasoning I don't mean logic. I mean the very opposite, for logic is the preservation of truth, while a style of reasoning is what brings in the possibility of truth or falsehood. Then I separate my idea of a style of reasoning from the incommensurability of Kuhn and Feyerabend, and from the indeterminacy of translation urged by Quine. Then I examine Davidson's fundamental objection to the supposition that there are alternative ways of thinking. He may refute subjectivity, as I understand it, but not relativity. The key distinction throughout the following discussion is the difference between truth-and-falsehood as opposed to truth. A second important idea is the looseness of fit between those propositions that have a sense for almost all human beings regardless of reasoning, and those that get a sense only within a style of reasoning.

Induction, Deduction

Neither deductive logic nor induction occur on Crombie's list. How strange, for are they not said to be the basis of science? It is instructive that no list like Crombie's would include them. The absence reminds us that styles of reasoning create the possibility for truth and falsehood. Deduction and induction merely preserve it.

We now understand deduction as that mode of inference that preserves truth. It cannot pass from true premises to a false conclusion. The nature of induction is more controversial. The word has been used in many ways. There is an important tradition represented alike by the philosopher C. S. Peirce and the statistician Jerzy Neyman: induction is that mode of argument that preserves truth most of the time. (Hacking 1980a shows how Neyman's theory of testing hypothesis connects with Peirce's theory of probable inference.)

Deduction and induction were important human discoveries. But they play little role in the scientific method, no more than the once revered syllogism. They are devices for jumping from truth to truth or from truth to probable truth. Not only will they give us no original contingent truth from which to jump, but also they take for granted the class of sentences that assert possibilities of truth or falsehood. That is why they do not occur in Crombie's list. In deduction and induction alike, truth plays the purely formal role of a counter on an abacus. It matters not what truth is, when we employ the mechanics of the model theory of modern logicians. Their machine works well so long as we suppose that the class of sentences that have truth values is already given. (Or, in the case of intuitionist logic, one supposes that the class of sentences that may, through proof, acquire truth values is already given.) Induction equally assumes that the class of possible truths is predetermined. Styles of reasoning of the sort described by Crombie do something different. When they come into being they generate new classes of possibilities.

Incommensurability and the Indeterminacy of Translation

Philosophers have recently given us two doctrines that pull in opposite directions. Both seem to use the idea of a conceptual scheme, a notion that goes back at least to Kant, but whose modern nominalist version is due to W. V. Quine. He says that a conceptual scheme is a set of sentences held to be true. He uses the metaphor of core and periphery. Sentences at the core have a kind of permanence and are seldom relinquished, while those on the periphery are more empirical and more readily given up in the light of "recalcitrant experience."

My talk of styles of reasoning does not mesh well with Quine's idea of a conceptual scheme (Quine 1960, ch. 2). In his opinion, two schemes differ when some substantial number of core sentences of one scheme are not held to be true in another scheme. A style of reasoning, in contrast, is concerned with truth-or-falsehood. Two parties, agreeing to the same styles of reasoning, may well totally disagree on the upshot, one party holding for true what the other party rejects. Styles of reasoning may determine possible truth values, but, unlike Quine's schemes, are not characterized by assignments of truth values. It is to be expected, then, that Quine's application of the idea of a conceptual scheme will not coincide with my idea of styles of reasoning.

Quine's most memorable thesis is the indeterminacy of translation. Let L and M be languages spoken by two truly disparate communities. Quine holds that there are indefinitely many possible but incompatible translations between L and M. No matter how much speakers of L and M might converse, there is in principle no way of settling on a definitely right translation. This is not a matter of settling on nuances; Quine means that you could take a sentence s of L and translate it by one system of translation into p of M, and translate it by another system into q of M, and p and q would, in M, be held to be incompatible.

As we shall see in the next section, Donald Davidson has noticed that the notion of conceptual scheme does not ride well with the indeterminacy of translation. For how are we to say that speakers of L have a scheme different from we who speak M? We must first pick out the true sentences from the core of the scheme of L, and show that many of these translate into sentences of M that we who speak M hold to be false. But what is to assure that this is the right translation? When translating, there is a strong instinct to render central doctrines of L as main truths of M. Once you focus on truth rather than truth-or-falsehood, you begin a chain of considerations that call in question the very idea of a conceptual scheme.

The thesis of indeterminacy of translation pulls in one direction and the idea of incommensurability pulls in another. We owe incommensurability to Kuhn and Feyerabend. For one slightly unusual version of this famous notion, see Feyerabend (1978, 65–70). The idea is that disparate systems of thought are not mutually expressible. Kuhn has tended to make the idea fit commonplace situations, while Feyerabend emphasizes the extreme. Thus Feyerabend's favorite example of incommensurability is the break between the cosmologies of archaic and classical Greece. Kuhn, in contrast, comes back to the idea of "no common measure" in the original meaning of the word, and applies it to more everyday "advances" in knowledge. When there has been a scientific revolution, the new science may address new problems and employ new concepts. There is no way of settling whether the new science does its job better than the old one, because they do different jobs. Kuhn finds this sort of incommensurability in all sorts of revolutions that strike the outsider as minor, while Feyerabend focuses on big shifts in human thought. Both writers had at one time suggested that incommensurability should be understood in terms of schemes and translation. Incommensurability meant that there would simply be no way of translating from one scheme to another. Thus this idea pulls in a direction exactly opposite to Quine's. Indeterminacy says there are too many translations between schemes, while incommensurability says there are none at all.

Would either the Kuhnian or the Feyerabendian idea of incommensurability apply if styles of reasoning were to supersede each other? The Kuhnian "no common measure" does not apply in any straightforward way, because when we reason differently, there is no expectation of common measure of the sort that successive Kuhnian paradigms invite. Hence it is to the more extreme, Feyerabendian, use of the term that we must look. That is surely the popular conception of incommensurability: the inability of one body of thought to understand another.

I do admit that there is a real phenomenon of disparate ways of thinking. Some styles of reasoning have been so firmly displaced that we cannot even recognize their objects. The renaissance medical, alchemical, and astrological doctrines of resemblance and similitude are well-nigh incomprehensible. One does not find our modern notions of evidence deployed in those arcane pursuits. There is very little truth in all that hermetic writing, and to understand it one cannot search out the core of truth that meshes with our beliefs. Yet that stuff may not be best described as incommensurable with our modern chemistry, medicine, and astronomy. It is not that the propositions match ill with our modern sciences, so much as that the way propositions are proposed and defended is entirely alien to us.

You can perfectly well learn hermetic lore, and when you do so, you end up talking the language of Paracelsus, possibly in translation. What you learn is not systems of translation, but chains of reasoning which would have little sense if one were not re-creating the thought of one of those magi. What we have to learn is not what they took for true, but what they took for true-or-false. (For example, that mercury salve might be good for syphilis because mercury is signed by the planet Mercury, which signs the marketplace where syphilis is contracted.)

Understanding the sufficiently strange is a matter of recognizing new possibilities for truth-or-falsehood, and of learning how to conduct other styles of reasoning that bear on those new possibilities. The achievement of understanding is not exactly a difficulty of translation, although foreign styles will make translation difficult. It is certainly not a matter of designing translations which preserve as much truth as possible, because what is true-or-false in one way of talking may not make much sense in another until one has learned how to reason in a new way. One kind of understanding is learning how to reason. When we encounter old or alien texts we have to translate them, but it is wrong to focus on that aspect of translation that merely produces sentences of English for sentences of the other language. With such a limited focus, one thinks of charitably trying to get the old text to say as much truth as possible. But, even after Paracelsus is translated into modern German, one still has to learn how he reasoned in order to understand him. Since the idea of incommensurability has been so closely tied to translation rather than reasoning, I do not use it here.

The indeterminacy of translation is an equally wrong idea. It is empirically empty, because we know that unequivocal translation evolves between any two communities in contact. As observed in the previous chapter, anecdotal counterexamples to this assertion do not stand up to scrutiny. Indeterminacy is the wrong theoretical notion, because it starts from an idea of truth-preserving matching of sentences. In fact, the possibilities available in one language are not there in the other. To get them into the second language one has to learn a way of reasoning and, when that has been done, there is no problem of translation at all, let alone indeterminacy.

There is perfect commensurability, and no indeterminacy of translation, in those boring domains of "observations" that we share with all people as people. Where we as people have branched off from others as a people, we find new interests, and a looseness of fit between their and our common-places. Translation of truths is irrelevant. Communication of ways to think is what matters.

Conceptual Schemes

In his famous paper "On the Very Idea of a Conceptual Scheme," Donald Davidson (1974) argues more against incommensurability than indeterminacy, but he is chiefly against the idea of a conceptual scheme that gives sense to either. He provides "an underlying methodology of interpretation" such that "we could not be in a position" to judge "that others had concepts or beliefs different from our own." He makes plain that he does not reach this result by postulating "a neutral ground, or a common coordinate system" between schemes. It is the notion of a scheme itself to which he is opposed. He rejects a "dogma of dualism between scheme and reality" from which we derive the bogey of "conceptual relativity, and of truth relative to a scheme."

Davidson distinguishes two claims. Total translatability between schemes may be impossible, or there may be only partial untranslatability. Even if we do not follow the intricacies of his argument, nor even accept its premises, we can, like Davidson, dismiss the idea of total untranslatability. As a matter of brute fact, all human languages are fairly easily partially translatable. The fact is closely connected with what I said earlier, that there is a common human core of verbal performances connected with what people tend to notice around them. But I said that there is a looseness of fit between that broad base of shared humanity and the interesting things that people like to talk about. That looseness leaves some space for incommensurability. It is not only the topics of discussion that may vary from group to group, but what counts as a point of saying something. Yet Davidson counters there too, and mounts a magnificent attack against even the notion of partial untranslatability between groups of people. Since in fact even partial untranslatability is chiefly a matter of coming to share the interest of another, and since lots of travelers are pretty sympathetic people, interests do get shared, so we should welcome an argument against partial untranslatability too. Yet since Davidson's argument may seem founded upon a lack of concern for alternative interests, we may fear his premises while we accept his conclusions. My diagnosis is that, like

Quine, he assumes that a conceptual scheme is defined in terms of what counts as true, rather than of what counts as true-or-false.

Truth Versus Truth-Or-Falsehood

Davidson concluded his argument against relativity with the words, "Of course the truth of sentences remains relative to a language, but that is as objective as can be." Earlier, he rightly stated what is wrong with the idea of making a sentence true:

> *Nothing* makes sentences and theories true: not experience, not surface irritations [he there alluded to Quine], not the world . . . *That* experience takes a certain course, that our skin is warmed or punctured . . . these facts, if we like to talk that way, make sentences and theories true. But this point is better made without mention of facts. The sentence "my skin is warm" is true if and only if my skin is warm. Hence there is no reference to a fact, a world, an experience, or a piece of evidence. (Davidson 1974, 16)

Davidson's example, "my skin is warm," serves me well. I urge a distinction between statements that may be made in any language, and which require no style of reasoning, and statements whose sense depends upon a style of reasoning. Davidson writes as if all sentences were of the former class. I agree that "my skin is warm" is of that class. When I once looked for the best example of a sense-datum sentence to be actually published in the annals of real science, I hit upon precisely this sentence, or rather, "my skin is warmed." It begins Sir William Herschel's investigations of 1800, which are said to commence the theory of radiant heat. He noticed that by using filters of some colors his skin was warmed, while in using other colors he had much light but little heat (Hacking 1983a, 171).

Herschel went on to pose a theory of invisible rays of heat, a theory that we now call correct, although his own experiments made him give it up. In the course of this reasoning he abandoned the following sentence: "The heat which has the refrangibility of the red rays is occasioned by the light of those rays." We can certainly write out a truth condition of the form "*s* is true if and only if *p*" for this sentence. But there arises a problem for the sufficiently foreign translator. It is not that words like "ray" and "refrangible" are mildly theoretical and the translator may have no such notions in his vocabulary. If another culture has acquired the styles of reasoning enumerated by Crombie, it can perfectly well learn Herschel's physics from the ground up—that is just what I do in making sense of Herschel's text. The problem is that the sufficiently foreign person will not have Herschel's kind of sentence as the sort of thing that can be true-or-false, because the ways of reasoning that bear on it are unknown. To exaggerate the case, say the translator is Archimedes. I do not choose him at random, for he wrote a great tract on burning mirrors and was a greater scientist than Herschel. Yet I say he would not be able to effect a translation until he had caught up on some scientific method.

I should repeat my opposition to usual versions of incommensurability. It is not that Herschel's science had some Newtonian principles about rays and refrangibility that determined the meaning of sentences in which those words occur, and so those sentences could not have the same meaning in another theory. On the contrary, Herschel's sentences were fairly immune to change in theory. They were up for grabs as true or false in 1800; Herschel thought first that a crucial sentence is true and later held it to be false; many years later the world agreed on the truth of the sentence. Herschel, then, first grabbed the right end of the stick and then grabbed the wrong one. My claim about a translator less well placed than Archimedes is that until he learns how to reason more like Herschel, there are no ends of a stick to grab.

Schemes Without Dogma

"Truth of sentences," writes Davidson, "remains relative to a language, but that is as objective as can be." I claim that for part of our language, and perhaps as part of any language, being true-or-false is a property of sentences only because we reason about those sentences in certain ways. Subjectivists put their worries in the form of saying that with different customs we could "rightly" take some propositions for true while at present we take them for false. Davidson has dealt sharply with all such formulations. But he has left a space for a relativist fear. The relativist ought to say that there might be whole other categories of truth-or-falsehood than ours.

Perhaps I am proposing a version of the conceptual scheme idea. Quine's conceptual schemes are sets of sentences held for true. Mine would be sets of sentences that are candidates for truth or falsehood. Does such a notion fall into the "dogma of scheme and reality" that Davidson resents? I do not think so. The idea of a style of reasoning is as internal to what we think and say as the Davidsonian form, "*s* is true if and only if *p*," is internal to a language. *A style is not a scheme that confronts reality.* I did speak earlier of styles of reasoning being applied to data and to the formation of data. But data are uttered and are subject to Davidsonian treatment. There is much to be said about the neglected field of study of experimental science, but it has nothing much to do with scheme/reality. My own work on the subject (Hacking 1983a) tries to show how experiment has a life of its own, unrelated to theories or schemes.

Anarcho-Rationalism

This chapter makes two assertions and draws some inferences from them. Each assertion and every inference is in need of clarification. To list them is to show how much more must be done.

(1) There are different styles of reasoning. Many of these are discernible in our own history. They emerge at definite points and have distinct trajectories of maturation. Some die out, others are still going strong.

(2) Propositions of the sort that necessarily require reasoning to be substantiated have a positivity, a being true-or-false, only in consequence of the styles of reasoning in which they occur.

(3) Hence many categories of possibility, of what may be true or false, are contingent upon historical events, namely the development of certain styles of reasoning.

(4) It may then be inferred that there are other categories of possibility than have emerged in our tradition.

(5) We cannot reason as to whether alternative systems of reasoning are better or worse than ours, because the propositions to which we reason get their sense only from the method of reasoning employed. The propositions have no existence independent of the ways of reasoning towards them.

This chain of reflections does not lead to subjectivity. It does not imply that some proposition, with a content independent of reasoning, could be held to be true, or to be false, according to the mode of reasoning we adopt. Yet this defeat of subjectivity seems hollow, because the propositions that are objectively found to be true are determined as true by styles of reasoning for which in principle there can be no external justification. A justification would be an independent way of showing that the style gets at the truth, but there is no characterization of the truth over and above what is reached by the styles of reason itself.

Can there not be a meta-reason justifying a style of reason? Can one not, for example, appeal to success? It need not be success in generating technology, although that does matter. Nor is it to be success in getting at the truth, for that would be circular. There can, however, be noncircular successes in truth-related matters. For example, following Imre Lakatos (1978, chs. 1, 2), one might revamp Popper's method of conjecture and refutation, urging that a methodology of research programs constantly opens up new things to think about. I have quoted Chomsky giving a similar meta-reason. On his analysis of the Galilean style, it has not only worked remarkably well, but also, in the natural sciences at least, we have no alternative but to go on using that style, although, of course, in the future it may not work. Although Chomsky does not make the distinction, his meta-reason is less that Galileo's style continues to find out the truth about the universe than that it poses new kinds of probing and answering. It has produced an open-ended dialogue. That might terminate in the face of a nature that ceased to participate in ways that the Galilean can make sense of. We know it might cease to cater to our interests, but at present (says Chomsky) we have no alternative.

Chomsky is saying that if we want to engage in certain pursuits (call them the natural sciences or even the pursuit of truth in our tradition), we must reason with our reasons. Other styles of reasoning may occur; some are current. Other people may have other interests. We ought at least to be cautious, in the social sciences, in looking for other styles of reasoning. Such considerations may lead the arch-rationalist to be a stick-in-the-mud, but since relativity does not imply subjectivity, he can carry on doing what we do with few qualms.

Some arch-rationalists may even find themselves agreeing that an anarcho-rationalism I have learned from Feyerabend is appealing. Our overall interests in truth and reason may well be served by letting other styles of reason evolve in their own ways, unfettered by a more imperial kind of rationalism. But that does not mean to say that I, as an anarcho-rationalist, will take up something so recently killed off in our own tradition as homoeopathic medicine and its appeal to similitudes. That is for others (though if they look healthier than me, I might join up). Anarcho-rationalism is tolerance for other people combined with the discipline of one's own standards of truth and reason. The anarcho-rationalist is at home with the sentiment expressed by Sartre (1980, March 10, 93) in his last interview:

> C'est ça ma tradition, je n'en ai pas d'autre.
> Ni la tradition orientale, ni la tradition juive.
> Elles me manquent par mon historicité.

12

"Style" for Historians and Philosophers

This essay is a substantial development of the ideas of Chapter 11. It was first presented in Corfu in May 1991, at a conference on "Recent Trends in the Historiography of Science," which benefited from the wonderful leadership and hospitality of Kostas Gavroglu and Aristide Baltas.

Relations between the history and the philosophy of the sciences are often debated and sometimes contested. My interest here is collaboration. I shall describe a new analytical tool that can be used by historians and by philosophers for different purposes. It is a specialized, indeed technical, version of an idea often used or abused elsewhere: "style." The historian of science A. C. Crombie had been writing about "styles of scientific thinking in the European tradition" since the mid-1970s, and his work finally came to fruition in three volumes (1994). I heard him lecture on the topic in 1978, and in chapter 11 adapted the idea to metaphysics and epistemology, changing the name slightly to "styles of reasoning." The two uses, by historians and philosophers, are complementary but to some extent asymmetric. The historian may conclude that the philosopher's use of the tool is bunk, irrelevant to understanding the past. But the philosopher needs the history, for if the tool does not provide a coherent and enlightening ordering of the record, then it has no more place in sound philosophy than would any other fantasy.

Crombie's idea is less about the content of the sciences than about their methods. The focus is on how we find out, not on what we find out. It is out of step with present fashion, which teaches us so much about the intricate details of incidents and relationships. It derives from a conception of the entire Western scientific tradition; we cannot help but recall that

Spengler (1918, 1922) too spoke of the "Western style." His use of the word *Stil* is so generous that his translator says, "The word *Stil* will therefore not necessarily be always rendered 'style'" (1926, 108). Be prepared, however, for surprise translations. For example, *die Expansionskraft der abendländischen Stil* (1922, 55) becomes, in translation, "the expansion power of the Western Soul" (1926, 46). Crombie's ambitious analysis should remind us more, however, of the cabinet than of Spengler's bandstand, for it draws upon a lavish array of citations spanning three millennia, plus dense references to secondary studies—the lifetime collection of an erudite.

One root source is, of course, the History of Art. Arnold Davidson (2001c) traces the passage from art history to epistemology. Phrases like "style of thinking" or "reasoning" occur naturally enough without specialist connotations. This is to be expected with a word like "style" that already has so many connotations. In chapter 11 I mentioned the cosmologist Stephen Weinberg and the theoretical grammarian Noam Chomsky. Both authors attribute their idea of a Galilean style of reasoning to Husserl. I. B. Cohen gave a more detailed account of the same kind of reasoning; he called it "the Newtonian style," a way of combining "two levels of ontology," the mathematical and the measurable.

> A case could perhaps be made out [he added] that this style is Galilean or Keplerian, rather than an invention of Newton's. In fact, Edmund Husserl has written at large concerning the "Galilean" style, essentially the mode of modern mathematical physics; from this point of view, the Newtonian style can be seen as a highly advanced and very much refined development of the Galilean. (Cohen 1982, 49).

Cohen and Weinberg were referring to §9 of Husserl (1970, part 2). In this very long section Husserl certainly did write, as Cohen puts it, "at large" about Galileo as the discoverer of a new kind of science, but I do not think that he used the words "Galilean style." In fact, I do not think he used the word "style" in the way any of those three writers do, or as I do. For example, the word is used six times on one page (Husserl 1970, 31), twice with emphasis in the original German, but in each case to refer to a feature of the "empirically intuited world."

Literary critics have long distinguished a "generalizing" and a "personalizing" use of the word "style." There is a Balzacian style and there is Balzac's style. Equally, in swimming, there is the Australian crawl and freestyle, as opposed to the style of Patti Gonzalez, that can be imitated but is inimitably hers. It is entirely natural to talk of the style of an individual scientist, research group, programme or tradition. Kostas Gavroglu, although taking the word "style" from myself and by derivation from Crombie, has quite legitimately put the word to its personalizing usage, for he contrasts the "style of reasoning" of two low temperature laboratories, and indeed of two men, Dewar and Kaemerlingh Onnes (Gavroglu 1990). Crombie and I instead intend something more attuned to Cohen, Chomsky, and Weinberg than to Gavroglu. And even if we put aside all obviously personalizing uses of "styles" of thinking, there are plenty of generalizing uses in the history or philosophy of science that differ from Crombie's. For example, Freeman Dyson's third Gifford lecture "is concerned with the history of science. It describes two contrasting styles in science, one welcoming diversity and the other deploring it, one trying to diversify and the other trying to unify" (Dyson 1988, 13).

For historians and philosophers, the most famous instance of another idea of style is in Ludwik Fleck's fundamental book of 1935, subtitled *Introduction to the Theory of the Thought Style and the Thought Collective* (Fleck 1979). By a thought style Fleck meant something less sweeping than Crombie, more restricted to a discipline or field of inquiry. Nevertheless, a thought style is impersonal, the possession of an enduring social unit, the "thought collective." It is "the entirety of intellectual preparedness or readiness for one particular way of seeing and acting and no other" (Fleck 1979, 64). Fleck intended to limn what it was possible to think; a *Denkstil* makes possible certain ideas and renders others unthinkable. Crombie and I fix on an extreme end of the spectrum of such permissible uses, and accordingly enumerate very few styles of thinking or reasoning. This is partly because our unit of analysis is very large in scope. There are many other units of analysis comparable to Fleck's, and which also deal with what it is possible to say. They are thoroughly impersonal, but more restricted in scope, in time and in space. For many purposes they may be, for that very reason, more instructive than something along the lines of Spengler or Cohen or Weinberg and Chomsky. We think for example of Michel Foucault's episteme and discursive formation, or Nicholas Jardine's not unrelated "questions" (Jardine 1991).

I prefer to speak of styles of (scientific) "reasoning" rather than Crombie's "thinking." This is partly because thinking is too much in the head for my liking. Reasoning is done in public as well as in private: by thinking, yes, but also by talking and arguing and showing. This difference between Crombie and myself is only one of emphasis. He writes that "the history of science has been the history of argument"—and not just thinking. We agree that there are many doings in both inferring and arguing. Crombie's book describes a lot of them, and his very title happily ends not with science but with "Sciences and Arts." He has a lot to say about architecture, clock making, and the doctrine that "knowing is making." Nevertheless, there may still be a touch too much thinking for my pleasure. He titled a 1988 prospectus for his book, "Designed in the mind" (Crombie 1988). Does one not hear the resonance of Crombie's somewhat Koyréan origins? Even my word "reasoning" has too much to do with mind and mouth and keyboard; it does not, I regret, sufficiently invoke the manipulative hand and the attentive eye. Crombie's last word in the title of his book is "Arts;" mine would be "Artisan."

But there's more to my preference for reasoning over thinking than that. It recalls me to my roots—I am talking about what Aristotle called rational, even if my analysis is better suited to the temper of our times than his. "Reasoning" recalls the *Critique of Pure Reason.* My study is a continuation of Kant's project of explaining how objectivity is possible. He proposed preconditions for the string of sensations to become objective experience. He also wrote much about science, but only after his day was it grasped how communal an activity is the growth of knowledge. Kant did not think of scientific reason as a historical and collective product. We do. My styles of reasoning, eminently public, are part of what we need to understand what we mean by objectivity. This is not because styles are objective (that is, that we have found the best impartial ways to get at the truth), but because they have settled what it is to be objective (truths of certain sorts are what we obtain by conducting certain sorts of investigations, answering to certain standards).

Crombie does not expressly define "style of scientific thinking in the European tradition." He explains it ostensively by pointing to six styles that he then describes in painstaking detail. "We may distinguish in the classical scientific movement six styles of scientific thinking, or methods of scientific inquiry and demonstration. Three styles or methods were developed in the investigation of individual regularities and three in the investigation of the regularities of populations ordered in space and time" (Crombie 1988, 10). These six are (I combine and select wording from several of his expositions):

(a) The simple method of postulation exemplified by the Greek mathematical sciences.

(b) The deployment of experiment both to control postulation and to explore by observation and measurement.

(c) Hypothetical construction of analogical models.

(d) Ordering of variety by comparison and taxonomy.

(e) Statistical analysis of regularities of populations, and the calculus of probabilities.

(f) The historical derivation of genetic development.

I am glad that he includes mathematics among the sciences, which is where they belong, whatever some of my recent philosophical predecessors may have thought. I do not mean that mathematics is empirical—only that it is a science. Note that styles do not determine a content, a specific science. We do tend to restrict "mathematics" to what we establish by mathematical reasoning, but aside from that, there is only a very modest correlation between items (a) through (f) and a possible list of fields of knowledge. A great many inquiries use several styles. For example, the fifth, statistical style is now used, in various guises, in every kind of investigation, including some branches of pure mathematics. The paleontologist uses experimental methods to carbon date and order the old bones. The "modern synthesis" of evolutionary theory is among other things a synthesis of taxonomic and historico-genetic thought.

I start with a canonical list of styles descriptively determined by a historian who, whatever his axes, is not grinding any of mine. As a philosopher I need to discover, from his examples, at least a necessary condition for there being such a "style." We are not bound to accept Crombie's preferred descriptions, nor to conclude with exactly his arrangement of styles. I shall list three related reasons why we may diverge and then give two examples.

(1) Crombie offers an account of the "classical scientific movement" and tailors his characterizations to the long period of time in which that movement was formed and firmed up. He tends to leave a given style at the date when it is securely installed. His discussions of mathematics end with Kepler's revivals of Greek mathematics. His exposition of the first three styles dries up at the end of the seventeenth century. Only the final style is developed for the nineteenth century, with Darwin being the major figure. But I as philosopher am decidedly Whiggish. The history that I want is the history of the present. That is Michel Foucault's phrase, implying that we recognize and distinguish historical objects in order to illumine our own predicaments. Hence I might modify Crombie's list not to revise his history but to view it from here.

(2) Crombie's (a) to (f) is itself a historical progression, each style beginning later than its predecessor in the list, and his presentation of each successive style concludes closer to the present than his descriptions of preceding styles. What strikes me, however, is the ahistorical point that all six styles are alive and quite well right now. I am writing about what styles of scientific reasoning do for us. What is important now may be different from what was important in the early days.

(3) Crombie did not intend to write down an exhaustive list of mutually exclusive styles. He transcribed what he found central and enduring in the formative period of the Western vision. Quite aside from any styles that we might properly want to call scientific, and which evolved largely outside the West, there might also be yet earlier styles of "science" found, say, in records of Babylonian computations, and not to be identified with a mere anticipation of (a). And certainly new styles may have evolved after the "classical" events Crombie recounts, just as new styles of reasoning may emerge in the future. There could also be mergings of two or more styles. I don't mean the truism that we commonly use more than one style in any modern inquiry, but that there may have evolved a style that is essentially composed of two classical styles, not a mixture but a compound, in the chemist's sense of the word—a new intellectual substance.

Now I turn to two examples. As a philosopher of mathematics, I see proof where Crombie sees postulation. His first style emphasizes the Greek search for first principles. It is there that he brings in Greek medicine, with its battle between empirics and dogmatists. We meet Aristotle during Crombie's discussion of (a)—even when the Stagyrite is canonizing what later becomes the taxonomic style (d). That is correct history, putting (a) and its contemporary correlatives first, in their place. Yet there is no doubt that what individuates ancient mathematics for us is that we recognize proof and to a limited extent calculation. Wilbur Knorr speculatively ordered segments of actual and lost texts by the development of proof procedures (Knorr 1975). Mathematics has the astonishing power to establish truths about the world independently of experience. That is the phenomenon that so astounded Socrates in the Meno, and has so vexed every serious epistemologist of mathematical science ever since. I will want my account of the mathematical style to help understand that phenomenon. Hence my emphases will differ from Crombie's.

For another example, the historical distinction between styles (b) and (c) is profoundly important. It has to do with the familiar tensions between today's experimenter and theoretician. The former is heir to the medical empirics, who insisted that we should never go beyond observables in our descriptions of the course of disease and its cure, while it was the dogmatists who introduced what we would now call theoretical entities that play so major a part in hypothetical modeling (c). Crombie speaks of "controlling postulation" in his summary description of (b), but the postulation is at the level of observables and measurable quantities. It is by and large the science of phenomena given or measured in nature that is not much tampered with. Something else began just about the end of the period for which Crombie describes (b) and (c). I call it the laboratory style, characterized by the building of apparatus in order to produce phenomena to which hypothetical modeling may be true or false, but using another layer of modeling, namely models of how the apparatus and instruments themselves work. The relationship between the laboratory style, call it (bc), and styles (b) and (c) is complex. Peter Galison (1998) describes it with the metaphor of a trading zone between the producers of analyzed data and the merchants of theoretical approximations. He took the idea from linguists studying the development of "Creole" or "pidgin" languages in which a new language develops, for purposes of trade and social intercourse, at the interface between two established languages. The trading-zone idea will be useful in the study of styles of reasoning when we begin to describe any inquiry that employs several styles. It is often not the case that a single investigator is at home in more than one style of reasoning. Instead, there is collaboration in which a person expert in style X makes use of a handy robust core of techniques from style Y. This is at its most obvious in "cookbooks" of statistical reasoning prepared for this or that branch of science, psychology, cladistic taxonomy, high energy physics, and so forth. With no understanding of principles, and perhaps using only a mindless statistical package for the computer, an investigator is able to use statistics without understanding its language in any meaningful way whatsoever.

To return to the laboratory style, I do not mean that it has supplanted Crombie's (b), experimentation, and (c) modeling. On the contrary, there are whole fields of specialization in which either (b) or (c) is in full play on its own. On the one hand, despite all the talk about intervening variables and the like, many of the social sciences operate only at the empirical level of (b). On the other hand, cosmology and cognitive science—none other than the chief modern instances of the Galilean style so admired by Weinberg and Chomsky—remain at the level of (c), hypothetical modeling.

Those sciences answer to observation, but experimental manipulation and intervention is almost never practicable. That is precisely why Weinberg and Chomsky invoke (a certain Koyréan vision of) Galileo to legitimate their own work. Cosmology and cognitive science remain sciences that represent; the laboratory style introduced sciences that intervene.

I judge that the laboratory style began about the time that Boyle made the air pump in order to investigate the spring of the air. It is characteristic of styles that they have popular myths of origin. Crombie's list strikes the right note just because it codifies familiar legend. How could it be otherwise if one is recapitulating European science from within? There was that legendary moment when, as Althusser put it, Thales "discovered the continent of mathematics" (Althusser 1972, 185). Next in the list of continents is "and Galileo discovered the continent of mechanics." Well, Galileo is everybody's favorite hero—not only for Chomsky and Weinberg but also for Husserl (for whom Galileo is simply The Hero of Science) and Spengler. Crombie's talk on styles of scientific thinking that aroused my interest long ago was about—Galileo. At that same conference, Winifred Wisan read a paper titled "Galileo and the Emergence of a New Scientific Style (Wisan 1981). All these authors referred chiefly to some aspect of style (c), so let us not forget that according to Stillman Drake, it was Galileo who, by the purest use of style (b), established the very first experimental and quantitative law of nature. Galileo is the stuff of myth, a point made by Crombie himself (1987). Althusser continued, "and Marx discovered the continent of history." Good myth, wrong man; I much prefer Michel Foucault's retelling with Bopp, Cuvier, and Ricardo. Cuvier, as many have noticed, is questionable, and we'd add a geologist, but Bopp's philology seems perfect as the start of the historico-genetic style. As for style (e), that too has its legends. "A problem about games of chance proposed to an austere Jansenist by a man of the world was the origin of the calculus of probabilities," or so wrote Poisson (1837, 1). And I take Schaffer and Shapin's book, subtitled *Hobbes, Boyle, and the Experimental Life* (1986), as setting out the myth of origin for the laboratory style. Their hero, as both Bruno Latour (1990) and I (1991) have observed, is not a person but an instrument, the apparatus, the air pump.

Styles, to continue Althusser's metaphor, open up new territory as they go. I am sure that the Indo-Arabic style of applied mathematics, little interested in postulation but dedicated to finding algorithms, is a distinct style with, of course, non-European origins. I call it the algorismic style, referring to yet another legend. "Al-gorismi" was the early European name for the Arab mathematician who flourished in the early ninth century. (Abu Ja'far Mohammed Ben Musa, native of Khwarazm, or al-Khowarazmi.) His book on algebra (which is also probably the source of our word "algebra") was the text from which Europeans learned the Arabic numerals—and the algorismic style of reasoning.

The algebrizing of geometry, the Arabicizing of the Greek, was an essential piece of territorial expansion. Every such expansion is contested. We can overhear today's battles. For example: are computer-generated concepts and proofs really mathematics? When I was a student, I went around with some topologists who would talk and draw pictures and tell tall stories; today, when I have topological house guests, the first thing they do is set up their Macs in my basement, not calculating but generating ideas to which real-time computation is integral. And I know others who say that my friends have stopped doing mathematics. That's how it is, when a style goes into new territory.

For all these differences in emphases, I do not differ significantly from Crombie, either in my individuation of styles or in how I describe them. Without his three-volume vindication of his canonical list, I would be left with dubious anecdotes and fables. I'm not claiming that I'm on solid non-ideological ground when I resort to a historian for an initial individuation of styles. I claim only a certain independence: his motivation is very different from mine, but the list he presents admirably suits my purposes. It is a good workhorse of a list that holds no surprises. To use yet another obsolete metaphor, it covers the waterfront, and provides a directory to the main piers, in a readily recognizable and fairly satisfactory way. And it could be the wrong waterfront for me. Maybe he was describing a once wondrous but now gutted Liverpool, or at any rate a dignified San Francisco that has taken up leisure pursuits like denim and tourism—harbors that history has passed by. Perhaps I should instead be attending to a bustling container port like Felixstowe or Oakland. Maybe science as we know it began late in the nineteenth century and the philosopher who is not an antiquarian should just forget about the olden times. I don't think so. The proof of my confidence that Crombie's list remains germane is, however, not a matter of principle but of the success of the resultant philosophical analysis.

Our differences lie not in the identity of styles or their description, but in the use to which we put the idea. Crombie's advance notice of his book began: "When we speak today of natural science we mean a specific vision created within Western culture, at once of knowledge and of the object of that knowledge, a vision at once of natural science and of nature" (Crombie 1988, 1). He said on the next page that,

> The whole historical experience of scientific thinking is an invitation to treat the history of science, both in its development in the West and in its complex diffusion through other cultures, as a kind of comparative historical anthropology of thought. The scientific movement offers an invitation to examine the identity of natural science within an intellectual culture, to distinguish that from the identities of other intellectual and practical activities in the arts, scholarship, philosophy, law, government, commerce and so on, and to relate them all in a taxonomy of styles. It is an invitation to analyse the various elements that make up an intellectual style in the study and treatment of nature: conceptions of nature and of science, methods of scientific inquiry and demonstration diversified according to subject matter, evaluations of scientific goals with consequent motivations, and intellectual and moral commitments and expectations generating attitudes to innovation and change.

This is history in the grand manner, an invitation to a comparative historical anthropology of thought. Regardless of interest, philosophical or historical, many of us may be glad that at a time of so many wonderfully dense and detailed but nevertheless fragmented studies of the sciences, we are offered such a long-term project. This is especially so for philosophers, to whom the most fascinating current historiography of the sciences is work of the "social studies of knowledge" schools of philosophically motivated history: the strong program, network theory, the doctrine of the construction of scientific facts by negotiation. Increasingly fine-grained analyses of incidents, sometimes made tape-recorder in hand, have directed the history of science towards the fleeting. On the other hand, many of my philosophical colleagues take it to the quasi-timeless end, as when Hilary Putnam writes of "the ideal end of inquiry." Crombie's styles may also seem to be edging off towards the excessively long run. But his intentions are plain, to conduct a historical investigation of that specific vision mostly created around the Mediterranean basin and then in more northerly parts of Europe, "a comprehensive historical inquiry into the sciences and arts mediating man's experience of nature as perceiver and knower and agent [that must] include questions at different levels, in part given by nature, in part made by man." Crombie was well aware of the need to establish the historical continuity of styles across periods of latency, of the need to understand "the intellectual and social commitments, dispositions and habits, and of the material conditions, that might make scientific activity and its practical applications intellectually or socially or materially easy for one society but difficult or impossible for another." He wanted to compare those now familiar items, "the numbers, social position, education, occupation, institutions, private and public habits, motives, opportunities, persuasions and means of communications of individuals," and so on: "military context," "rhetorical techniques of persuasion." The grand view need not neglect the fashionable topics of the moment, nor on the other hand ignore philosophical chestnuts like the existence of theoretical entities. That conundrum is described in the mandarin manner, as you will have noticed from my other quotations: "distinguishing the argument giving rational control of subject-matter from an implication of the existence of entities appearing in the language used" (that is, the polarizing electron gun works, but do electrons exist?).

I have hardly begun to enumerate Crombie's historiographic aims. How can a philosopher make use of so expansive an idea of a style of scientific thinking or reasoning in the European tradition? First, I notice the way in which styles become autonomous. Every style comes into being by little microsocial interactions and negotiations. It is a contingent matter, to be described by historians, that some people with disposable time and available servants should value finding something out. Yet each style has become independent of its own history. We can forget the history or enshrine it in myth. Each style has become what we think of as a rather timeless canon of objectivity, a standard or model of what it is to be reasonable about this or that type of subject matter. We do not check to see whether mathematical proof or laboratory investigation or statistical studies are the right way to reason: they have become (after fierce struggles) what it is to reason rightly, to be reasonable in this or that domain.

I assert neither that people have decided what shall count as objectivity, nor that we have discovered what does the trick. I am concerned with the way in which objectivity comes into being, and shall shortly state how to address the question of what keeps certain standards of objectivity in place. Why do I not say that we have simply discovered how to be objective, how to get at the truth in a long haul? This is because there are neither sentences that are candidates for truth, nor independently identified objects to be correct about, prior to the development of a style of reasoning. Every style of reasoning introduces a great many novelties including new types of:

> objects
> evidence
> sentences, new ways of being a candidate for truth or falsehood
> laws, or at any rate modalities
> possibilities.

One will also notice, on occasion, new types of classification and new types of explanations. We should not envisage first a style and then the novelties. That is one of the many merits of the word "style." We did not first have fauvism, and then Matisse and Derain painting fauve pictures in 1905. The style comes into being with the instances, although (as the example of the fauves makes plain) the recognition of something as new, even the naming of it, may solidify the style after it has begun. What the word "style" does not make plain is why fauvism fades almost as soon as named, while a few styles of reasoning become autonomous of their origins and their originators. That is a pressing philosophical issue in the study of styles of reasoning.

Each style, I say, introduces a number of novel types of entities, as just listed. Take objects. Every style of reasoning is associated with an ontological debate about a new type of object. Do the abstract objects of mathematics exist? That is the problem of Platonism in mathematics. Do the unobservable theoretical entities of the laboratory style really exist? That is the problem of scientific realism in the philosophy of the natural sciences. Do the taxa exist in nature, or are they, as Buffon urged, mere artifacts of the human mind? Are there objects, such as languages, to be understood in terms of their historical derivation, or are they just a way of organizing a mess of complexity on top of the only reality, a postulated innate universal grammar? Are coefficients of correlation or the rates of unemployment real features of populations, or are they products of institutional arrangements of classification and measurement?

Each style of reasoning has its own existence debate, as illustrated, because the style introduces a new type of object, individuated by means of the style, and not previously noticeable among the things that exist. Indeed, the realism-antirealism debates so familiar in recent philosophy will now be understood in a new and encyclopedic fashion, as a by-product of styles of reasoning. That is not true of questions of global idealism, mind versus matter debates, which are not engendered by this or that style of reasoning.

Objects are only one kind of novelty. One may run down my list of novelties checking that each style introduces these novelties. That, I argue, is an essential and definitive feature of a style of reasoning, accounting for the relatively small number of styles on Crombie's list. Hence we are in a position to propose a necessary condition for being a style of reasoning: each style should introduce novelties of most or all of the listed types, and should do so in an open-textured, ongoing, and creative way. Mathematicians do not just introduce a few sorts of abstract objects, numbers, and shapes, and then stop; the type "abstract object" is open-ended once we begin reasoning in a certain way. Note that on this criterion, logic, be it deductive, inductive, or abductive, does not count as a style of reasoning. This is as it should be. Crombie did not list the branches of logic, and no wonder. People everywhere make inductions, draw inferences to the best explanation, make deductions; those are not peculiarly scientific styles of thinking, nor are they Mediterranean in origin.

I use my list of novelties as a criterion, as a necessary condition for being a style of reasoning. I've mentioned the ontological debates arising from one sort of novelty, the new types of objects; now I shall say a little more about new types of sentences. Each new style, and each territorial extension, brings with it new sentences, things that were quite literally never said before. That is hardly unusual. That is what lively people have been doing since the beginning of the human race. What's different about styles is that they introduce new ways of being a candidate for truth or for falsehood. As Comte put it—and there is a lot of Comtianism in my philosophy—they introduce new kinds of "positivity," ways to have a positive truth value, to be up for grabs as true or false. Any reader who fears too much early positivism should know also that I took the word "positivity" in the first instance from Michel Foucault, whose influence on my idea of styles of reasoning is more profound than that of Comte or Crombie. I should repeat for philosophers what was said in chapter 11, that his idea of positivity falls far short of what Michael Dummett calls bivalence, of being definitely true, or definitely false. Bivalence commonly requires far more to be in place than a style of reasoning. It may demand a Foucauldian episteme, some of Jardine's questions, or even, as Gavroglu argues, an entirely personal research style localized in a single laboratory. And even after all that, as Dummett has well taught, even when similarities in the surface grammar and in possible ways of inquiry may make us think that sentences we investigate using them are beyond question bivalent, closer scrutiny abetted by a stern theory about meaningfulness may make us skeptical.

The kinds of sentences that acquire positivity through a style of reasoning are not well described by a correspondence theory of truth. I have no instant objection to a correspondence theory for lots of humdrum sentences, what we might call pre-style or unreasoned sentences, including the maligned category of observation sentences. But I reject any uniform all-purpose semantics. The instant objection to correspondence theories, for sentences that have positivity only in the context of a style of reasoning, is that there is no way of individuating the fact to which they correspond, except in terms of the way in which one can investigate its truth, namely by using the appropriate style. As J. L. Austin showed, that objection does not so instantly apply, for example, to "observation sentences" in subject-predicate or subject-relation-object form. I reject the first dogma of traditional anglophone philosophy of language, that a uniform "theory of truth" or of "meaning" should apply across the board to an entire "language." That is a fundamental lesson to draw from Wittgenstein's talk of different "language-games." Among shop-soiled theories of truth and meaning, the one that best fits sentences of a kind introduced by a style of reasoning is a verification theory.

The truth of a sentence (of a kind introduced by a style of reasoning) is what we find out by reasoning using that style. Styles become standards of objectivity because they get at the truth. But a sentence of that kind is a candidate for truth or falsehood only in the context of the style. Thus styles are in a certain sense "self-authenticating." Sentences of the relevant kinds are candidates for truth or for falsehood only when a style of reasoning makes them so. This statement induces an unsettling feeling of circularity.

The statement is closely connected with the claim that styles of reasoning introduce novelties, including new kinds of sentences. There simply do not exist true-or-false sentences of a given kind for us to discover the truth of, outside of the context of the appropriate style of reasoning, The doctrine of self-authenticating styles is distinct from "constructionist" accounts of scientific discovery. For in those accounts individual facts of a typically familiar kind become constructed-as-facts in the course of research and negotiation. There was no fact "there" to discover until constructed. According to my doctrine, if a sentence is a candidate for truth or falsehood, then by using the appropriate style of reasoning we may find out whether it is true or false. There is more to say here, connected with the difference between a sentence having positivity and bivalence, but I may have said enough to show how my doctrine falls a long way short of constructionism.

The apparent circularity in the self-authenticating styles is to be welcomed. It helps explain why, although styles may evolve or be abandoned, they are curiously immune to anything akin to refutation. There is no higher standard to which they directly answer. The remarkable thing about styles is that they are stable, enduring, accumulating over the long haul. Moreover, in a shorter time frame, the knowledge that we acquire using them is moderately stable. It is our knowledges that are subject to revolution, to mutation, and to several kinds of oblivion; it is the content of what we find out, not how we find out, that is refuted. Here lies the source of a certain kind of stability. Some years ago, when I published a brief paper about the stability of the laboratory sciences, I could refer only to some observations by S. S. Schweber and to some work on "finality in science" done by a group in Frankfurt (Hacking 1988b). Now the topic of stability is positively trendy, and at the time of writing this had occupied the correspondence pages of the *Times Literary Supplement* for several weeks (Durant 1991, cf Hacking 1999a, 84–92).

I believe that understanding the self-authenticating character of styles of reasoning is a step towards grasping the quasi-stability of science. I doubt that Crombie agreed with this. If so, our difference would not be between a historical judgment and a philosophical one, but rather a philosophical difference between two students, one a historian and one a philosopher. Other historians, of a more constructionist bent, will hold that my doctrine of self-authentication does not go far enough; in any event, the issues are philosophical, not historical.

In respect of stability I do wholly endorse one much used lemma from the strong program in the sociology of knowledge. The truth of a proposition in no way explains our discovery of it, or its acceptance by a scientific community, or its staying in place as a standard item of knowledge. Nor does being a fact, nor reality, nor the way the world is. My reasons for saying so are not Edinburgh ones; they are more reminiscent of very traditional philosophy. I would transfer to truth (and to reality) what Kant said about existence, that it is not a predicate, adding nothing to the subject. I may believe that there was a solar eclipse this summer because there was one in the place I was then staying; the eclipse is part of the explanation of my belief (a view which might be resisted in Edinburgh), along with my experience, my memory, my general knowledge, the folderol in the newspapers, etc. But the fact that there was an eclipse, or the truth of the proposition that there was an eclipse, is not part of the explanation, or at any rate not over and above the eclipse itself. This is no occasion to develop that theme, except to say that anyone who endorses the Edinburgh conclusion, that truth is not explanatory, should want an understanding of the stability of what we find out, and not settle for "because that's the way that the world is." I shall now sketch how the theory of styles of reasoning may provide such an understanding.

The idea of self-authentication is only a step, a fingerpost, towards an understanding of the quasi-stability of some of our knowledge. We shall not progress further by thinking about method in general, let alone "science" in general. Each style of reasoning has its own characteristic self-stabilizing techniques. An account of each technique requires detailed analysis, specific to the style, and it is aided by vivid historical illustration. Each is a long story. I have published three papers about the statistical, the mathematical, and the laboratory styles (Hacking 1991a, 1992a, 1995b). There is little overlap between these essays, because the techniques and the histories involved differ substantially from case to case.

Almost the only thing that stabilizing techniques have in common is that they enable a self-authenticating style to persist, to endure. Talk of techniques that I describe are quite well known, but, I claim, inadequately understood. For example, Duhem's famous thesis about how to save theories by adjusting auxiliary hypotheses is (by one measure) exactly 1/14th of the stabilizing techniques that I distinguish in the laboratory sciences. I owe much more to recent work by Andrew Pickering, to whom I would attribute another 3/14th (Pickering 1989). Overall we are concerned with a mutual adjustment of ideas (which include theories of different types), materiel (which we revise as much as theories) and marks (including data and data analysis). All three are what Pickering calls plastic resources that we jointly mold into semi-rigid structures. I should emphasize that, although I use Duhem, this account does not go in the direction of the underdetermination of theory by data (Quine's generalization of Duhem's remarks). On the contrary, we come to understand why theories are so determinate, almost inescapable. Likewise my account of the stability of the mathematical style owes much to two unhappy bedfellows, Lakatos and

Wittgenstein. It introduces an idea of "analytification"—of how some synthetic if *a priori* propositions are made analytic: thus the logical positivist doctrine of the *a priori* is historicized. But we no more arrive at the radical conventionalism or constructionism sometimes read into *Remarks on the Foundations of Mathematics* than we arrive at the underdetermination of theory by data (Hacking 2000).

A happy by-product of this analysis is that not only has each style its own self-stabilizing techniques, but also some are more effective than others. The taxonomic and the historic-genetic styles have produced nothing like the stability of the laboratory or the mathematical style, and I claim to be able to show why. On the other hand, although Mark Twain, Disraeli, or whoever could, in the earlier days of the statistical style, utter the splendid canard about lies, damn lies, and statistics, the statistical style is so stable that it has grown its own word that gives a hint about its most persistent techniques: "robust." In the case of statistics there is an almost too evident version of self-authentication (the use of probabilities to assess the probabilities). But that is only part of the story, for I emphasize the material, institutional requirements for the stability of statistical reasoning. Indeed, if my accounts deserve to be pegged by any one familiar philosophical "-ism," then it is materialism. That is most notably true of my account of the laboratory style, despite my incorporating the idealist "Quine-Duhem thesis" as an adjunct.

Techniques of self-stability return us to the question of how to individuate styles. We began with an ostensive definition, Crombie's list. Then we moved to a criterion, a necessary condition: a style must introduce certain novelties, new kinds of objects, laws, and so on. But now we get closer to the heart of the matter. Each style persists, in its peculiar and individual way, because it has harnessed its own techniques of self-stabilization. That is what constitutes something as a style of reasoning.

This three-stage definition of styles must be treated with caution. Consider for example the question of whether some styles of reasoning have simply died out, after a robust life in recorded history. In chapter 11 I suggested one extinct style, the Renaissance reasoning by similitudes so well represented by Paracelsus. My characterization of styles above began with a historian's classification of styles, not intended to be exhaustive: of course that allows that some styles are no longer with us. I don't know what Crombie thought about Renaissance medicine, but I know of nothing in his published writing to exclude it as participating in an additional style that has now been abandoned. So the possibility of "dead" styles is unproblematic for the first, ostensive, definition of styles. Barry Allen (1996) has suggested witchcraft as another.

Next I gave a philosopher's necessary condition for being a style, in terms of introducing a battery of new kinds of objects. That too allows that some styles die out. It is at least arguable that the reasoning of a Paracelsus satisfies this criterion. Finally I have suggested—and here, only suggested—a more analytic definition, in terms of a style being constituted by self-stabilizing techniques. There arise two questions: first, whether hermetic medicine of those times did have such techniques, and then, if the answer is yes, why this style of reasoning has been so brusquely displaced. I believe that the answer to the first question is a qualified affirmative—but see my observation above about some techniques being more effective than others. The second question leads into dense history; recall complaints addressed to Michel Foucault that he never explained why epistemes die out, in particular why his Renaissance episteme of resemblance expired. I do not believe that one can give purely internal explanations of why we abandon certain practices, but have no confidence in external explanations either. It does not discredit the philosopher's use of styles of reasoning that it leads directly to such historical chestnuts; the contrary, I should imagine.

The historian will want to distinguish several types of events. There is the extinction of a style, perhaps exemplified by reasoning in similitudes. There is the insertion of a new style that may then be integrated with another, as has happened with algorismic reasoning, combined with geometrical and postulational thought. There is the challenge offered by a new style, the laboratory style, to an old one, the postulational style, and the ensuing triumph of the new. I am inclined to go with the contingency theorists among historians on all these points. It is altogether contingent that there have been such replacements, and the concept of style is of no aid in explaining what happened. Style is a more metaphysical concept, important for understanding truth-or-falsehood once a style has become autonomous.

More pressing to the philosopher than dead, merging, or emerging styles are questions posed in the present by a number of special-interest groups. What are the other styles of reasoning? Historical reasoning? Legal reasoning? Mystical reasoning? Magical reasoning? John Forrester (1996) makes a case for the "case," in psychoanalysis, as a style of reasoning. Arnold Davidson (1996) has a more general argument for the whole of psychiatry.

We may even, in a modest way, get a grip on Richard Rorty's question,

"Is Science a Natural Kind?" (Rorty 1988) without being reduced to his view that there is only the largely undifferentiated conversation of mankind. We can do so without embracing the opposed idea of Bernard Williams, that science leads us to something worth calling an absolute conception of reality (Williams 1984, 214 and 1985, 138–139). The very mention of styles, in the plural, corrects the direction of the debate: we shall stop talking of science in the singular and return to that healthy nineteenth-century practice of William Whewell and most others: we shall speak of the history and philosophy of the sciences—in the plural. And we shall not speak of the scientific method as if it were some impenetrable lump, but instead address the different styles (Hacking 1996). On the other hand, once we have a clearer understanding of what, from case to case, keeps each style stable in its own way, we shall not think that there are just endless varieties of Rortian "conversation." My doctrine of self-authentication, which sounds like part of the current mood for sceptically undermining the sciences, turns out to be a conservative strategy explaining what is peculiar about science, distinguishing it to some extent from humanistic and ethical inquiry.

A proposed account of self-stabilizing techniques begins by observing that a style becomes autonomous of the local microsocial incidents that brought it into being. Then there is the detailed account of how each style does stabilize itself. That is not the end of the matter. It is a contingent fact about us and our world that the techniques work at all—that we can analytify the sentences of mathematics or create phenomena in the laboratory to which our models are true. The persistence of a style demands some brute conditions about people and their place in nature. These conditions are not topics of the sciences, to be investigated by one or more styles, but conditions for the possibility of styles. An account of them has to be brief and banal, because there is not much to say. What we have to supply are, to quote Wittgenstein, "really remarks on the natural history of man: not curiosities, however, but rather observations on facts which no one has doubted and which have only gone unremarked because they are always there before our eyes" (Wittgenstein 1981, 47). Wittgenstein and others also called this (philosophical) anthropology (cf Bloor 1983). The resonance is with Kant's *Anthropologie* rather than the ethnography or ethnology commonly studied in departments of anthropology or sociology. Crombie's "comparative historical anthropology of thought" is by and large historical ethnology, a comparative study of one profoundly influential aspect of Western culture. Wittgenstein's philosophical anthropology is about the "natural history of man," or, as I prefer to put it, about human beings and their place in nature. It concerns facts about all people, facts that make it possible for any community to deploy the self-stabilizing techniques of styles of reasoning. It is in philosophical anthropology that we slough off the Eurocentrism with which this study began.

We should be wary of giving grand names to our modest projects. In 1990, two works were subtitled "Towards an Anthropology of Science." They were written a few hundred meters apart, at the École Polytechnique and the École des Mines in Paris. They were both published in England (Atran 1990, Latour 1990). They are both written from perspectives at right angles to Wittgenstein's. My own abuse of what Wittgenstein meant by anthropology has more in common with Atran than with Latour. This is because Atran is concerned with—among many other things in his extraordinarily versatile book—what made possible the taxonomic style (d). He also has a Chomskian vision of an underlying, innate, universal structure for what he calls folk-taxonomy. In contrast, Latour's projected anthropology of science is profoundly anti-innatist, anti-universalist. These two authors do, however, have one important thing in common, as distant as possible from Wittgenstein's *Anthropologie* or natural history of mankind. Atran does real ethnography, studying classification systems used by Mayan peoples in the jungles of Guatemala. Latour too was trained as an ethnographer, and his study of the synthesis and identification of a tripeptide was conceived of as an ethnography of the workplace, the laboratory (Latour and Woolgar 1979). That work now serves as a role-model—or as horrid cautionary tale—for a generation of trainee anthropologists whose field site is a laboratory. (I myself think it is a plausible example of a less plausible general thesis about constructionism; Hacking 1988d.)

What should we call my inquiry, less ambitious than philosophical anthropology, namely the detailed study of the stabilizing techniques used by a given style? If we are to use the suffix "-ology," then a fitting name for the study of self-stabilizing techniques would be philosophical technology. This label does not carry its meaning on its face, for I am not talking about what we usually mean by "technology," namely the development, application, and exploitation of the arts, crafts, and sciences. What I mean by philosophical technology is the philosophical study of certain techniques, just as philosophical anthropology is the study of certain aspects of man, epidemiology of epidemic diseases.

We have finally reached the fundamental difference between the historian's and the philosopher's use of the idea of a scientific style of thinking or reasoning, a difference that has nothing to do with disagreements about history or divergence in philosophies. Crombie led us to a comparative historical anthropology (moved, he also told us, by the experiences of teaching in Japan, and of crossing parts of Asia and its oceans when visiting his native Australia). I invite what I call philosophical technology: a study of the ways in which the styles of reasoning provide stable knowledge and become not the uncoverers of objective truth but rather the standards of objectivity. And when asked how those techniques could be possible at all, I fall back on a few and very obvious remarks about people, of the sort to which Wittgenstein has already directed us. Less all-encompassing histories will provide the social conditions within which a style emerged and those in which it flourished; less ambitious essays in philosophical technology will describe, in a more fine-grained way, the ways in which a style took on new stabilizing techniques as it pursued its seeming destiny in new territories. Comparative historical anthropology is a fundamentally different enterprise from either philosophical anthropology or philosophical technology.

I began by saying that the philosopher requires the historian. If Crombie's three volumes did not present a coherent ordering and analysis of European scientific practice and vision, then my talk of self-authenticating styles and of philosophical technology would be suspect. That is why I called the relation between the history and the philosophy of the sciences asymmetric. The philosopher who conceives of the sciences as a human production and even invention requires the historian to show that analytic concepts have application. After learning from the historian's analysis, I turn to a different agenda, which, you will have noticed, summons all the old gang: truth, reality, existence. But also, as is always the case in philosophy, we are directed to a complementary range of entirely new topics, such as philosophical technology.

For all the manifest differences of endeavor between the historian and the philosopher, they have this in common: we share a curiosity about our Western "scientific" vision of objectivity. That is as central a philosophical concern as could be: the core question of Kant's first critique. Crombie's volumes will, I hope, be read in part as an account of how conceptions of objective knowledge have come into being, while the philosopher can describe the techniques which become autonomous of their historical origins, and which enable styles of reasoning to persist at all. Yet I would not push this division of labor too far. As I said in chapter 1, objectivity, in its several guises, is a hot topic for active historians of science such as Lorraine Daston, Peter Galison, Theodore Porter, and many others. Even when objectivity is not explicitly in view, however much the historian may abjure philosophical issues, every sound history is imbued with philosophical concepts about human knowledge, nature, and our conception of it. And aside from central shared concerns, there is a more general predicament that the historian and the philosopher experience. Crombie was powerfully aware of the reflexive elements of his volumes. He knew that he who describes a certain vision of ourselves and our ecology has that vision himself. More constraining, although more difficult to come to coherent terms with, philosopher and historian alike are part of the community of living things that has been transformed by bearers of that vision in their interactions with nature as they saw it.

CHAPTER 13

Leibniz and Descartes:
Proof and Eternal Truths

This, the earliest piece in this collection, was given in 1973 at the British Academy as a Dawes Hicks Lecture in the history of philosophy. Here is the first attempt to practice what in chapter 2 was called "one way to do philosophy." One way is only one way among many. This lecture appeared in print at about the same time as my totally a-chronistic account of Leibniz's theory of infinitely long proofs, in which I explicate them in terms of the transfinite proofs in Gerhardt Gentzen's theory of natural deduction (Hacking 1974).

References to works by Leibniz are given as follows: *P = Die philosophische Schriften* (Leibniz 1875–90) and *M = Mathematische Schriften* (Leibniz 1849–1863), both edited by Gerhardt; *O = Opuscules et fragments inédits* (Leibniz 1903), edited by Couturat. References to Descartes may be identified in any standard edition.

Leibniz knew what a proof is. Descartes did not. Due attention to this fact helps resolve some elusive problems of interpretation. That is not my chief aim today. I am more interested in prehistory than history. Leibniz's concept of proof is almost the same as ours. It did not exist until about his time. How did it become possible? Descartes, according to Leibniz, furnished most of the technology required for the formation of this concept, yet deliberately shied away from anything like our concept of proof. I contend that Descartes, in his implicit rejection of our idea of proof, and Leibniz, in his excessive attachment to it, are both trying to meet a fundamental malaise in seventeenth-century epistemology. I speak of a malaise rather than a problem or difficulty, for it was not formulated and was perhaps not formulable. But although these unformulated preconditions for

200

the concept of proof are forgotten and even arcane, many facts of the resulting theories of proof are familiar enough. Leibniz was sure that mathematical truth is constituted by proof, while Descartes thought that truth conditions have nothing to do with demonstration. We recognize these competing doctrines in much modern philosophy of mathematics. The way in which the two historical figures enacted many of our more recent concerns has not gone unnoticed: Yvon Belaval deliberately begins his important book on Leibniz and Descartes with a long chapter called "Intuitionisme et formalisme" (Belaval 1960). There are plenty more parallels there for the drawing. I find this no coincidence, for I am afflicted by a conjecture, both unsubstantiated and unoriginal, that the "space" of a philosophical problem is largely fixed by the conditions that made it possible. A problem is individuated only by using certain concepts, and the preconditions for the emergence of those concepts are almost embarrassingly determining of what can be done with them. Solutions, countersolutions, and dissolutions are worked out in a space whose properties are not recognized but whose dimensions are as secure as they are unknown. I realize that there is no good evidence for the existence of conceptual "space" nor of "preconditions" for central concepts. Nothing in what follows depends on succumbing to the conjecture that there are such things. The annual Dawes Hicks lecture is dedicated to history, and I shall do history, but I do want to warn that my motive for doing so is the philosophy of mathematics and its prehistory.

In saying that Leibniz knew what a proof is, I mean that he anticipated in some detail the conception of proof that has become dominant in our century. He is commonly said to have founded symbolic logic. He occupies the first forty entries in Alonzo Church's definitive *Bibliography of Symbolic Logic*. I do not have that logical activity in mind. Most seventeenth-century wrestling with quantifiers, relations, combinatorics, and the syllogism seems clumsy or even unintelligible to the most sympathetic modern reader. In contrast, Leibniz's ideas about proof sound just right.

A proof, thought Leibniz, is valid in virtue of its form, not its content. It is a sequence of sentences beginning with identities and proceeding by a finite number of steps of logic and rules of definitional substitution to the theorem proved. He said so explicitly to Conring in March 1678 (*P.* I, 194) and to Tschirnhaus in May (*M.* IV, 451; cf. *P.* VII, 194 and *O.* 518). He experimented with various rules of logic and sometimes changed his mind on which "first truths" are admissible. He was not able to foresee the structure of the first order predicate logic. He unwittingly made one of our more beautiful theorems—the completeness of predicate logic—into a definition through his equivalence between provability and truth in all possible worlds.

My claim for Leibniz is only that he knew what a proof is. He was not even good at writing down proofs that are formally correct, for by nature he was hasty, in contrast to Descartes, who despised formalism and who is nearly always formally correct.

The Leibnizian understanding of proof did not much exist before his time. Yet so well did Leibniz understand proof that he could offer meta-mathematical demonstrations of consistency using the fact that a contradiction cannot be derived in any number of steps from premises of a given form. One example is the notes he wrote in November 1676 to prepare himself for a discussion with Spinoza (*P.* VII, 261). He understood that a proof of a necessary proposition must be finite, and made an important part of his philosophy hinge on the difference between finite and infinite proofs. We owe to him the importance of the definition of necessity as reduction to contradiction, and the corresponding definition of possibility as freedom from contradiction, understood as the inability to prove a contradiction in finitely many steps. Proof is not only finite but computable, and the checking of proofs is called a kind of arithmetic. Leibniz even saw the importance of representing ideas and propositions by a recursive numbering scheme (*Lingua generalis,* February 1678; *O.* 277). His invention of topology is motivated by a theory of the notation needed for valid proof (To Huygens, 8 September 1678; *M.* II, 17; cf *P.* V, 178). He is not alone in any of these observations, but he did have the gift of synthesizing and stating some of their interconnections. In asking how these ideas became possible, it is immaterial whether they are the ideas of a single man. It suffices that they were novel and had become widespread in the era of Leibniz, but it is convenient to have an Olympian figure who so perfectly epitomized this new understanding.

Leibniz himself has a plausible explanation of why the concept of proof emerged at this time. Insight into the nature of proof is not to be expected when geometry is the standard of rigor. Geometrical demonstrations can appear to rely on their content. Their validity may seem to depend on facts about the very shapes under study, and whose actual construction is the aim of the traditional Euclidean theorems. A Cartesian breakthrough changed this. Descartes algebrized geometry. Algebra is specifically a matter of getting rid of some content. Hence in virtue of Descartes's discovery, geometrical proof can be conceived as purely formal. Leibniz thought that Descartes had stopped short, and did not see his way through to a completely general abstract Universal Characteristic in which proofs could be conducted,

> and which renders truth stable, visible and irresistible, so to speak, as on a mechanical basis . . . Algebra, which we rightly hold in such esteem, is only a part of this general device. Yet algebra accomplished this much— that we cannot err even if we wish and that truth can be grasped as if pictured on paper with the aid of a machine. I have come to understand that everything of this kind which algebra proves is due only to a higher science, which I now usually call a *combinatorial characteristic*. (To Oldenburg 28 December 1675; *M.* I, 84)

"Nothing more effective," Leibniz ventures to say, "can well be conceived for the perfection of the human mind." Insight becomes irrelevant to recognizing the validity of a proof, and truth has become "mechanical." Two trains of thought parallel this conception of proof. One has long been known: Leibniz's belief that there exists a proof, possibly infinite, for every truth. Sometimes readers have inferred that the Universal Characteristic was intended to settle every question, whereas in fact Leibniz continues the letter quoted above saying that after the Characteristic is complete, "men will return to the investigation of nature alone, which will never be completed." The second train of thought concerns probability. Leibniz did often say that when the Characteristic is available, disputes would be resolved by calculation. Sometimes these calculations would be *a priori* demonstrations, but more usually they would work out the probability of various opinions relative to the available data. In surprisingly many details Leibniz's program resembles the work of Rudolf Carnap on inductive logic (Hacking 1971). I shall argue at the end of this chapter that the Leibnizian conceptions of proof and probability have intimately related origins. For the present I shall restrict discussion to proof.

Although the conception of proof and probability is partly familiar, there is a point at which most admirers of Leibniz stop:

> Every true proposition that is not identical or true in itself can be proved *a priori* with the help of axioms or propositions that are true in themselves and with the help of definitions or ideas. (*P.* VII, 300)

"Every" here includes all contingent truths. Moreover, Leibniz thought one does not fully understand a truth until one knows the *a priori* proofs. Since the "analysis of concepts" required for proof of contingent propositions is "not within our power," we cannot fully understand contingent truths. In these passages Leibniz is not giving vent to some skeptic's claim that only what is proven is reliable. Leibniz is no skeptic. He is not even an epistemologist. You need a proof to understand something because a proof actually constitutes the analysis of concepts which in turn determines the truth, "or I know not what truth is" (to Arnauld, 14 July (?), 1686, *P*, II, 56.). Moreover, a proof gives the reason why something is true, and indeed the cause of the truth. Truth, reason, cause, understanding, analysis, and proof are inextricably connected. It is part of my task to trace the origin of these connections. The connections are not automatic then or now. To illustrate this we need only take the contrasting doctrines of Descartes.

Leibniz thought that truth is constituted by proof. Descartes thought proof irrelevant to truth. This comes out nicely at the metaphorical level. Leibniz's God, in knowing a truth, knows the infinite analysis and thereby knows the proof. That is what true knowledge is. Leibniz's God recognizes proofs. Descartes's God is no prover. A proof might help a person see some truth, but only because people have poor intellectual vision. It used to be held that angels did not need to reason. Although commendably reticent about angels, Descartes has just such an attitude to reasoning. He is at one with the mathematician G. H. Hardy, "Proofs are what Littlewood and I call gas, rhetorical flourishes designed to affect psychology . . . devices to stimulate the imagination of pupils" (Hardy 1929, 18). Naturally Descartes says little about demonstration. Much of what he says is consistent with the doctrines advanced in the *Regulae*. Intuition and deduction are distinguished. Elementary truths of arithmetic can be intuited by almost anyone. Consequences may also be intuited. Deduction requires the intuition of initial propositions and consequential steps. The modern reader tends to equate intuition and deduction with axiom and theorem proved, but this is to see matters in a Leibnizian mold. The Cartesian distinction is chiefly psychological. One man might require deduction where another would intuit. In either case the end product is perception of truth. Some Cartesian scholars have recently debated whether the *cogito ergo sum* is inference or intuition or something else again (Frankfurt 1966, 333; Kenny, 1970, ch. 3; Hintikka 1962). I most closely agree with André Gombay (1972), from whose conversations about Descartes I have much profited.

Descartes does give varying accounts of this famous *ergo,* but it is completely immaterial to him whether one person needs to infer where another intuits directly. The point of the *cogito,* as the *Discourse* informs us, is to display a truth one cannot doubt. Then one may inquire what, in this truth, liberates us from doubt. The intuition/inference/performative controversy is misguided because Descartes is indifferent to what sort of "gas" induces clear and distinct perception. However you get there, when you see with clarity and distinctness you note that there is no other standard of truth than the natural light of reason. Leibniz, although granting some sense to "what is called the natural light of reason" (to Sophia Charlotte, 1702, P. VI, 501), inevitably observed what Descartes "did not know the genuine source of truths nor the general analysis of concepts" (to Philip, Dec. 1679, P. IV, 282).

The Cartesian independence of truth from proof is illustrated by Descartes's unorthodox view on the eternal truths. These comprise the truths of arithmetic, algebra, and geometry, and usually extend to the laws of astronomy, mechanics, and optics. Contemporary authorities like Suárez's *Disputationes Metaphysicae* of 1597 taught that eternal truths are independent of the will of God. All the eternal verities are hypothetical. If there are any triangles, their interior angles must sum to two right angles. Since God is free to create or not to create triangles, this hypothetical necessity is no constraint on his power (Cronin 1987, 154). Descartes, although cautious in expressing opinions at odds with received doctrine, disagreed. The eternal truths depend upon the will of God, and God could have made squares with more or fewer than four sides. As we might express it, the eternal truths are necessary, but they are only contingently necessary. "Even if God has willed that some truths should be necessary, this does not mean that he willed them necessarily, for it is one thing to will that they be necessary, and quite another to will them necessarily" (To Mesland, 2 May 1644. Other texts on eternal truths are as follows. To Mersenne, 6 May and 27 May 1630 and 27 May 1638. Reply to *Objections* V and VI. *Principles* xlviii–xlix.)

I very much like the way that Emile Bréhier (1937, 15) uses this theory about eternal truth in order to explain away the Cartesian "circle" alleged, in the first instance, by Arnauld. The circle goes like this: from the clarity and distinctness of the third meditation it follows that God exists, but clarity and distinctness can be counted on only if there is a good God. Many commentators interrupt this simple-minded circle by saying that God's veracity is not needed when we are actually perceiving truth with clarity and distinctness. God comes in only when we turn our minds to another thought. This leaves open the question of the role that God plays when we are thus distracted. There are several competing interpretations. André Gombay (1988) uses this comparison. In moments of passionate love, a man (such as the husband in Strindberg's play, *The Father*) cannot doubt that his wife is faithful. But at more humdrum moments he doubts her love. What is his doubt? (*a*) His memory is playing tricks; the feeling of passionate certainty never occurred. (*b*) He remembers correctly his passionate conviction, but subsequently feels that he was misled by his passion. No matter how convinced he was then, he was wrongly convinced. (*c*) She was true to him at that passionate moment, but is no longer so. In the case of Cartesian doubt, recent commentators correctly rule out doubts of kind (*a*): God is no guarantor of memory. Gombay, probably rightly, favors (*b*). But doubt of kind (*c*) is instructive. Bréhier proposes that God is needed to ensure that an "eternal truth," once perceived clearly and distinctly, *stays* true.

No set of texts tells conclusively for or against the Bréhier reading. This in itself shows how far Descartes separates proof from truth. What would happen to the proof of *p* if *p*, previously prove, went false? We can imagine that in the evolution of the cosmos Euclid's fifth postulate was true, relative to some assigned metric, and subsequently ceased to be true. At least this remains, we think: if a complete set of Euclidean axioms is true, the Pythagorean theorem is true too. That necessary connection between axiom and theorem cannot itself be contingent. Descartes disagreed. God is at liberty to create a Euclidean non-Pythagorean universe. We owe to Leibniz the clear statement that if not-*p* entails a contradiction, then *p* is necessary and indeed necessarily necessary. Descartes grants that it is unintelligible how *p* can entail contradiction and still be true. But this unintelligibility shows the weakness of our minds. In the *Monadology*, §46, Leibniz caustically dismisses this view of modality. It betrays, he thought, a lack of comprehension of the very concepts of necessity, contradiction, and proof.

Not only did Descartes acknowledge no dependence of necessary truth on proof; he also challenged accepted modes of presenting proof. He favored "analysis" rather than "synthesis." His doctrine is sufficiently hard to understand that Gerd Buchdahl (1969, ch. 3) distinguishes radically different Cartesian meanings for "analysis," but even if Descartes ought to have distinguished meanings of the word, he intended to be unequivocal. Synthesis is deduction, whose paradigm is Euclid. Deduction may bully a reader into agreement, but it does not teach how the theory was discovered. Only analysis can do that. At the end of the second set of *Objections,* Descartes subscribed to the standard myth that the Greeks had a secret art of discovery. The new algebraic geometry rediscovered it. He called it analytic geometry, as we still do. As he put it at the beginning of his *Geometry,* its method is to:

> suppose the solution already effected, and give names to all the lines that seem needful for the construction . . . then, making no distinction between known and unknown lines, we must unravel the difficulty in any way that shows most naturally the relations between these lines, until we find it possible to express a quantity in two ways.

Then we solve the equation. Analysis is a mode of discovery of unknowns, and the arguments of the *Geometry* show how solutions can be obtained. Descartes thought that the physicist postulating causes on the basis of observed effects may be doing analysis, and he maintained that the *Meditations* furnish another example of analysis.

The Cartesian notion of analysis underwent strange transformations. The fact that Euclidean synthesis was deemed to depend on content as well as form is well illustrated by Descartes's own observations that in geometry the primary notions of synthetic proofs "harmonize with our senses." The point of all those "minute subdivisions of propositions" is not even to ensure that the proof is sound. It is to render citation easy "and thus make people recollect earlier stages of the argument even against their will." Synthetic proofs work partly because we have sensible representations of what we are proving and are thus unfit for metaphysics which uses abstract concepts. Yet by a strange inversion, it is Cartesian analysis that enables Leibniz to argue that proof is entirely a matter of form, and to apply this thought to deductive proof in general, including synthesis. Moreover, what he calls the analysis of concepts proceeds by what Descartes would have called synthetic demonstration!

Descartes wanted good ways to find out the truth and was indifferent to the logical status of his methods. This is well illustrated by yet another kind of analysis. Traditionally science was supposed to proceed by demonstration of effects from causes stated in first principles. In practice, the more successful scientists were increasingly guessing at causes on the basis of effects according to what we can now call the hypothetico-deductive method. When challenged, Descartes said that his too is a kind of "demonstration," at least according to "common usage," as opposed to the "special meaning that philosophers give" to the word "demonstration." In reality, says Descartes, there are two kinds of demonstration, one from causes to effects, in which we prove the effect from the cause, and the other from effect to cause, in which we explain the effect by postulating a cause (To Morin, 13 July 1638).

There was a pressing practical problem for the second kind of so-called demonstration. As his correspondent put it, "nothing is easier than to fit a cause to an effect." To which Descartes replied that "there are many effects to which it is easy to fit separate causes, but it is not always so easy to fit a single cause to many effects." This thought was worked up by Leibniz into the theory of "architectonic" reasoning (*Tentamentum Anagogicum,* 1696, P. VII, 270). We seek those hypotheses that would be attractive to the Architect of the World, who has a mania for maximizing the variety of phenomena governed by laws of nature, while minimizing the complexity of those laws.

On such questions of method there does not seem, in perspective, very much at issue between the two philosophers. But they have radically different theories of what they are finding out. Leibniz supposes that truths are constituted by proof, and so proof is essentially linked to truth, while Descartes imagines that truths exist independently of any proof. However, we shall not find the origin of this difference in what might be called the philosophy of mathematics, but in what we should now call the philosophy of science. The very success of scientific activity in the early seventeenth century had created a crisis in man's understanding of what he knows. In the medieval formulations, adapted from Aristotle, knowledge or science was arrived at by demonstration from first principles. It demonstrated effects from causes, and its propositions were universal in form and were necessarily true. In giving the causes, it gave the reasons for belief, and also the reasons why the proposition proved is true. As well as arithmetic and geometry, science included astronomy, mechanics, and optics. This did not mean that one was supposed to do all one's mechanics *a priori,* for it might need ample experience to grasp the first principles of the universe. Francis Bacon furnishes a good example of a thinker trying to preserve this old ontology, insisting that instead of being dogmatic, the scientist must survey large quantities of experiences before he ventures to guess at the axioms, common notions, and first principles. What one is aiming at, however, is a body of universal and necessary axioms which will, when recognized and understood, have the character of self-evidence.

Bacon's methodology is a despairing attempt to save the old theory of truth on its own ground. Increasingly, men of science are not doing what they are supposed to be doing. Among what I shall call the high sciences, astronomy, mechanics, and optics, there is a dogmatic school maintaining the Aristotelian physics. It is shattered by new theories which do not merely contradict the old physics but do not even have the same kind of propositions that the old physics sought after. Moreover, among the low sciences, medicine and alchemy, whose practitioners are what Bacon scornfully called the empirics, there has developed a set of practices and concepts that are unintelligible on the old model of knowledge.

Descartes's curious assertions about "false hypotheses" illustrate how far he has come from traditional views. He says at length in his *Principles,* and throughout his life to various correspondent, that the chief hypotheses of his physics are strictly false, and may be regarded as a kind of fable (*Principles,* xliii–xlvii, and, e.g., To Mesland, May 1645). It is common to construe this as a safety net spread out after the Galilean scandal. Is it? Hypotheses serve as the basis for deducing true effects, but are not themselves to be asserted as true. Many ancient writers, including Archimedes, base their demonstrations on hypotheses that are strictly false, or so Descartes says. Perhaps he is merely seeking bedfellows in support of political caution. I see no reason to think so. Leibniz says that if they worked, Descartes's "false hypotheses" would be like cryptograms for solving the regularity of phenomena (To Conring, 19 March 1678, *P.* I, 194). He also says that Descartes is just wrong in changing the direction of physics to a search for false hypotheses. In short, the Cartesian view was taken literally by the next generation of readers.

If Descartes means what he says, everything has been turned upside down. Science was to make the world and its truths intelligible. From universal first principles concerning essence and cause and the true being of things one was to deduce the effects and their reasons, making intelligible the variety of general phenomena present to us. The first principles were to get at the very core of truth. But now the core evaporates, turns into a mere sham, a cryptogram of falsehoods. New merits have to be found for science, chief among them, in the seventeenth century, being the virtue of predictive power. In the traditional theory of truth, predictive power did not matter much because science was demonstrating necessities. When it abandons its ability to give reasons and causes by way of first principles, all it can do is provide us with predictions.

The evaporation of truth is what I have called the malaise or even the crisis in the early seventeenth century. We have been accustomed, especially in Britain, to notice the epistemological worries of the period. In fact, men wrote treatises not of epistemology but of methodology. The methodology was an attempt to tell how to do what was in fact being done, and how to do it better. The Cartesian titles such as *Rules for direction of the mind,* or *Discourse on Method,* are characteristic of the time. Underneath these works runs not the problem of British empiricism-scepticism, "How can I ever know?" It is rather, "What is knowledge, what is truth, are there such things?"

Reconsider the situation of Descartes. We have usually read him as an ego, trapped in the world of ideas, trying to find out what corresponds to his ideas, and pondering questions of the form, "How can I ever know?" Underneath his work lies a much deeper worry. Is there any truth at all, even in the domain of ideas? The eternal truths, he tells us, are "perceptions . . . that have no existence outside of our thought" (*Principles,* I. xlviii). But in our thought they are, in a sense, isolated perceptions. They may be systematized by synthesis, but this has nothing to do with their truth. The body of eternal truths which encompassed mathematics, neo-Aristotelian physics, and perhaps all reality, was a closely knit self-authenticating system of truth, linked by demonstration. For Descartes, there are only perceptions which are ontologically unrelated to anything and moreover are not even candidates for having some truth outside my mind. One is led, I think, to a new kind of worry. I cannot doubt an eternal truth when I am contemplating it clearly and distinctly. But when I cease to contemplate, it is a question whether there is truth *or* falsehood in what I remember having perceived. Bréhier suggested that demonstrated propositions may go false. It seems to me that Cartesian propositions, rendered lone and isolated, are in an even worse state. Perhaps neither they nor their negations have any truth at all. They exist in the mind only as perceptions. Do they have any status at all when not perceived? When demonstration cannot unify and give "substance" to these truths, the constancy of a veracious God who wills this truth suddenly assumes immense importance. We have long been familiar with the role of God as the willing agent that causes Berkeley's perceptions. We know Leibniz required the mind of God as the arena in which the essences of possible worlds compete for existence, saying in "The Radical Origination of Things" that "neither the essences nor the so-called eternal truths about them are fictitious but exist in a certain region of ideas, if I may so call it, namely in God himself" (*P.* VII, 305). I am suggesting that Descartes's veracious God is needed not just to guarantee our beliefs, but also to ensure that there is some truth to believe. I do not claim this as a worked out Cartesian thought, but rather as an underlying response to the breakdown in the traditional conception of knowledge.

Descartes was almost ingenuously radical. Faced by the fact that the new science was not Aristotelian knowledge or *scientia*, he abolished the traditional concepts even where they did work, namely in arithmetic and geometry. Leibniz, in contrast, was ingeniously conservative. The merit of the old system was that it gave us some understanding of the nature and interconnection of truths. The demerit was the inadequacy of the implied methodology of doing physics by deduction. So Leibniz grafted a new methodology on to the old theory of demonstration. Demonstration was formerly the key to both ontology and method. Leibniz restricts it to the former. It is turned into the theory of formal proof. In the old tradition only universal propositions are subject to demonstration. In the new practice, only what we now call pure mathematics fits this model. But Leibniz, making proof a matter of ontology, not methodology, asserts that all true propositions have an *a priori* proof, although in general human beings cannot make those proofs. This is to resolve the open question as to the nature of truth. Hence his careful distinction between finite and infinite proofs, the importance of form over content, and all the rest of Leibniz's rendering truth "mechanical." The universal characteristic, you will recall, "renders truth stable, visible, and irresistible, as on a mechanical basis." The new science that was not *scientia* had made truth totally unstable. The concept of formal proof was intended to restore the balance.

The ingenuity of Leibniz's eclecticism shows itself in another direction. The Universal Characteristic, as I have said, was to be the vehicle of finite deductions and of probability calculations of inductive logic. Whereas demonstration is the tool of what was traditionally called knowledge, probability, in medieval times, pertained to a quite different realm, opinion. The low sciences of alchemy and medicine are the artisans of opinion and the forgers of probability—or so I argue at length in *The Emergence of Probability* (1975a). Those thoroughly alien hermetical figures of the Renaissance did more: they actually engendered a concept of inconclusive evidence derived from facts, as opposed to testimony. The high sciences related to experience in a hypothetico-deductive or one might say Popperian way. That is, they concerned themselves with the deductive connections between experienced effects and conjectured causes. The low sciences were too inchoate for that, and created what, in recent times, has been called probability and induction. Leibniz puts the antique theory of demonstration into the realm of ontology. Finite demonstrations become the topic of mathematics, now rendered formal. Architectonic reasoning is his version of the hypothetico-deductive method. Inductive logic is the rationalization of what Bacon dismissed as mere empiricism. The vehicle for all these parts of methodology is the Universal Characteristic. It is a vehicle that cheerfully carries finite proofs and calculations of probability, and yet is a coarse and inadequate mirror of the very nature of truth, the infinite proof.

Carnap and Popper have re-enacted the tension between Leibniz's inductive logic and his architectonic reasoning. My topic is proof, not probability. I claim that the concept of formal proof was created in the time of Leibniz to overcome quite specific breakdowns in traditional ontology. The Cartesian concept of anti-proof has the same origin. These concepts were devised, almost unwittingly, to fill a vacuum. We still employ those concepts but live in a vacuum that those concepts cannot fill. Consider the sterility of modern philosophy of mathematics—not the collection of mathematical disciplines now called the foundations of mathematics, but our conflicting theories of mathematical truth, mathematical knowledge, and mathematical objects. The most striking single feature of work on this subject in this century is that it is very largely banal. This is despite the ample fertilization from the great programs and discoveries in the foundations of mathematics. The standard textbook presentations of "Platonism," constructivism, logicism, finitism, and the like re-enact conceptual moves which were determined by an ancient and alien problem situation, the disintegration of the concept of *scientia* and the invention of the concept of evidence, culminating in the new philosophy of the seventeenth century. We have forgotten those events, but they are responsible for the concepts in which we perform our pantomime philosophy.

Take, for example, the most seemingly novel, and also the most passionately disparate of contributions, Wittgenstein's *Remarks on the Foundations of Mathematics*. He invites us to destroy our very speech, and abandon talk of mathematical truth and knowledge of mathematics and its objects. We are asked to try out language in which mathematics is not "true," our discoveries are not "knowledge" and the "objects" are not objects. Despite this fantastic and perplexing attempt to get rid of all these inherited notions, Wittgenstein ends up with a dilemma that is essentially Leibniz-Cartesian. On the one hand he suggests, in quite the most radical way, that mathematical "truth" is constituted by proof, and on the other he is obsessed by just the intuitions that so impressed Descartes. Hardly anyone thinks he achieved a synthesis of these notions. There is a reason for this. He rejects that antique tryptich, truth, knowledge, and objects, but works in the space created by that earlier period, and is driven to employ the concepts created then for the solution of quite other problems, and which are fettered by their need to solve those other problems. The "flybottle" was shaped by prehistory, and only archaeology can display its shape.

14

Wittgenstein as
Philosophical Psychologist

The two volumes of Ludwig Wittgenstein's *Remarks on the Philosophy of Psychology* were published only in 1980. *The New York Review of Books* sent them to me, along with armfuls of recent books about Wittgenstein. The idea was that I should write a survey article. I did. It went on and on. Happily it had to be cut, and I ended up writing only about Wittgenstein.

Ludwig Wittgenstein wrote his *Remarks on the Philosophy of Psychology* about thirty-five years before they were published in 1980, rather late in a long sequence of posthumous books. The two volumes are successive attempts to sort out the same ideas. He was never fully satisfied by them, but they may well turn out to be his most enduring secondary work, fair companions to the only books that Wittgenstein did cast into final form: *Tractatus Logico-Philosophicus,* finished in 1918, and Part I of *Philosophical Investigations,* done by 1945.

Wittgenstein's reflections on the human mind are central to his later philosophy. He pairs off quite nicely with Descartes, his predecessor by exactly three centuries, and the founder of philosophical psychology. Although great philosophers never come two of a kind, these men are strikingly alike. The similarity may seem a bit surprising, since Wittgenstein is often presented as the very opposite of Descartes, and even as the man who brought the Cartesian era of philosophy to an end.

Each man chose to be an émigré. The Viennese Wittgenstein made his base at Cambridge University, while the French Descartes worked in Holland. Each lived in the midst of a foreign language but wrote most of his thoughts in his native tongue. Each soldiered in yet other countries. Both not only settled abroad but also set off for very strange parts. Wittgenstein traveled to the Soviet Union in 1935, possibly intending to become a doctor in Siberia. Descartes finally accepted the bidding of Queen Christina and went off to Sweden to die of the cold.

Both philosophers were secretive about their work, holding it back for years. Each could be furious if any of it was leaked prematurely to the public. Their eccentricities were legion, but each had a personality that dominated, nay, obsessed, close friends. Both men told us never to hurry with their work. The few pages of a Cartesian *Meditation* are to be reread on successive days. Only when you have made them your own should you move on to the next thought. Wittgenstein: "My work must be read *slowly*." He ensured that if you do read it, you do so slowly. Eclectics can dip into this or that choice fragment speedily enough, but if you read the matter systematically you have to take your time.

Wittgenstein wrote in numbered paragraphs, a few of which pursue the same topic and then may abruptly switch to something different. Even a single paragraph may be a series of quick exchanges between Wittgenstein and an interlocutor. A topic that has been dropped will reappear many paragraphs later. Strange possibilities are described and the same phenomenon will be held up again and again to be glimpsed from new perspectives. This style fits the content, for Wittgenstein's thought keeps on illustrating related themes from successive vantage points, shooting off, recollecting, transcending, backsliding. It is not unlike a mind that talks to itself in a half dozen different conversations at once, but the successive paragraphs are the subtly organized, intensely disciplined product of unending toil. Both Descartes and Wittgenstein are remarkably graceful authors, graceful not only in the seemingly relaxed flow of words, but also in the meticulous sequencing of ideas that lies beneath the charm of the sentences.

It is a commonplace that the "philosophical psychology" of Descartes and that of Wittgenstein are totally different, the one the very negation of the other. That is half right and half wrong. What's right is that Descartes starts from inside himself, while Wittgenstein begins in the world of human communication. The Cartesian philosophy says that I best know my own mind. All my knowledge is based upon my private experiences, sensations, and thoughts. Thought is the movement of ideas in the mind. Wittgenstein holds in contrast that shared practices, actions, reactions, and interactions among people provide the foothold upon which all such self-description of our mental life must rest. Language is first of all public and firmly rooted in what we do together. He rightly resented casual readers who would dismiss him as a behaviorist:

> Then is it misleading [Wittgenstein asks himself] to speak of man's soul, or of his spirit? So little misleading, that it is quite intelligible if I say "My soul is tired, not just my mind." But don't you at least say that everything that can be expressed by means of the word "soul," can also be expressed somehow by means of words for the corporeal? I do not say that. But if it were so—what would it amount to? For the words, and also what we point to in explaining them, are nothing but instruments, and everything depends on their use.

To ask whether Descartes believes in the human soul, while Wittgenstein does not, is simply to put a bad question. "Do I *believe* in a soul in someone else, when I look into his eyes with astonishment and delight?" Wittgenstein thought that it is not a question of belief founded on evidence at all.

Descartes held that mind and body are distinct substances and wondered how they interact. That doctrine, called dualism, has obsessed much Western philosophy. It will be said that Wittgenstein was no dualist, thus emphasizing his fundamental difference from his predecessor. I do not agree. The contrast is, I think, wrongly understood. Wittgenstein certainly did not hold that mind and body are two "substances," or that "mind" names a special kind of thing. But in many essentials, he is just as much a dualist as Descartes. Both hold that psychology requires forms of description and methodology quite different from those called for in natural science. Reflection on thinking is not remotely like the study of the inhuman world of spatial, mechanical objects.

Descartes took a word—*cogitare, penser,* "think"—and gave it an extended sense in which it captured all the disparate but roughly mental activities such as hoping and remembering and seeing and hurting. Where Descartes unifies, Wittgenstein mercilessly divides. Something different may have to be said about each mentalistic verb. Hence there is a long sequence of items that jut out in an index to the two volumes of *Philosophy of Psychology:* believing, calculating, expecting, experiencing, feeling, intending, and so on. Precisely such a list might be used to elucidate Descartes's portmanteau term "thinking." Both philosophers understood that descriptions of these items will be unrelated to anything that goes on in the material, space-occupying organs of the body such as the brain. At the same time, Wittgenstein rejects the very possibility of any doctrine about Cartesian thought-in-general.

Before looking at Wittgenstein's descriptions of the mental, one needs to place them within the rest of this work. Three decades separate the completion of his *Tractatus* and the final form of Part I of *Philosophical Investigations*. These masterpieces are usually said to represent his early and his later philosophy. Both are worth calling philosophies of language. In the Cartesian epoch, language had been a wonderful system of signs for conveying thoughts from one mind to another, but language was always secondary to ideas in the mind. There came at last the strange reversal; language became a necessarily public institution within which human selves are formed and by which people constitute the world they live in. The switch from the primacy of private thought to that of public discourse is not the work of Wittgenstein. In 1868, C. S. Peirce, founder of pragmatism, had published in a St. Louis philosophy magazine the remarkable sentence: "My language is the sum total of myself." That was twenty-one years before Wittgenstein was born, and the same thoughts were circulating elsewhere about that time.

Wittgenstein no more invented the idea of human beings and their world being constituted in language than Descartes invented the mind-body problem. Both philosophers are historical personages whose writings turn the claptrap of their time into monuments. Insofar as Wittgenstein had an earlier and a later philosophy, his monuments face away from each other. The *Tractatus* had a vision of a single role for language, while the *Investigations* tells of innumerable language games, each of which is embedded in its own web of activities.

The *Tractatus* is written as if language had but one function: representing the world. That creates a problem to which the book addresses itself. How is it possible to represent a nonlinguistic world in words? The opening sentences begin the answer. "The world is the totality of facts, not of things." When the penknife is to the left of the snuffbox, we tend to think of two things, the knife and the box. We think of a world made up of things like penknives that can be arranged in various ways. Not so, says Wittgenstein: the world consists simply of a set of facts, like the fact that the knife is to the left of the box. This is not to deny that there are things, such as penknives. It says only that the totality of facts is all there is to the world. Once that totality is given, you add nothing more by saying, "and there are things too, such as snuffboxes." This idea of the world begins to explain how representative language is possible. Propositions represent the world by picturing the structure of the facts. This idea has been called "the picture theory of meaning."

A theory of language as essentially representative excludes an enormous amount of discourse. Much of life most dear to us, including beauty, philosophy, and moral worth, has nothing to do with representation. Although values can be lived, acted out, or displayed, they cannot, on Wittgenstein's early account, literally be stated. This is not for the simpleminded reason later expounded by positivists, that values are mere expressions of feeling, and thus neither true nor false. On the contrary, we can represent facts about feeling just as well as any other facts, and there are truths and falsehoods about the inner world just as much as the external one. Wittgenstein's difficulty is that neither a value nor a philosophical thesis is a representation at all, and so is not something that can be "said." It is only something that can be "shown" by saying or doing something else. The *Tractatus* is written as a sequence of numbered propositions. It concludes by showing its own impossibility. This very philosophy cannot be a series of propositions at all. It, too, can at best be shown. The book ends by recommending silence.

Among the many themes in that strange and powerful book, I would here emphasize only its unified conception of the role of language: representation of facts by propositions. That vision is abandoned in the later philosophy. Wittgenstein came to see that language is not one monolithic system of representations for picturing reality. Instead, it is composed of myriad fragments that loosely overlap and intersect. Most of these are not used to represent anything. We are told to look at little bits of real or invented discourse to see what nonlinguistic activity—what social context or use—must accompany each one in order for it to make sense. A case in point of this approach is the way in which *Remarks on the Philosophy of Psychology* replaces the Cartesian concept of "thinking" by detailed study of lots of different mentalistic verbs—introspecting, calculating, remembering, intending—each of which demands its own social setting.

Philosophical Investigations begins by imagining a game in which builders call out a few words such as "block," "pillar," "slab," or "beam," thereby indicating to their helpers what materials they want where. Actions and words are formed in a language game from which the words take their meaning. Later, we learn that what we say about knowing and feeling and pain are likewise a mélange of small language games, each with its own family of preconditions and applications. Collectively, these display how wrong it is to seek a single model for language. They show us the *disunity* of language.

The game of the builders began an attack on the idea that words work chiefly as names. We are led through many related themes, including the famous maxim, "Don't ask for the meaning, ask for the use." One point of that slogan is: don't ask for objects that might serve as meanings of our words. Meanings are not objects that are expressed by words. Consider what we do with words, not what they represent. That comes out even in my long *Philosophy of Psychology* quotation about the soul, above. It is part of the reason that Wittgenstein could doubt that we use the words "soul" or "mind" to name a thing.

Philosophical Investigations is also famous for its "private language argument," that there cannot be a language that is in principle inaccessible to anyone else. There can, for example, be no language with names for just *my* sensations. A word like "pain" does not get its use by first naming something that we feel, and then telling others about it. Instead, it is necessarily embedded in various kinds of things we do in connection with being hurt. That is not to say that there is no pain without behavior, or that pain is a kind of behavior. But the idea of stoically concealed pain is nested in and parasitic upon more public ways of talking about pain—evincing it, wincing, trying to comfort the victim or relieve the suffering. We must particularly resist the idea of a private object (pain) that is named by the word "pain." *Remarks on the Philosophy of Psychology* imaginatively applies this line of thought to all kinds of mental goings-on. For example, knowing is not in general a state named by the "know"-words, nor does "I know" have the same family of uses as "he knows." Again, Wittgenstein asks, "Why can a dog feel fear but not remorse?" Not because there is something in the dog's mind correctly named by the word "fear" while there is nothing in the dog's mind to which the word "remorse" applies.

Many philosophers nowadays make eclectic use of these and many more ideas. Wittgenstein may, however, have hoped that his thoughts would one day be understood less for his theses than for his method and attitudes. He had a gloomy view of scientific culture and a deep pessimism about the possibility of his work's being understood in the darkness of his times. Maybe he was right. After his death, his thought was briefly quite fashionable among leading philosophy teachers, but now it is not. It continues to attract young people, and the name "Wittgenstein" is often enough invoked in high culture. Yet most serious philosophers seem to have put him aside, tending to find his concentration on diverse cases unproductive for the systematic analyses that philosophers have traditionally preferred. The other day, I heard a distinguished older philosopher, no "Wittgensteinian" herself, say crossly: "Really, it is astonishing. It is just as if Wittgenstein had never lived!"

Wittgenstein carefully preserved his work in tin boxes. His literary executors have edited it piece by piece in what sometimes seems haphazard order. They will be made fun of (or insulted) when a later generation prepares an Academy Edition of the Great Man's Work, but the somewhat personal style of editing may well coincide with the author's own intentions. At any rate, chunks of Wittgenstein's writings have appeared every year or so since his death in 1951. They have the effect of time-release capsules. This is salutary if you think, as I do, that many of us skim his words and forget.

He filled notebook after notebook. Often he clipped out the paragraphs and rearranged them. The same paragraph can appear in different settings. When he was confident of an arrangement, he would write it all down again and then dictate it to a typist. Volume I of these *Remarks* was dictated in the fall of 1947, and Volume II a year later. A third later and shorter survey was used by the editors to form a sixty-page "Part II" of *Philosophical Investigations,* but aside from a remarkable discussion of "seeing as," it has neither the tightly knit craftsmanship of Part I nor the wealth of examples discussed in the two previous but newly published typescripts under review.

What is Wittgenstein's philosophical psychology? We can see at once a number of things that it is not. It is not experimental psychology. A famous remark that concludes *Philosophical Investigations* runs thus:

> The confusion and barrenness of psychology is not to be explained by calling it a young science—the existence of experimental methods makes us think we have the means of solving the problems that trouble us; though problems and methods pass one another by.

Philosophical psychology is not introspection, whose noblest practitioner was William James. James is the only psychologist (besides some of the Gestalt people) to whom Wittgenstein regularly alludes. The vigor of James's writing is used to make plain the bizarre paths into which we are led by the very idea of a faculty of introspective knowledge. The danger here lies in postulating that there is an exclusively subjective means of gaining self-knowledge.

Philosophical psychology is certainly no cousin of psychoanalysis. "Freud's fanciful pseudo-explanations (precisely because they are so brilliant) perform a disservice. Now any ass has these pictures available to use in 'explaining' symptoms of an illness."

Philosophical psychology is not cognitive psychology, which seeks models of what goes on in the brain when we think, know, talk, perceive. Cognitive psychology nowadays most often means the study of how mental representations are connected with cognitive functions in the brain. Wittgenstein would have been quite hostile to this. "I don't care whether his brain goes green or red when he thinks of that."

Even when cognitive psychology does not postulate representations in the brain, it still seeks *explanations* of what is going on in the head when we act or think or talk. That is just what Wittgenstein resists. "People who are constantly asking 'why' are like tourists who stand in front of a building reading Baedekker and are so busy reading the history of its construction that they are prevented from *seeing* the building." "The tendency to explain instead of merely describing" gives only bad philosophy. *Describing:* that is what he would like to be doing. "Not to explain, but to *accept* the psychological phenomenon—that is what is so difficult."

> Mere description is so difficult because one believes that one needs to fill out the facts in order to understand them. It is as if one saw a screen with scattered color-patches and said: the way they are here, they are unintelligible; they only make sense when one completes them into a shape.—Whereas I want to say: Here *is* the whole. (If you complete it, you falsify it.)

I find this conception of philosophical psychology oddly congenial to Descartes. That's odd, because Descartes was a great explainer. He did make explanatory models of how the body works, of the movements of the blood, even in the brain. He was fabled to have made a human robot, thrown overboard during a storm on the last voyage to Sweden because the sailors thought it was a Jonah. He was, then, intrigued by speculations about how the body works. The mind, however, is something else. He thought it is not in the same ballpark, or in another ballpark, either: mind and body are about as different as the Oakland A's and the letter A. That is, they are not open to remotely the same styles of description, and whereas the Oakland A's often need explanation, it is obscure what it would mean to try to explain the letter A.

Descartes was very cagey about the relationship of mind to body. He did not like the ancient formulation that "I am in my body as a pilot in his ship." He wrote that instead "I am most tightly bound to my body, and as it were intermingled with it, so that it and I form a unit." An interviewer asked what he meant by that. Descartes tartly replied: "It is very difficult to explain; but our experience is enough, since it is so clear on this point that it cannot be gainsaid. This is evident in the case of the feelings and so on." It is possible to put some of Descartes's descriptions of love, yearning, and desire alongside those of Wittgenstein and not quite know whose is which. "I find my arms reach out as if to embrace something; my soul is thereby moved to join itself willingly to this object." "One really always thinks of the stance of the body towards an object. The stance of the soul to the image is just what one might represent in a picture: the man's soul, as it leans with gestures of longing towards the picture (an actual picture) of an object." The first remark was written in 1647, the second in 1947.

It seems to me that Descartes wants to say not only that all this is "very difficult to explain," but also that one ought not to try to explain the way in which events in the brain are associated with feelings. There is a whole domain of descriptions about how one feels thirsty, sees trees, grieves, and so forth, where one would be making some sort of conceptual error to ask for explanations of a materialistic sort. This is the important sense in which Wittgenstein and Descartes are equally dualistic.

I would never urge that a person cannot learn from both philosophical and cognitive psychology. I say only that they are different enterprises, of which only the latter could ever be explanatory. Human interests are commonly so narrow that you won't find many people who, like Descartes, could take pleasure and profit from both kinds of endeavor. But we must not let differences in taste or in life-projects make us think that one of these enterprises is right-minded while the other is wrong-headed.

We must not imagine that Wittgenstein, in rejecting explanation, randomly describes a "screen" of scattered mental events, refusing to "complete" it for fear that he might "falsify it." His paragraphs are never unmotivated. They turn out always to be directed at "the problems that trouble us." He means conceptual problems and confusions. I shall take only one example, a sustained discussion of "imaging" in Volume II, pages 13–28. "Imaging" is the best the English translator can do for the activity of forming images. The word "image" translates *Vorstellung*, as central a term of art as exists in the whole of German philosophy. It is a word variously translated as "representation" or "idea," but Wittgenstein uses it more in the sense of "image," like the English translation. Indeed, the opening shot is fired not at a German thinker but at a Scotch one. "Auditory images, visual images—how are they to be distinguished from sensations? Not by vivacity."

The target is David Hume, who, like Descartes, would have liked to build up all knowledge from our immediate mental experiences. He badly wanted a way to tell mere ideas (which would include visual images) from sensations and sense impressions. "They differ," Hume wrote, "only in their different degrees of force and vivacity." To call sensations more lively than images is to suppose that they are the same sort of thing, all bits of that global Cartesian "thought." That is so wrong that we should not even assert that seeing and imaging are *different* phenomena. Better to say that neither is a phenomenon, and that "image" and "sense impression" do not name kinds of entities.

Wittgenstein is very thorough. He gently probes the idea that still lures many a person: a sense impression and an image might have the same "experiential content." He does not sarcastically urge (as did the Oxford Philosopher J. L. Austin in *Sense and Sensibilia*, 1962) that an "image" and a "sense impression" of the Taj Mahal would never look the same. On the contrary. Could I not form a detailed image of a face, and later see exactly that face in real life? Would not my earlier image have the same "experiential content" as my later seeing? (Wittgenstein often hands his interlocutor a better example than we read in his real-life opponents.) He holds that "one can *not* say the two are not the same on the grounds that an image and an impression never look alike." We might even draw just one picture to illustrate what first one imaged and later saw. If you like, you can call that very picture—the one you drew on the paper—the "experiential content" of both events. "Only one mustn't allow oneself to be deceived by the myth of the *inner picture*." It was of course just that myth that forced Hume to distinguish images and sense impressions in terms of their vivacity.

Instead, consider what may be essential to our usage of words such as "image" and "see." I call Wittgenstein a philosopher of language, but he is not a "linguistic philosopher" of the sort once dominant in Oxford, and who studied, often with great panache, the actual uses and nuances of English words and phrases. Wittgenstein directs us often to imagined language games to get at what is essential to this or that concept. So imagine two games. In one of them people say, "Look at that figure!" perhaps pointing to a cube in a book of geometry. In the other they say, "Imagine that figure!" One game goes along with other instructions such as "Look over there!"—said holding up the book. The other might have, "Shut your eyes." The verb "see" will have a role in one, but need not in the other. ("A language game comprises the use of *several* words." But only several.)

We are not to think of seeing and imaging as being different phenomena in themselves, but as verbs distinguished by the ways in which they "relate to a host of important kinds of human behavior, to the phenomena of life." The phenomena are not the seeing and the imaging, but the practices in which they are embedded. Wittgenstein's examples include: "closing one's eyes to form an image, straining to see something, following a moving object with the eyes."

In the mere fifteen pages devoted to this topic, numerous considerations weave in and out. Imaging, for example, seems subject to the will while seeing is not. We can call up, form, or banish images, but seeing is not like that. Is that the real difference between the two kinds of thing? No. Wittgenstein tells a story where we might say that sense impressions are as subject to the will as are images, but that does not reduce them to the same kind of thing. We are led back to the more general point: "With the sentence 'images are voluntary, sensations are not,' one differentiates not between sensations and images, but rather between the language games in which we deal with these concepts."

"In philosophizing," wrote Wittgenstein, "we may not *terminate* a disease of thought. It must run its natural course, and *slow* cure is all important." My speedy snippets from a few pages are no substitute for slow reading, especially since they cannot adequately illustrate Wittgenstein's thesis of disunity—that we engage in endless loosely overlapping language games. Once we have described imaging, other stories must be told for other mental activities such as hoping, wishing, describing, hearing, and so forth. His remarks about "cures," alas, are too often overemphasized. We are sometimes told of a Wittgenstein as therapist who would gladly bring philosophy to an end. He certainly did think that we are prone to certain kinds of conceptual mistakes, and he detested philosophers who feel good being quick, clever, and flashy, three arguments on the blackboard and a hundred more in the pockets. From none of that does it follow that Wittgenstein either ends philosophy or stands outside it. My little example about imaging reminds us how much he stands in our own tradition. He himself did not quit, but kept on filling up notebooks on new topics until he was on his deathbed. His last written thoughts were about concepts of color. They are published in a short book, *Remarks on Colour* (Wittgenstein 1977), and are very much an instance of work in progress.

Emotions, intentions, and ever so many more aspects of being alive are illumined in these two volumes of *Remarks*. Why, he asks, may sorrow and grief be so naturally described as gray, or as a heavy cloud descending from the sky? Such an array of particulars does not, however, stay put as a row of isolated insights. There *are* general implications. For example, many of our leading philosophers at present debate the merits of this or that proposed systematic and general theory of meaning for a natural language. This takes many forms. There is no current work by an American philosopher that I more admire than that of Donald Davidson—as may be seen from my review of his papers on language (Hacking 1984a). His account of meaning, truth, understanding, and translation, combined with his theory of human action, has an enormous range of consequences. It starts with a precise version of the idea that language, action, and belief are to be approached as a whole. Our evidence may be piecemeal, but our interpretation of another person's speech is a theory about one unified thing.

Michael Dummett at Oxford has for some years been mounting an "atomistic" attack against Davidson, holding that we confer meanings upon our words almost one by one, situation by situation. Even he, although once strongly influenced by Wittgenstein, has fallen prey to the idea that there could be such a thing as a "theory of meaning" in general, and that there could be a general theory of the conditions under which what we say is true. I think that Wittgenstein's theme of the disunity of life, reason, and language runs counter even to Dummett, let alone Davidson. Neither of these men nor their students will be much moved by the disunity aspect of *Remarks on the Philosophy of Psychology*, but in the end Wittgenstein's little guerrilla army of unlike examples may begin to tell against the big guns.

More immediately, the disunity thesis helps vindicate the claim that there is a legitimate project to be called philosophical as opposed to cognitive psychology. It even connects with a phenomenon familiar to ethnographers, namely that once you have ceased being flummoxed by an inability to recognize phonemes and "words" in a really foreign language, you can make quick headway with translation. But as soon as you get to interesting concepts, things go poorly. You may find that hoping or expressions of anger or joy don't have a place in that culture, thanks to a lack of the same array of practices that we have in ours. Likewise for *their* important concepts. Moreover, having grasped "hope," the other people needn't by analogy grasp our "joy" or "anger," for each is embedded in its own web. This may even be true for speech acts, like promising or even stating, that are sometimes held out as neutral between cultures. Moreover, the disunity thesis is germane not just to psychology, but also to the "motley of mathematics" which Wittgenstein did discuss at length, and to the manifold styles of scientific reasoning about which he was silent.

15

Dreams in Place

This paper was first given in April 1998 at a conference in Toronto in celebration of my colleague André Gombay, who is fascinated by both Descartes and Freud. Dreams seemed the right way for me to connect the two enthusiasms. André gave me a copy of Michel Foucault's *Madness and Civilization* early in 1968, when we were both teaching in Uganda—and thus set in motion the chain of thoughts contained in this chapter. In June of 1998 I substantially revised the text; it has now been published in the *Journal of Aesthetics and Art Criticism,* 59 (2001), 245–260.

Objectivity has its home in the waking life; dreams welcome unreason. So much is familiar to all good rationalists in the Western tradition. Yet there are ways to weave dreams into knowledge, evidence, and proof, a fabric beloved by Aristotle, sought after by the Enlightenment, and respected by a host of small-time, old-time rationalists like myself. How do we do it? By putting dreams in places, or places in dreams. But it is a slippery operation. I shall end by wondering if it is not the dreamer who has made the place for objectivity, and still runs it behind the scenes.

Dreams are either significant or not—and "significant" itself can have many meanings. Significant dreams, in the cultural tradition with which I identify, are characteristically associated with place, although, as is the way with dreams, the role of place is protean; the place may be the place in which the dream is dreamt, or a place in the dream; "place" is itself a trope that is freely moved about. There seem to be no compelling reasons why dreams and places should be so related. We do know that reasoners from time immemorial dismiss dreams and fail to locate them; the anti-reasoners take dreams seriously, and as part of their strategy seem always to fit them into place, generously understood. That is how, in any world with a craving for objectivity, dreams are made "objective"—by embedding them in place, or by embedding places in them. Descartes, who wrote down three dreams at the moment of his epiphany, took them to be highly significant as portents of his future life as a philosopher. I argue that his dreams fit well into my theme of place, and that Descartes created reason for himself out of this unreason.

I intend to discuss some aspects of dreams in what I will call my culture, namely relatively high European literate culture, as traditionally conceived, with Greek and Judaic origins. More specifically for present purposes, my culture includes classical Greece, biblical Israel, the *Roman de la rose*, Descartes, Freud, and the Stanford sleep laboratories. That list lumps together distinct civilizations in a way that may be traditional but is hardly fashionable. One principle of lumping is that this is a sequence of groups or individuals that prize writing.

There are now many ethnographic accounts of dreaming. They all emanate from "my" culture. As in so many other social domains, universalism and localism compete. Some students find that features of dreaming are shared by all peoples. Under the influence of Freud or Jung, they detect a universal symbolic system. Even structuralist anti-Freudians, taking a cue from Lévi-Strauss, discover a logic of dream scene-switching, a mechanism of the mind or its languages exemplified in all societies (for example, Kuper 1989). Conversely, a great deal of recent ethnographic work on dreams expresses the view that almost everything about dreaming differs from culture to culture. I take no stand on such issues, but my opening presumption is that until we are given compelling reasons to the contrary, a great many aspects of dreams will be peculiar to the society in which the dreamer dreams, remembers the dream, tells the dream, acts out the dream, behaves in the light of the dream, and incorporates the dream into waking life (or excludes it). That is why I say I am discussing "my" culture, a rag-bag of snippets familiar to most of us. One important difference between my culture and what appears to be the case in many others is that there is a definitive break between waking and dreaming life. When someone's dreams and waking life flow into each other, the person is considered mad.

Descartes's Three Dreams

I know of my culture because it is a written culture. The peoples of West Asia were peoples of the book. Hence we know a lot about dreams in Israel, in Islam, and even in Mani, the prophet Mani being undoubtedly the most dream-inspired founder of a great religion. Needless to say, to write is already to place—on the page, the parchment, the tablet, the stele.

Writing plays a remarkable role in some classic dreams of my culture. For example, Descartes (to whom I shall return several times) had three dreams during the night of 10 November 1619, when he was 23. Yes, the night of the *poêle*, the stove on which he was sleeping. He wrote down these dreams. The text itself is lost, but his first biographer, Baillet, did see the text in a notebook, as did Leibniz. The text is called the *Olympica*. It has been helpfully reprinted and re-examined in two recent books (Cole 1992 and Hallyn 1995).

The first was a bad dream, then a short dream of sparks that I like to think of as the strobe dream, and then a good dream. I shall say more about the bad dream later. I have nothing to say about the strobe dream, the dream in which there is a bolt of lightning and the room is full of scintillating sparks. I imagine the sparks are like the flashing of a stroboscopic light. John Cole (1992, 146) attends to a different aspect of the dream and calls this the Thunder Dream. Descartes has had such dreams before. He has learned to blink hard and wake himself up. The sparking goes away and he falls asleep.

The third dream is a dream of written words. Some commentators state that the dream is a literary composition, on the ground that dreams like this are commonly reported around 1600, especially in describing or announcing radical changes in one's life. Hence Descartes had ample literary models on which to draw in order to compose his own contribution to this literary genre of a decisive life choice being enacted or represented in a dream. (A *Raptus Philosophicus* of 1619, by Rodophilus Staurophorus, has been mentioned in this connection. Boethius is cited as a root source for the genre.) At the strongest: Descartes never dreamt this dream at all; he composed it while awake, or at any rate dressed it up while awake.

The fact that Descartes told a dream according to a genre is no proof that he did not dream the dream. All of our own dreams that we tell, we tell according to the genres of our time and place. Of course Descartes could have made up the third dream. But dreams are mimics. Descartes could equally well (if there is a truth of the matter) have had exactly the dream he wrote down, a dream that aped a familiar literary form.

In the third dream Descartes saw a book on a table. He opened it and saw that it was some sort of dictionary or encyclopedia, and was overwhelmed by the hope that it would be very useful. But at that moment he found another book to hand. It was an anthology of poetry. Opening the book he found the verse *Quod vitae sectabor iter?* (What life shall I lead?) Immediately a man he did not know gave him a piece of verse beginning *Est et non* (it could be expressed as "Yes and No"). Descartes said this was from the *Idylls* of Ausonius, which are in the anthology on the table. But then he found the dictionary (encyclopedia) was less complete than it was at first viewing, and he could not find the verses *Est et non*. The words were not in their proper place!

There is much more, including Descartes's attempts, while dreaming, to interpret what he has just dreamt, and knows, while dreaming, to be a dream. Plato's debate between poetry and philosophy is enacted in the play between the verses and the dictionary. Here I emphasize only the role of writing, and the difficulty of locating the writing, of finding it in place. Descartes cannot obtain the text he wants in the anthology, he is thrust towards the dictionary, and so on. There are also other elements connected with printing, if not writing. Descartes sees certain copperpoint plates that he cannot identify. Throughout there is both the recognition of the word or the image and yet the inability to grasp exactly what it is.

The same inability appears in the most famous dream of modern times, Freud's *Irma* dream of 23–24 July, 1895. (Yes, one could develop a subsidiary theme, that not only are dreams in place, but dreams, or at any rate the most memorable dreams, occur at precisely recorded dates, such as 16 November 1623, or 23 July 1895.) "This is the first dream," Freud wrote in a footnote, "that I subjected to so exhaustive an interpretation." It was the starting point for *The Interpretation of Dreams* and for full-fledged psychoanalysis. "We were directly aware, too, of the origin of the infection. Not long before, when she was feeling unwell, my friend Otto had given her an injection of a preparation of propyl, propyls . . . propionic acid . . . trimethylamin (and I saw before me the formula for this printed in heavy type)" (Freud 1954, 107). Here we have two dreams, one of which inaugurates the Enlightenment, and the other, psychoanalysis. In both cases there is a writing that the dreamer cannot quite locate or make out. You might say that these are frustration dreams. Certainly. What is notable is that the frustration is precisely an inability to make out a text, to find it in the right place.

I said that Descartes was dreaming in a genre of dreaming, and telling his dream in a genre of telling. Descartes and Freud are more typical than unique. These are not only frustration dreams but inaugurating dreams, initiation dreams, remembered in tranquility at the beginning of a career that is almost superhuman. The genius who begins an age suffers from no false modesty. For another example, take Wordsworth's *Prelude.* That was his retrospective vision of the origin of the poet, and, we might say, of the romantic movement in Britain. Book V has a dream analogous to the two just described. Had Wordsworth been reading Descartes, of whom he was to present a pastiche? Certainly he had been reading Cervantes. "At length / My senses yielding to the sultry air, / Sleep seized me, and I passed into a dream." He dreams an Arab knight, a "semi-Quixote" who holds a stone under one arm and a shell in the other hand. The stone, he continues,

> Was "Euclid's Elements;" and "This," said he,
> "Is something of more worth;" and at the word
> Stretched forth the shell, so beautiful in shape,
> In colour so resplendent, with command
> That I should hold it to my ear. I did so,
> And heard that instant in an unknown tongue,
> Which yet I understood . . . (*The Prelude*, V, 89–93)

The shell speaks, and foretells the destruction of the earth by flood. Yet although it speaks, the stone and the shell are "two books" that the Arab will bury (line 102). The dreamer never "doubted once but that they both were books" (113), though he saw plainly that one was a stone and one a shell. The book of geometry "wedded soul to soul in purest reason", while the other had the "power / To exhilarate the spirit, and to sooth, / Through every clime, the heart of human kind." Philosophy and poetry strike again! The dreamer begs for the two books, but the knight rides off into the "illimitable waste" with a wild flood pursuing him. Once again, frustration, unattainable words in other languages, books that will be buried or drowned.

Realism and Positivism in the Telling of Dreams

Almost everything that can be important *in* a dream can also be important, in some changed or even reversed modality, in the telling of the dream. For example, we see that writing not only occurs in these dreams, but also that we know about them because they have been written down. One of the things that is constant, in my culture, is that in order to be preserved, dreams must be rehearsed. We must recite the dreams to ourselves, we can tell them out loud, even to other people, or we can write them down upon awakening or after they are recalled by some chance incident of the following day. Otherwise they are lost.

This may not be a universal. Some peoples have a rather short repertoire of dreams to tell. It is really not very hard for them to recall what they dreamt, because there are relatively few dreams to tell. Is this small repertoire a narrative convention or a fact about their dreams? This question is useful for distinguishing two extreme attitudes to dreams.

Realist: It might be true, although it would be hard to find out without interfering with the ways in which these people dream, that their dreams are vastly more rich than the reports they give. So these people might have dreams as varied and unpredictable as mine, but the conventions of their community determine that they report only a small group of rather stylized dreams. The genre, on this view, is in the telling of the dream, but not necessarily in the dream itself. The realist position is the common sense of my culture, and, I suspect, of every human society that has ever existed.

Positivist: There is in general no fact of the matter, as to whether a dream differed from a dreamer's report of it. Better: it usually makes no sense to ask if the report accurately tells the dream. Of course on any one occasion a person may lie about what was dreamt. But in general, says the positivist, the way the dream is told *is* the dream. This is not because people truly report dreams (a contingent matter of fact), but because the report constitutes the content of the dream, by and large—and this is an analytic truth.

Norman Malcolm's slim volume *Dreaming* (1959) is one authoritative representative of such an attitude. He is entirely uncompromising. There is no more to the content of a dream than the report (or successive reports) of a dream. Forms of words such as "I am dreaming now" make no sense, because there are no criteria for their correct application. Malcolm's argument derives from his understanding of Wittgenstein (Hacking 1975b, chap. 5). But his immediate aim was to challenge the takeover of dream studies by the recently triumphant work on Rapid Eye Movement, which for a short time made it a law of nature that you dream if and only if you are asleep and your eyes are oscillating wildly. Hilary Putnam (1962) defended the scientists against the disciple of Wittgenstein, incidentally setting in motion his own highly regarded account of the meaning of "meaning" (1975a). Dreaming, seemingly so inconsequential, has the curious attribute of leading us on into deeper and deeper philosophical topics.

Whatever Malcolm's motivation, and wherever it leads, he provides the perfect example of what I am calling the positivist attitude to dreams. In Malcolm's opinion, it is an analytic truth that the dream as told is the dream. Freud, in contrast, was merely what we may call a methodological positivist. "We can help to overcome the defect of the uncertainty of remembering dreams if we decide that whatever the dreamer tells us must count as his dream, without regard to what he may have forgotten or altered in recalling it" (1953, 85). We *decide* that the dream as told *is* the dream.

I feel the force of both extremes, realist and positivist. But we should not limit ourselves to a formal choice between positivism and realism. All dream reporting is in a larger framework. The Brazilian ethnographer Eduardo Viveiros de Castro told me about an Amazonian people with a small, specific repertoire of narrated dreams. Here is an example of a type of dream, by no means peculiar to this group, and cheerfully cited by anti-Freudians, which a man would dream who wants to win a position of social power and leadership in the community. This is foretold by his dreaming of copulating with his mother, so he spends some time before falling asleep preparing for this dream, which is one of a couple of dozen possible dreams to have. (Dreams of incest were generally held to be auspicious in ancient Greek culture too, Sophocles notwithstanding. Plato was the odd man out, holding in Book IX of the *Republic* (571–2) that such dreams were disgusting and betrayed the foul instincts of the dreamer.)

In the Amazonian group dreams are integral to the whole of life. Our sharp distinction of dreaming/waking does not make much sense to them. They plan their dreams before they fall asleep, in the hope that they have the right (fortunate) dream that bodes well for some future concern. When they wake up, they immediately recite what they dreamt—from a small range of possible dreams. How different from my own life! I would be deemed to be a total bore, and doomed to be one, if I told my dreams every morning, especially if there were nothing odd or curious about them.

To return to my culture and Descartes: some critics say that the third dream must be a literary composition, given such a genre. The realist says that there is a real fact of the matter as to the extent to which the actual dream is correctly described by what Descartes wrote down. The positivist says that although of course Descartes could have been outright lying, in general the report given, even if highly stylized according to the conventions of the day, cannot properly be distinguished from what Descartes dreamt.

Losing Dreams: The Book of Daniel

We all know that we lose dreams. That is, we wake up with the conviction of having dreamt, but with only the foggiest recollection of what. Or we wake up with a goodish memory, but unless we at once rehearse the dream, it is usually forgotten a few moments later. At best, an incident during the day may trigger a recollection or reporting of a lost dream. Although these facts are so familiar, I should like to recall the greatest forgotten dream, in *Daniel* 2.

> And in the second year of the reign of Nebuchadnezzar, Nebuchadnezzar dreamed dreams, wherewith his spirit was troubled, and his sleep brake from him. Then the king commanded to call the magicians, and the astrologers, and the sorcerers, and the Chaldeans, for to shew the king his dreams. So they came and stood before the king. And the king said unto them, I have dreamed a dream, and my spirit was troubled to know the dream. Then spake the Chaldeans to the king in Syriack [viz: old Aramaic] O king, live for ever; tell thy servants the dream, and we will shew the interpretation.
>
> The king answered and said to the Chaldeans. The thing is gone from me: if ye will not make known unto me the dream, with the interpretation thereof, ye shall be cut in pieces, and your houses shall be made a dunghill. But if ye shew the dream and the interpretation thereof, ye shall receive of me gifts and great honours; therefore shew me the dream and the interpretation thereof.

"The thing is gone from me." This is, to my mind, the most powerful reminder of the fact that we lose dreams. Moreover, no one can tell another's dream. Yet Daniel did pull it off. In a "night vision" he saw what Nebuchadnezzar dreamt. (He re-dreamed Nebuchadnezzar's dream?) The king accepted what Daniel said. Cynics among us will say that Daniel was a great confidence trickster. He knew the king could not remember, so he invented the king's dream, and then interpreted it.

The dream of Nebuchadnezzar seems never to be mentioned by Freud. He would have known the book of Daniel, perhaps the greatest book of recorded dreams before *The Interpretation of Dreams* itself. Is this because there is a lot of Daniel in Freud, the man who learned to tell other people's dreams to their faces?

Read the book of Daniel for much more fascinating material on dreams. Note how words too play their role in the book. Daniel's biggest triumph is at Belshazzar's feast, where the words *Mene, Mene, Tekel, Upharsin* appear on the wall. Or rather, some signs that none can read appear on the wall. Daniel both pronounces them and interprets them. Indeed, the signs resemble dreams, which only he can tell, and only he can interpret. Here we do not have a forgotten dream, but letter-like marks devoid of meaning, terribly scary. (Or are they part of a dream after all?) In one of his most marvelous paintings, Rembrandt dares to paint the semblance of marks-without-meaning that Daniel will invest with meaning. Susan James (1997) used a detail from it for the cover of her recent book about the emotions; I would put the whole on the cover of a book about Freud.

The book of Daniel describes events of about the seventh century BCE. The book is almost entirely about dreams. An unusual idea about it has been suggested to me in conversation: the book is derived from a much older Sumerian tradition that starts around 2200 BCE. In Sumerian civilization dreams played a central role, with the court going from dream site to dream site around the kingdom, in order to have dreams at each site. If there is some truth in this suggestion, then the most dream-filled book of the Hebrew Bible may in part be an attempt to establish authority by recalling an ancient tradition, in which the place of the dream is central to its significance.

Dream Sites

The way in which dreams are told is an integral part of the dream. In Greek antiquity there was a fairly sharp distinction between significant and insignificant dreams. That was the solution to a problem of objectivity. The significant dreams have some objective character and help foretell the future. But the insignificant dreams mean nothing; they merely reflect personal concerns of the dreamer.

In a significant dream a god, or goddess, or some other significant other, stands at the head of the dreamer, and the dream is enacted by this other, who speaks to the dreamer. Even if you have never gone further than Book II of the *Iliad*, you will recall that Zeus sends to "Agamemnon, son of Atreaus, / a wooly menace, a Dream" that is just such a dream. My description is not quite right, for apparently the several Greek words for dreaming do not take propositional clauses as in our "I dreamt that" followed by a proposition. Instead they take objects; one dreams a person.

> The Dream stood above [Agamemnon's] head. It looked
> Like Nestor, the old man that Agamemnon
> Respected most, looked just like Nestor
> And this dream that was a god addressed the king. (Homer 1997, 21)

You might want, at least occasionally, to dream a significant dream. How do you do that? It was widely believed that there were certain sites, sacred sites, suitable for significant dreams. The best known was Epidaurus, favored by the healer Asclepius. In Epidaurus you might dream Asclepius standing over you. If he dreamt you as healed, you would awake with a memory of that, and be healed.

Many classical scholars take the highly stylized character of significant dreams to indicate that these dream reports are not to be understood literally. These reports, they say, simply do not have the feel of dreams (meaning, of "our" dreams). I react differently. I have no trouble imagining my dreaming such a dream, and have recently trained myself to dream dreams something like that. But they are not truly like that, because such dreams have no meaning, no life, within my present community. To repeat what I said about Descartes: dreams conform to the dream genres of the day. The realist and the positivist give different spins to this. The positivist is inclined to say, "these people told what they dreamt, so that is what they dreamt (in general, allowing for occasional lies)." The realist keeps open the unknowable option that what was actually dreamt was different from what was narrated. I do not take sides on that issue. Instead, I emphasize the importance of place to significant dreams.

The Greek philosophers had their own, rather skeptical line on dreams. They rejected the possibility of significant dreams, and paid little heed to place, either in or around dreams. Aristotle is closest to a modern rationalist sensibility, but even his texts about sleep, dreaming, and divination in dreams form a strange mix. There is a recent consensus that *On Sleep and*

Waking, On Dreams, and *On Divination through Sleep* are among the last of the Aristotelian corpus to be composed (Gallop 1990). Even though he is skeptical, Aristotle allows that possibly some dreams truly foretell the future. But he is convinced that dreams are not of divine origin. Even animals dream; gods would not impart dreams to animals, including humans. He thus implicitly undoes the distinction between significant and insignificant dreams, because one could save the divine origin of significant dreams by holding that animals dream only insignificant ones.

Aristotle's rational account of apparently precognitive dreams would serve any modern rationalist. We dream of things that interest us. Images are prompted by recent experience, but dreams re-order events and people. By coincidence, some dreams will match the future. Only those dreams that match are later recalled, and so mere coincidence gets turned into clairvoyance. Nothing is significant in itself, and nothing is dreamt in place. There is a good deal of medical lore, especially about how the state of one's digestion, and the amount of wine one has drunk, affects the content of dreams.

Aristotle did not completely give up on divination. We may be more aware of our bodily states when asleep, so dreams may help a physician detect an illness that has not yet become serious in waking life. We may form intentions while dreaming, if only by moving our limbs in ways that foreshadow how we may move them when we are later awake. Democritus conjectured that sleepers pick up "emanations" from moving objects. Perhaps, on one reading of the texts, he meant that they pick up the thoughts of others, a sort of ancient version of the telepathy imagined by psychic researchers at the end of the nineteenth century. Aristotle swallows just this much of the idea: motions of bodies elsewhere may transmit movements in the air or water that a sleeper may detect, and hence know what is going on elsewhere to a very slight extent. Stupid people with few thoughts will be more liable to be receptive to such feeble stimulations, and so it is that divination, if it does occur, is to be had from the mouths of simpletons. Nowhere is the site of the dream ever mentioned, and so no place is made for significant dreams.

Stories and Pictures

Dreams have to be told, and, if not written down, at least rehearsed, in order to be preserved. Narration provides stability for dreams. There may be an unexpected dependence in the reverse direction. Take Chaucer, the man commonly taken to have given English a new genre, the written-down tale, as opposed to epic, saga, history, myth, or religious foundation. We read the *Canterbury Tales* with such avidity that we seldom recall Chaucer's earlier (1370–1380, say) long poems such as *The Book of the Duchess, The House of Fame, The Parliament of Fowls.* These, and others such as *Dido,* are all dream poems, that is to say, stories that are cast in the form of dreams.

This genre was widespread throughout Europe, the most famous model being the *Roman de la rose.* Chaucer's dream-tellings are full of philosophical speculation—said to be strongly influenced by Boethius—about the nature of truth and objectivity. What can one believe? The senses? Dreams? (a question posed within a dream). Books? Revelation? Books in dreams? Written-down revelations that are dreamt? Revelations gained by reading a book in a dream? The inside/outside play is phenomenal: a regular pressure from the outside to tell which dreams are objective, significant, true predictors, but in Chaucer's dream poems, this question of objectivity is debated within the dream.

Then Chaucer had a brilliant idea (Boccaccio was there before him). It enabled him, on the occasion of being temporarily out of work because of a change in patronage, to write down the *Canterbury Tales.* He discovered that we can leave out the framework of telling a dream, and simply have the telling. The telling is still framed, but not as dream: each pilgrim must tell a story. That is where secular, fictional narrative begins in early English. Dreams must be told as narratives so as not to be forgotten, and, reciprocally, the genre of telling a fictional story is derived from the telling of dreams.

Chaucer himself may have felt quite liberated. He put only one dream into the *Tales:* the "Nun's Priest's Tale." Surely it is deliberate that this is a secondary tale, told by one whose role is to accompany someone else. In this tale the dreamer is a rooster, one Chantecleer, whose favorite hen, Pertelote, is a skeptic about dreams. Chantecleer believes that dreams foretell, a doctrine that Pertelote ridicules. He then dreams of dangers, but he does not heed his own theory of signification. So he is tricked by a fox, who carries him off to a wood. Luckily he tricks the fox at the last moment.

Some schools of psychotherapy encourage a disturbed person, especially a child, to draw dreams directly. That too is a way of telling a dream. Stepping up one level, how do we represent in a picture that someone is dreaming, and at the same time, the content of what is being dreamt? We have conventions, as illustrated in the comic strip. The speaker's words are in a bubble coming out of the mouth, a bubble with a firm boundary. Thoughts come out with a less firm boundary, connected to the head by small soap bubbles. The same convention is used for dreams, but the dreamer is portrayed as asleep, and in the big bubble there is a picture of what is being dreamt.

What about earlier conventions? Francesco Salviati (Francesco de' Rosso), 1510–1563, was one of the first of the "mannerist" painters and a great admirer of Michelangelo. He has done some striking works, like a painting of the three Graces as three men in drag. In Florence, Cosimo I started a tapestry factory to make 20 giant tapestries for Salle de Due Cento in the Palazzo Vecchio. Salviati was hired to make one of Joseph interpreting Pharaoh's dream of the seven fat years followed by seven lean ones. Pharaoh is on a couch (yes, really) with Joseph nearby, manifestly interpreting the dream, but how to portray the dream? In the tapestry there is a Renaissance window, properly framed, in which one sees seven lean cattle devouring seven fat ones. One corner of the frame is posed just off Pharaoh's shoulder. Salviati also made a small cartoon Salviati in preparation for the tapestry (reproduced in Monbeig Goguel 1998). In the cartoon the corner of the frame is posed exactly at Pharaoh's head. A picture is made to be a picture of a dream by being put in the right place.

The tapestry was hung on 16 May 1548. It has been conjectured that it was a contribution to the great debate about the paragon of the arts that excited Florence in 1547. Which is the greater art, sculpture or painting? Here is one way in which painting is superior. You can easily represent a dream in a painting, by putting it in the proper place on the canvas or cloth. But there is no such way to represent dreaming in sculpture. That is a simple consequence of physics and the strength of materials: a sculpted dream attached to Joseph's shoulder would break off (unless it were on a frieze, which is the inferior mode of sculpture).

Back to Descartes

In the first major collection of ethnographic papers on dreams, one editor wrote that in the modern era inaugurated by Descartes, "We have less need of our dreams" (Callois and Grunebaum 1966). Yet this lessening of the need for dreams had been going on long before Descartes. (And Aristotle had no need of dreams! There were lots of Aristotelians between Aristotle and Descartes.) One might say of Chaucer and some of his contemporaries that they had less need of their dreams. And in a literal sense, Chaucer had less need of dreams when he stopped writing dream poems and started writing tales. Nevertheless Descartes is pivotal. This is not because he introduced skepticism with an argument from dreams. Noting the familiarity of dream arguments, Hobbes tartly objected to the first Meditation: "I am sorry that so excellent an author of new speculations should publish this old stuff." (That is the racy—and accurate—translation of Anscombe and Geach (Descartes 1964).)

Why then should Descartes be pivotal, if he is merely regurgitating tiresome old platitudes? Because at the age of 23 he had that epiphany, his dreams. He wrote them down in the notebook in which he kept many serious thoughts. I think he took them seriously for the rest of his life. I believe (against most commentators) that dream skepticism is a *live* skepticism for Descartes: that is, not a mere philosophical position, but genuine doubt. Moreover, this is in part because of the content of those three dreams, to which I shall return.

What do I mean by *live* skepticism? I introduced the term in Hacking (1993b), adapting the adjective "live" from William James. I mean that one is genuinely in doubt, and terrified that one's doubt might be well warranted. All of us can understand dream skepticism, but hardly any of us are genuinely moved by it for any length of time. But suppose one took it seriously. Compare solipsism. David Pears (1987–88) has argued that Wittgenstein actually felt or experienced solipsism, which most of us think of as a mere philosophical stance. Louis Sass, a philosopher with a thorough training in psychiatry, goes further in his book subtitled *Wittgenstein, Schreber and the Schizophrenic Mind* (1994). (Daniel Paul Schreber was the high court judge of Saxony whose book-length report of his own madness [1955] served Freud as his paradigm of paranoid schizophrenia.) Sass compares the mental conditions of Wittgenstein and Schreber, arguing that they are similar, and that Wittgenstein's philosophy is a troubled but sane response to that condition of mind which incidentally produces a live skepticism about the very existence of other minds—and which drove Schreber mad. For a profoundly moving version of this idea, one should read Thomas Bernhardt's single-paragraph novella, *Wittgenstein's Nephew* (1986). The eponymous nephew appears to be a strange merging of the two men, Ludwig Wittgenstein and Daniel Paul Schreber. Live skepticism is close kin to madness.

I suggest that Descartes and dreaming are comparable to Wittgenstein and solipsism, and that Descartes at least for a time experienced a live skepticism about dreams. In the convoluted replies to the seventh set of objections, Descartes observes that he was "the first philosopher to over-turn the doubts of the skeptics" (AT VII 554). Well, perhaps this mis-states matters. I agree with Myles Burnyeat (1982), who has argued that Des-cartes introduced a wholly new level of skepticism, unknown in the Greek tradition. I add the thought that Descartes did not only make this intellec-tual step forward (or backward into chaos); he also experienced it as a live doubt, not as a paradoxical conundrum.

On this view, Descartes was right and Hobbes was wrong. He was the first to overturn a wholly new skepticism about dreams, his own. Hobbes did not see the point, because he could not experience the new skepticism. Only at the very end of the *Meditations* could Descartes laugh at his worry about dreams. Is it the aftershock giggle of someone who was truly scared?

> The exaggerated doubts of the last few days should be dismissed as laugh-able. This applies especially to the principal reason for doubt, namely my inability to distinguish between being asleep and being awake. For I now notice that there is a vast difference between the two, in that dreams are never linked by memory with all the other actions of life as waking expe-riences are . . . when I distinctly see where things come from, and when I can connect my perceptions of them with the whole of the rest of my life without a break, then I am quite certain that when I encounter these things I am not asleep but awake and I ought not to have even the slight-est doubt of their reality if after calling upon all of the senses as well as my memory and my intellect in order to check them, I have no con-flicting reports from any of these senses.

Coherence arguments like that are two a penny in the history of philoso-phy. What is remarkable is not the argument, but that it comes as the dénouement of one of most powerful European texts of all time.

One does sympathize with Hobbes. Why does Descartes find dream skepticism so exciting? Hobbes was fascinated by dreams, but as a question of physiology and psychology, not as epistemology and metaphysics. My answer is that Descartes was that rare thing, a philosopher who invents and experiences live philosophical skepticism. At the end of the *Meditations* he recites the old stuff, the coherence argument, but only because by then he has convinced himself that he no longer experiences live skepticism.

Another Young Man Aged 23

Descartes had his dreams when he was 23. (Spinoza was excommunicated when *he* was 23, and dreams were not in the forefront of his thought.) But here is what another thoroughly modern young man wrote about dreams when he was 23, Leibniz, in 1669:

> We have this criterion for distinguishing the experience of dreaming from being awake—we are certain of being awake only when we remember why we have come to our present position and condition and see the fitting connection of the things which are appearing to us, and to each other, and to those which preceded. In dreams we do not grasp this connection when it is present, nor are we surprised when it is absent. It is to be noted, however, that now and then the dreamer himself observes that he is dreaming, yet the dream continues. Here he must be thought of as if he were awake for a brief interval of time, and then, once more oppressed by sleep, returned to the previous state. It is also to be noted that some men can wake themselves up, and it is a familiar experience of mine that, when some pleasing vision presents itself, I notice that I am dreaming and try my eyes and pull them open with my fingers to admit the light. We should also think about the cause of sensations of falling out of bed, which are popularly ascribed to lapses into sin, and which occur sometimes, and to some people, almost between the limits of sleep and waking, so that they are suddenly awakened at the very moment of falling asleep. Sometimes when this has happened to me, I can scarcely persuade myself to fall asleep all night. For in the first moment of falling asleep, I suddenly recollect myself, and, sensing this fact, leap up. Nor ought we to overlook the spontaneous ejection of semen without any contact in sleep; in wakers it is expelled only when they are strongly agitated, but in sleep the spirits are moved internally by a strong imagination alone and without any rubbing of the members. I have also heard this confirmed by a physician. (Leibniz, 1975, 2, 276–8)

Leibniz and Descartes both gave a coherence criterion to distinguish dreaming from waking life. But Leibniz never entertained live skepticism about dreaming. He even granted that we could have a coherent lifelong dream, but then it would not matter that it was a dream. This thought is in the same vein as his seemingly solipsistic remark in the *Monadology* §6, that it would make no difference to me if there were nothing else in this world except this monad, me; in fact it would make no difference to anything, except God. Leibniz was completely untroubled by solipsism or any other kind of philosophical skepticism such as dreaming.

Leibniz found dreams totally ordinary, unsurprising, in almost every respect except one: he was amazed at the inventiveness of dreams, the way in which we, or at any rate he, could dream quite extraordinary visions of brilliant architecture, noble towers, intricate tracery, "while in waking it would be difficult for me and I could succeed only with enormous difficulty in framing the idea of the simplest house." Not to mention "all the wonderful speeches, books, letters, and moving poems which I have never read but have encountered in my dreams." The structures that Leibniz dreamt were so extraordinary, so beautiful, that they must be derived from the Art of Invention in its most sublime form, as intimations of the mind of God itself—from which, the young Leibniz seems to have opined, we ought to be able to construct an argument for the existence of God. I believe that he continued in this attitude. Certainly the dream of Descartes that interested Leibniz most was the very one that interests me least—the strobe dream. He seems to have thought that the scintillating sparks, like nothing on earth, might be one of those intimations of divinity.

In the vein of vision dreams, parenthetically, one building is famous in a poem presented as a dream, the most famous poem in English allegedly recovered from a dream under opiates. But even before the building we have a place. The dream is not dreamt in a site, but is the dream of a site, a building site, witness again to the malleability of the role of place, consistent with place having a role.

> In Xanadu did Kubla Khan
> A stately pleasure dome decree
> Where Alph the sacred river ran
> Through caverns measureless to man
> Down to a sunless sea.

Scholars agree that Coleridge crafted *Kubla Khan* when he was stone sober, and reject as romantic myth the story of the poem being written down on awakening. That does not preclude Coleridge's having dreamt the perfect architectural dream in the perfect site. And even if he did make up the whole thing, Coleridge knew the significance of place to dreams that aimed at significance.

Lucid Dreams (i)

For some readers the most interesting bit of my quotation from Leibniz will be the mention of dreams in which the dreamer is aware that he is dreaming. And recall that towards the end of this third dream Descartes started interpreting the early parts of the dream, knowing them to be a dream. Today this is called "lucid dreaming." In mid-nineteenth century, a sinologist at the Collège de France, Hervey de Saint-Denis, became fascinated by this phenomenon, which for Leibniz is commonplace. I think Hervey's profession as scholar of Chinese culture is relevant, for he thought that there were certain Chinese sects who made great use of such dreams. He tried to cultivate lucid dreams, for he thought they were a profound guide to some other reality, even if it was only a reality inside ourselves. Moreover, he thought we could gain some control over our dreams, increasing our awareness of them as we were dreaming (Hervey 1982). The label "lucid dreaming" did not become entrenched in English until 1913, when the Society for Psychical Research in London learned it from a Dutch psychiatrist, Frederick van Eeden, who was familiar with Hervey's essay. Like Hervey, van Eeden (1913b) was able to direct his dreams. The London SPR was, at that time, much involved in survival after death and medium contact with the other world. Van Eeden told how he directed his dreams, so that in them he was able to meet a number of dead people. A psychiatrist by profession, he was cautious in explaining his experiences and first wrote them up as a novel (van Eeden, 1913a). The practice of directing one's dreams was seldom explored, at least in print, but see Dumas (1909) for another example. Today, however, it has achieved cult status, and, as we shall see, makes use of the latest (pseudo) technology.

Dream direction is part of the ongoing subculture of lucid dreaming, which produces a stream of arcane books that continue to intersect with spiritism and parapsychology. How about this title (Godwin, 1994): *The Lucid Dreamer: A Waking Guide for the Traveller between Two Worlds?* Or this (Green 1990): *Lucid Dreaming: The Paradox of Consciousness during Sleep?* Where the cult of lucid dreams finds paradox and supernatural experience, Leibniz, the prototypical modern man, saw nothing paradoxical about lucid dreaming. The phenomenon was a rather trifling part of the natural world of everyday experience, and had a common-sense explanation.

The Bad Dream of Descartes

Back again to Descartes and dreams that matter. The story of Descartes's three dreams reads like pure Borges. The young man inscribes the dreams in his notebook. The notebook, much like my own notebook, begins at both ends, with comments on different topics, and has entries, separated by blank pages, on various topics. Who read the notebook? His biographer, and one other, Leibniz. Leibniz has much of the notebook copied, but barely mentions the dreams. The book is lost. We rely on the biographer's version, already a problem because the notes on dreams were in Latin, and Baillet published his summary of the dreams in French. Cross-checking with Leibniz's Latin transcriptions, we know that Baillet took some mild liberties with other parts of the text. To complete the circle of readers, Baillet's text was sent to the elderly Freud for analysis. Could Borges improve on that?

Freud began by being true to psychoanalysis. One had to know the associations that the dreamer would make on the basis of the manifest content. There was no way we can do that, so forget it. But then Freud was untrue to himself, for the sake of universalism. He suggested that some items in dreams have such a universal significance that one can draw a few inferences. The first dream caught his attention.

That dream begins with terrifying phantoms. As Descartes tries to drive them away, he experiences a terrible weakness in his right side. There is a great wind and he is whirled around on his left foot. He cannot stand up straight, for he is constantly blown to the left. He tries to get to a college chapel to pray, but realizes he has passed a man whom he knows but has not acknowledged. He is thrown against the chapel wall by the wind. Someone else calls out his name and tells him that he should seek Mr. *N*, who will give him something. Descartes thinks that this something is a melon from a far country. The man is surrounded by people who can stand up straight, despite the wind. The wind lessens, he wakes, he feels pain in his left side.

Descartes thought the melon signified the solitary life. His eighteenth-century readers thought the melon was a capital joke. Freud abandoned his resolve not to comment. The sinister bending to the left while others stand up straight, the stranger who is bringing the melon from afar, these all add up to one thing: Descartes' fear of his homosexual inclinations. When I related the dream to my wife, she said immediately, "oh, that melon. I suppose he has got someone pregnant." A whole new field for Cartesian research opens up. John Cole has offered the most convincing chain of associations between the melon and songs, saws, and sayings of the day. Here is one of several examples, current between 1585 and 1630, in translation:

> Friends in the present day
> Have this in common with the melon:
> You've got to try fifty
> Before you get a good one. (Cole 1992, 142)

Cole finds two preoccupations in the dream. The first is readily recognized: Descartes' break with his filial obligation to become a lawyer. The second is more personal. Descartes had a deep emotional attachment to his older friend and mentor, Isaac Beeckman. Descartes felt betrayed by Beeckman's unenthusiastic response to some of his sketched mathematics; hence the melon; his mentor was no true friend.

Something else is more interesting than the androgynous melon. Descartes was mercilessly buffeted by the wind, which thrust him against the wall of the chapel. At the end of his dreaming Descartes (as rendered by Baillet), thought that, "Le vent qui le poussait vers l'Église du collège, lorsqu'il avait mal au côté droit, n'était autre chose que le mauvais Génie qui tâchait de le jeter par force dans un lieu où son dessein était d'aller volontairement" (Hallyn 1995, 37). (The wind that blew him toward the chapel wall while his right side hurt was none other than the evil genius/spirit, which tried to throw him by force against the place where he intended to go voluntarily.) In the margin Baillet wrote what is presumed to have been Descartes original Latin: *A malo Spiritu ad Templum propellabar.* F. Hallyn (1995, 14) remarks that "the Latin text states that an evil spirit pushes the dreamer towards the chapel, while the French account mentions an evil *Genius.*" One may well ask what was the Latin equivalent of the other occurrences of "genius" in Baillet's version. For example, Descartes awakes convinced that, in his own words, *quelque mauvais génie* is the cause of the pain he feels in his left side. Baillet's words are: *que ce ne fût l'opération de quelque mauvais génie qui l'aurait voulu séduire* (. . . that it were not the work of some evil genius that wanted to lead him astray).

What were the words of Descartes? Allow me to imagine that Baillet did get things more or less right. Then there is a truly remarkable inversion. The first surfacing (of which we know) of the evil genius that Descartes uses to create a doubt more hyperbolic than dreaming was actually experienced as the product of the first of the dreams that Descartes himself says set him on his career.

That is highly contentious. Here is an acerbic comment by Geneviève Rodis-Lewis (1992, 328, n.29): "Whereas *malus spiritus* clearly refers to the spirit of evil *(l'esprit du mal),* Baillet's translation leads to confusion with the very much later *malin génie,* the deceiver of the *Meditations,* the instrument of supreme doubt. This confusion skews the entire interpretation offered by J. Maritain, *Le Songe de Descartes,* Paris, 1932."

Actually, Maritain seems to have been more interested in the "Spirit of Truth," identified as the lightning that sets off the strobe dream and which, Descartes thought in retrospect, *"had forecast these dreams to him before he retired to his bed."* He continues: "The historians of rationalism ought to settle for us once and for all, the identity of this genius. Could it be by any chance a cousin of the *Malin Génie of the Meditations?"* (Maritain 1946, 116, original italics). Has not the historian answered, in the person of Rodis-Lewis? She says, in effect, that there is not a chance that we have even a distant cousin here. I should say that I have quoted the only occasion on which Maritain appears to make a comparison with the malicious demon of the *Meditations,* either in the essay called "Le Songe de Descartes," or in the collection of essays which bears that name. I would hardly want to defend Maritain in general; his final paragraph in his final essay (on the Cartesian heritage) begins, "I have often said that Descartes (or Cartesianism) has been the great French sin in modern history"—and he urged the Russians to, as people now say, deconstruct Hegel, while the English and Americans should deconstruct Locke, each people taking upon itself the sin of its intellectual father. Not my cup of tea, but it is hardly debunked in its entirety by pointing to a single question asked by Maritain about whether the *malin génie* is cousin to a benevolent spirit of truth.

I am suggesting something far more radical than Maritain ever allowed himself in print, and I am not fully dissuaded by the historian. Rodis-Lewis does not quite convince me that we should never allow ourselves to speculate that the Baillet version, although using a French phrase that Descartes did not use in 1619 *(mauvais génie),* did capture Descartes's thought about his dream, a thought that lasted him the rest of his life.

Why is the evil genius—or, to use a better translation, a malicious demon—needed in the first Meditation? Why won't dreaming suffice for skeptical doubt?

The trouble seems to be this: "Whether I am awake or asleep two and three added together are five, and a square has no more than four sides." Even in dreams two plus three equals five, and squares have four sides. So dreaming skepticism is not enough. But why cannot I dream that I go to geometry class and learn that squares have five sides? In the next class (in my dream) I learn that two plus three equals four. Moreover, I dream that what I am taught is right, and I myself see that two plus three equals four. Why not? I suggest it is because the telling of such a dream ceases to be intelligible. "You can dream those words, if you want, but you cannot dream a square with five sides!" What we have is a constraint less on what is dreamt, but on what can be told as dream. The evil genius, descendant of that terrible wind in the original first dream, is then invoked to create a new kind of doubt that goes even deeper than dream skepticism.

The malicious demon does not enter until the page after the reflection on the truths of arithmetic and geometry. He is an all-purpose demon who can create doubt about anything, particularly the truth that I have a body, that I have a head and arms. *This* doubt, about my very body, is in fact strikingly close to some manifestations of what is called paranoid schizophrenia. A real live felt skepticism is close to genuine madness.

The Couch

Dreams, place, and significance are profoundly connected, but never, or almost never, in straightforward ways. I mentioned Epidaurus, a holy place in which the healing cult of Asclepius encouraged you to dream. That is straightforward. You go to a place to dream. The holy site for dreams, in the twentieth century, has of course been the couch. It is not that you dream on the couch, but you tell your dream on the couch, and free-associate thereon. Let the problem be: how can we make a dream *significant?* Solution: not to dream in a holy place, but to tell the dream in a sacred place, in this case, the couch. And Freud was not satisfied with the couch; he insisted that the room in which it sat was sealed off from the consulting room by double doors, each lined with felt. The temple at Epidaurus with its altar; the felt-insulated room with its couch.

Freud's couch and the double doors were unique, but they have become generic as psychoanalysts copied the layout of the analytic chamber. Some time before Freud set the pace in analytic interior decoration, he had another fixation with a place that he wanted to be hallowed, namely the building in which he first formed his theory of dream interpretation, 15 Bergasse. He wrote to his then closest friend, Wilhelm Fliess, "Do you suppose that some day one will read on a marble tablet on this house:

> Here, on 24th July, 1895
> The Secret of the Dream
> Revealed itself to Dr. Sigm. Freud.

The plaque was duly erected on 6 May, 1977 (Freud 1985, 417).

An Experiment with (Space)-Time

Between the two world wars, the writing down of waking memories of dreams was much encouraged in the English-speaking world by a strange book by J. M. Dunne, *An Experiment with Time* (1927). Perhaps influenced by Bergson and by the Cambridge philosopher McTaggart's reflections on time, Dunne believed that we live in all time, all the time, although we are primarily conscious of a shortish (roughly two-day) moving segment of time; the moments that we are conscious of in waking life are experiences of the middle of such a segment. But in dreams we blend together events that we experienced when awake during the whole of time surrounding a dream, both past and future, with events closer in time being more salient than those further away. We can establish this by writing down our dreams as soon as we wake (we must keep pencil and paper by the pillow). A day after recording a dream, we read it through, as an impersonal account, and notice many events, of a purely personal sort (reading about a volcano in the newspaper, rather than experiencing a volcano) that took place either preceding *or following* the recording of the dream. This is no precognition but cognition, in dreams, of the larger segment of time that we experience when dreaming.

Dunne was an eccentric innovator. Kenton Kröker told me that Dunne was among other things an engineer who built one of the first flying machines, and certainly the first swept-wing or "delta" aircraft, in the first decade of this century. He tried to sell it to the British military. They seem not to have been interested. He then flew the machine to France and apparently sold it to the French government. But his ideas about dreams really did take off. The middle classes of Great Britain were much taken by his practice of inscribing dreams. J. B. Priestley was so interested by Dunne's ideas that he used them in three plays that ran successfully in the West End of London (Priestley 1937a, b, 1939; cf. 1964). In 1939 Benjamin Britten composed a Suite for orchestra inspired by the third play, *Johnson over Jordan* (Britten 1993). A later thriller with Dunnean overtones, *The Inspector Calls* (1946), is still performed in repertory.

One reason for the success of Dunne's bizarre theory of time was its intimation of immortality. It presented a vision of existence in which we are, albeit dimly, aware of events in the whole of time, eternity, both past and future. This was a comforting thought for the myriad aging parents, widows, and spinsters who had lost their sons, husbands, or lovers in the Great War.

Dunne's writing down of his dreams was a terribly lonely, solitary event, made public and fascinating only when embedded in a bizarre theory about time. Indeed, Dunne wonderfully fits my theme of dreams in place. He wrote in the era in which his readers were fascinated by four-dimensional Minkowski space-time, even if they did not much understand it. Dunne made dreams significant by embedding them in an entirely novel "location" in this new hyperspace.

Internet Dreams

I should update my remarks about loneliness and the writing down of dreams. The telling of dreams has been totally transformed in the past decade. The Internet is now full of dream sites—bulletin boards and web sites in which to write dreams. Apparently people wake up in the morning and scurry off to write down their dreams. And other people in cyberspace comment, discuss, elaborate, interpret these dreams, and in exchange present their own. I said that I would be deemed to be a total bore, and doomed to be one, if I told my dreams every morning. Certainly that would be true if I did it to my nearest and dearest, but in the massive impersonality—or is it a new way to have a personality—of the Internet, I can tell my dreams to everyone, and leave to electronic space itself the question of who is reading, listening, attending, replying. It has been a subtheme of mine that writing moves around in connection with dreams; it has, in the past decade, moved afresh—to writing that is promiscuously available to everyone, and to no one. How is it that all these people, writing down their dreams on their keyboards, can imagine that the dreams are of the slightest significance? Because they tell them in that new place that they call cyberspace.

Between the couch and the Internet, the other holy place for dreaming in the twentieth century has been William Dement's sleep laboratory at Stanford, and others like it. Here we have far stranger practices than were ever conducted at Epidaurus. You are wired up, and a whole bunch of electrodes are attached to your face, and often to other parts of your body, to determine the movements of your eyes in sleep. Actually it is not so hard to observe eye movement while watching a sleeper in a suitably illuminated room. But the movements became significant only when a sacred place came into being, a sleep lab with a lot of expensive electrical equipment wired to your body.

The sleep labs produced one of the strongest claims ever made about dreams. For some time scientists believed that people are not dreaming *at all*, unless their eyes are moving in a way that would be detected in the sacred place, the sleep lab. The place certified the discovery of the rapid eye movement (REM) phenomenon. Kenton Kröker (2000) has confirmed in personal interviews with leading researchers that rapid eye movements can be readily detected without any apparatus at all. But in fact they were only attended to when experimental subjects were hooked up to apparatus in an uncomfortable laboratory. Kröker argues that the apparatus was necessary to embed dream study within a tradition of physiology research that descends from the electroencephalograph. That must be right, but I repeat the importance of the place, the special site where the sleeper is observed.

In fact, the simplistic identity of rapid eye movements and dreaming has not fared very well. Quite a number of physiological states during sleep have been distinguished. One of the original motivations was to be able not only to determine the time when one dreamed, but also to draw inferences about the content of the dream: remember that in 1953, when REM research took off, Freudian psychoanalysis held sway in the psychiatry departments of American medical schools. Since that time, correlations between the character and content of dreams reported when sleepers are aroused from these various states have become increasingly suspect.

There are more serious problems. Rapid eye movement is most common in the fetus. If REM were a mark of dreaming, we would have to grant a vigorous prenatal dream life. After birth, REM is only a little less common in the newly born infant. Among adults, movements are most rapid late in the sleep cycle. A recent paper may explain this. It appears to establish that rapid eye movements circulate the aqueous material so as to enable oxygen to get to the cornea when the eyes are closed. Hence the fetus needs constant washing of the cornea, since its eyes are never open to air; infants need a lot, as they sleep much, and adults need REM after they have had their eyes closed for a long time (Maurice 1998). That does not prove that dreams are not associated with rapid eye movement. It does take REM out of the domain of dreaming into ordinary experimental physiology. The core phenomenon is that our corneas need oxygen all the time, and sleeping eye movements, which can be determined in many ways, are useful for bathing the eye when it is shut. Dreams drop out, and so does the original sleep lab, the sacred place.

Lucid Dreams (ii)

The sleep lab, or its descendants, have not disappeared for people who take dreaming seriously. The lucid-dream seekers have always favored some sort of holy site, but have not agreed what it should be. The rapid eye movement detectors may be a godsend. Thus Keith Hearne (1990), who self-describes as "the world's leading researcher in 'lucid' dreaming," has a sleep laboratory in Manchester. He has gone one further than the early enthusiasts who held that you dream when and only when you have rapid eye movements. He has adapted the technology to determine times at which you are having lucid dreams. Suitable simple electronics either wake you up (because telling lucid dreams is an overwhelmingly profound experience) or reward you in sleep by reinforcement so you will go on dreaming lucidly.

The lucid-dream people adapt the technology of the sleep lab in environments that simulate the laboratory. Amusingly, some maintain that the easiest way to identify rapid eye movements is by certain changes in the moisture in the nose. Devices in the nostril are now used to detect these changes, and wake the dreamer up when the changes indicate REM and "hence" that dreaming is going on. All this is to serve the ends that the lucid-dream people think of as a path towards what they call (using the very word) *enlightenment*. This enlightenment is patterned on some ill-understood and romantic model of the wisdom of the East. That is, dreams are systematically worked upon, using the seeming paraphernalia of reasoned experimental science, in order to provide an anti-science, an anti-reason. We get the Janus-faced sense of the word "enlightenment": the enlightenment of the East that transcends reason, and the Enlightenment of Western Europe that elevates reason.

I am no Freud-basher, but I put that superb dialectical reasoner, Sigmund Freud, on the side of anti-reason. Dreams are interpreted to uncover, among other things, the repressed drives that are at work in the unconscious, the very drives that reasonable and civilized humanity will not own up to. Freud is not provoking an anti-science, but a science of anti-reason. He used that sacred place, the couch, to indulge the free associations arising from dreams. That is the deliberate cultivation of incoherence, of breakdown in pattern, in order to create a pattern. Dreams and the uses we have made of them since 1619 are not so much the mirrors of reason as the mimics of reason, which use the simulacra of reason to bring unreason to the surface.

We do not commonly attend to the sites of philosophy. Yes, there is old Kant taking his daily constitutional in Königsberg, by which people set their watches. And so on with other manifestly accidental anecdotes. Perhaps only in *Phaedrus* is there a true sense of place, and even that is because the place is a large prop, a stage setting, what the Japanese, in describing sacred sites, call "borrowed scenery." But one site in the whole of philosophy is different: the *poêle*, the stove. I put it to you that this, the site of Descartes's dreams, was wittingly constructed as a sacred place, so that his dreams should be significant. The man who would vanquish the skeptical threat that we might be dreaming had that place for the dream in which the evil genius constantly tried to knock him over—and then found the way to a base from which even the genius of evil could not knock him over into unreality. All that required a place. If the Cartesian room with the stove were still intact in a village on the banks of the Danube, we could erect a plaque there to the effect that,

Here, on 10th November, 1619
The Secret of Method
Revealed Itself to René Descartes.

Part of Descartes's entire project was to put dreams behind us, outside of us, forever. We feel that he succeeded with a vengeance. But dreams have a habit of creeping back in. The Enlightenment view, or the enlightened view, is that dreams are *nothing*, physiological productions that at most jumble up some recent memories. They are at most chance weavings of images or thoughts, many of which are connected to events of the preceding day. The essence of the dream is incoherence. But dreams have a habit of mimicking the coherent life, making mockery of it. If the coherent life is the life of reason, then dreams are anti-reason. But suppose reason got there by anti-reason?

My remarks about dreams have, with some deliberation, mimicked dreamscapes themselves, abruptly switching from scene to scene. Think of them as the work of a dreamer. My view of dreams, at least in my culture, is that each of us has a dreamer, or perhaps many dreamers. Dreamers play with us, as I have, slightly, played with the reader. Play? If I ask a class of first-year undergraduates to keep a dream diary for a month, they come back amazed. Not a one of them has had a dream for a week. But when I decided to keep them company with my own dream diary, my dreamer, who knows I know about censorship, maliciously counterattacked, allowing me to wake up with enough fully remembered dreams that it would take me an entire day to write them all down. People standardly remark that Freud's patients dream Freudian dreams (and Jung's, Jungian). But it is much more complicated than that. My dreamer deliberately plants Freudian puns, most of which are quite funny, to get me to focus on them, and not to listen to what else is being dreamt. The dreamer, for me, filches Freud's baton, while for another person it filches the holy electrodes and plays games with them. The dreamer, one might say, is always one step ahead of the culture, making fun of it. It was the brilliance of Descartes to trick his dreamer, reversing the reversal of roles, turning the *malus spiritus*, the wind, into a hyperbolic trickster in order to demolish him.

Many are happy to say that the era of Descartes brought in a gamut of new types of demonstration, tests, and proof—brought in a new sense of objectivity, a new feel for what is significant. It is part of that objectivity that dreams are ruthlessly excluded from real life, and cease to be signifiers at all. But the dreamer may have won after all. If that objectivity arose by reversing a dream held in a sacred place, is not the dreamer still in charge of objectivity?

Works Cited

Aarsleff, Hans. 1981. Vico and Berlin. *The London Review of Books* 3 (5–18 November): 6–8.

———. 1982. *From Locke to Saussure: Essays on the Study of Language and Intellectual History.* Minneapolis: University of Minnesota Press.

———. 1988. Introduction. In Humboldt (1988), vii–lxv.

Allen, Barry. 1993. Demonology, styles of reasoning, and truth. *International Journal of Moral and Social Studies* 8: 95–121.

Althusser, Louis. 1972. *Politics and History: Montesquieu, Rousseau, Hegel, Marx.* London: New Left Books.

Anscombe, G. E. M. 1957. *Intention.* Oxford: Blackwell.

———. 1976. The question of linguistic idealism. *Acta Philosophica Fennica* 28: 188–215.

Atran, Scott. 1990. *Cognitive Foundations of Natural History: Towards an Anthropology of Science.* Cambridge: Cambridge U.P.

Austin, J. L. 1962. *Sense and Sensibilia.* Oxford: Clarendon Press.

———. 1970. A plea for excuses. In his *Philosophical Papers,* edited by J. O. Urmson and G. J. Warnock. Oxford: Clarendon Press, 175–204.

Bachelard, Gaston. 1928. *Essai sur la connaissance approchée.* Paris: Vrin.

———. 1953. *Le Matérialisme rationnel.* Paris: Presses Universitaires de France.

Barnes, Barry, David Bloor, and John Henry. 1996. *Scientific Knowledge: A Sociological Analysis.* London: Athlone.

Barnstorff, J. 1895. *Youngs Nachtgedanken und ihr Einfluss auf die deutsche Literatur.* Bamburg: C. C. Buchner.

Belaval, Yvon. 1960. *Leibniz, critique de Descartes.* Paris: Gallimard.

Benjamin, Walter. 1966. *Briefe.* Edited by G. Scholem and T. Adorno. Stuttgart: Suhrkamp.

Bennett, Jonathan. 1964. *Rationality: An Essay towards an Analysis.* London: Routledge & Kegan Paul.

———. 1971. *Locke, Berkeley, Hume: Central Themes.* Oxford: Oxford U.P.

————. 1976. *Linguistic Behaviour*. Cambridge: Cambridge U.P.

————. 1984. *A Study of Spinoza's Ethics*. Indianapolis: Hackett.

————. 1988. *Events and Their Names*. Indianapolis: Hackett.

Berlin, Isaiah. 1977. *Vico and Herder: Two Studies in the History of Ideas*. New York: Random House.

————. 1981. Reply to Hans Aarsleff, "Vico and Berlin." *The London Review of Books* 3 (5–18 November): 8–9.

————. 1991. Two concepts of nationalism: An interview with Isaiah Berlin. *The New York Review of Books* 37 (21 November): 19–23.

————. 1993. *The Magus of the North: J. G. Hamann and the Origins of Modern Irrationalism*. Edited by Henry Hardy. London: J. Murray.

Bernhardt, Thomas. 1986. *Wittgenstein's Nephew*. Translated by Eward Oser from the German of 1976. London: Quartet.

Bloomfield, L. 1933. *Language*. New York: Holt, Rinehart & Winston.

Bloor, David. 1983. Mathematics, an anthropological phenomenon. Chapter 5 of Bloor's *Wittgenstein, A Social Theory of Knowledge*. London: Macmillan, 81–111.

Boswell, John. 1982–1983. Towards the long view: Revolutions, universal and sexual categories. *Salmagundi* 58–59: 89–114.

Bourdin, C. E. 1845. *Du suicide consideré comme maladie*. Paris: De Hennuyer & Turpin.

Brecht, Bertholt. 1967. Notizen zur Philosophie 1929 bis 1941. In *Gesammelte Werke in acht Bänden*. Frankfurt am Main: Suhrkamp, 8: 681–734.

Bréhier, Emile. 1937. La creation des verités éternelles. *Revue Philosophique* 112: 15–29.

Britten, Benjamin. 1993. *Johnson over Jordan. A Suite for Orchestra: 1939*. London: Faber Music.

Buchdahl, Gerd. 1969. *Metaphysics and the Philosophy of Science*. Oxford: Blackwell.

Buchwald, Jed Z. 1994. *The Creation of Scientific Effects: Heinrich Hertz and Electric Waves*. Chicago: University of Chicago Press.

————. 2000. How the ether spawned the microworld. In Daston (2000a), 203–225.

Burnyeat, Myles. 1982. Idealism and Greek philosophy: What Descartes saw and Berkeley missed. *Philosophical Review*, 92: 3–40.

Callois, Roger and G. E. Von Grunebaum, eds. 1966. *The Dream and Human Societies*. Berkeley and Los Angeles: University of California Press.

Canguilhem, Georges. 1967. Mort de l'homme ou épuissement du *Cogito? Critique* 21: 600–618.

Chomsky, Noam. 1966. *Cartesian Linguistics: A Chapter in the History of Rationalist Thought*. New York: Harper & Row.

————. 1980. *Rules and Representations*. New York: Columbia.

Chomsky, Noam and Michel Foucault. 1974. Human nature: Justice versus power. (A television debate between the two men). In *Reflexive Waters: The Basic Concerns of Mankind,* edited by Fons Elders. Gateshead, U.K.: Condor, 133–199.

Clifford, James. 1986. On ethnographic self-fashioning: Conrad and Malinowski. In Heller et al. (1986): 140–162.

Cohen, I. B. 1992. The *Principia,* universal gravitation, and the "Newtonian Style," in relation to the Newtonian revolution in science: Notes on the occasion of the 250th anniversary of Newton's death. In *Contemporary Newtonian Research.* Dordrecht: Reidel, 21–108.

Cole, John. 1992. *The Olympian Dreams and Youthful Rebellion of René Descartes.* Urbana: University of Illinois Press.

Comte, Auguste. 1830–1842. *Cours de philosophie positive.* 10 vols. Paris: Bachelier.

Condillac, Etienne Bonnet de. 1998. *Essai sur l'origine des connaissances humaines: Ouvrage ou l'on réduit à un seul principe tout ce qui concerne l'entendement humain.* Edited from the original of 1746 by Michèle Crampe-Casnabet. Paris: Alive.

Crombie, A. C. 1981. Philosophical perspectives and shifting interpretations of Galileo. In *Theory Change, Ancient Axiomatics and Galileo's Methodology: Proceedings of the 1978 Pisa Conference in the History and Philosophy of Science,* edited by J. Hintikka et al. Dordrecht: Reidel, 271–286.

———. 1987. Alexandre Koyré and Great Britain: Galileo and Mersenne. *History and Technology* 4: 81–92.

———. 1988. Designed in the mind: Western visions of science, nature and humankind. *History of Science* 24: 1–12.

———. 1994. *Styles of Scientific Thinking in the European Tradition.* 3 vols. London: Duckworth.

Cronin, Timothy J. 1987. *Object Being in Descartes and in Suarez.* New York: Garland. (Reprinted from *Analecta Gregoriana* 154 [1966].)

Dailey, Abram H. 1894. *Mollie Fancher, the Brooklyn Enigma.* Brooklyn: Eagle Publishing.

Daston, Lorraine. 1991a. Baconian facts, academic civility, and the prehistory of objectivity. *Annals of Scholarship* 8: 337–364.

———. 1991b. Objectivity and the escape from perspective. *Social Studies of Science* 22: 597–618.

———. 1995. The moral economy of science. *Osiris* 10: 2–24.

——— (ed.). 2000a. *Biographies of Scientific Objects.* Chicago: University of Chicago Press.

———. 2000b. The coming into being of scientific objects. In Daston (2000a), 1–14.

Daston, Lorraine and Peter Galison. 1992. The image of objectivity. *Representations* 40: 81–128.

Daston, Lorraine and Kathleen Parks. 1998. *Wonders and the Order of Nature.* New York: Zone Books.

Davidson, Arnold. 1996. Styles of reasoning, conceptual history, and the emergence of psychiatry. In Galison and Stump (1986), 75–100.

———. 2001a. *The Emergence of Sexuality: Historical Epistemology and the Formation of Concepts.* Cambridge, Mass.: Harvard U.P.

———. 2001b. Closing up the corpses: Diseases of the mind and the emergence of psychiatric styles of reasoning. In Davidson 2001a, 1–29. This paper was written by 1983, but was first published only in 1999 in a Festschrift for Hilary Putnam.

———. 2001c. Styles of reasoning: From the history of art to the epistemology of science. In Davidson 2001a, 125–141.

Davidson, Donald. 1974. On the very idea of a conceptual scheme. *Proceedings and Addresses of the American Philosophical Association* 47: 5–20.

Descartes, René. 1964. *Descartes: Philosophical Writings,* edited and translated by G. E. M. Anscombe and Peter Geach. London: Nelson.

Dixon, R. M. W. 1980. *The Languages of Australia.* Cambridge: Cambridge U.P.

Douglas, Jack D. 1967. *The Social Meanings of Suicide.* Princeton: Princeton U.P.

Dreyfus, Hubert L. and Paul Rabinow. 1983. *Michel Foucault: Beyond Structuralism and Hermeneutics; with an Afterword by and Interview with Michel Foucault.* Second edition. (The first edition lacks the interview). Chicago: University of Chicago Press.

Dumas, Georges. 1909. Comment on gouverne les rêves. *Revue de Paris* 16: 344–367.

Dummett, Michael. 1976. *Truth and Other Enigmas.* London: Duckworth.

———. 1991. *The Logical Basis of Metaphysics.* Cambridge, Mass.: Harvard U.P.

Duncan, A. R. C. 1957. *Practical Reason and Morality: A Study of Immanuel Kant's Foundations for the Metaphysics of Morals.* London: Nelson.

Dunne, J. M. 1927. *An Experiment with Time.* London: Macmillan.

Durant, John. 1991, Is science only an invention? *Times Literary Supplement* (15 March): 19. Cf. subsequent letters on this topic: Mark Weatherall, 29 March; Durant, 12 April; Neil Hirschson, 12 April; and Alan Gross, Christopher Lawrence, and Steven Shapin, 19 April.

Dyson, Freeman, J. 1988. *Infinite in All Directions: Gifford Lectures Given at Aberdeen, Scotland, 1985.* New York: Harper & Row.

Esquirol, E. 1812–1822. Suicide. Vol. 53: *Dictionnaire des sciences medicales.* Paris: C. L. F. Pancouck.

Ferrand, Gabriel. 1905. *Dictionnaire de la langue de Madagascar, d'après l'édition de 1658 et l'Histoire de la grande isle Madagascar de 1661.* Paris: E. Leroux.

Feyerabend, Paul. 1975. *Against Method.* London: New Left Books.

———. 1978. *Science in a Free Society.* London: New Left Books.

Flacourt, Etienne de. 1658. *Histoire de la grande isle Madagascar.* Paris: G. de Luyne. (Reprinted Sainte Clotilde, La Réunion: A. R. S. Terres créoles, 1991).

———. 1661. *Histoire de la grande isle Madagascar.* Paris: G. Clouzier. (Edited and reprinted by C. Allibert, Paris: Relire, 1995).

Fleck, Ludwik. 1979. *Genesis and Development of a Scientific Fact.* Translated by T. J. Trenn and R. K. Merton from the German of 1935. Chicago: University of Chicago Press.

Forrester, John. 1996. "If *p,* then what?" Thinking in cases. *History of the Human Sciences* 9 (3): 1–25.

Foucault, Michel. 1965. *Madness and Civilization.* Abridged version of *Folie et déraison: Histoire de la folie à l'âge classique.* Paris: Libraire Plon, 1961. Translated by Richard Howard. London: Tavistock.

———. 1970. *The Order of Things: An Archaeology of the Human Sciences.* Translated from the French ed. of 1966. London: Tavistock.

———. 1971. *The Archaeology of Knowledge.* Translated by A. M. Sheridan Smith from the French of 1969. New York: Pantheon.

———. 1973. *The Birth of the Clinic: An Archaeology of Medical Perception.* Translated by A. M. Sheridan Smith from the French of 1963. London: Tavistock.

———. 1975. (In collaboration with Blandine Barrett-Kriegel et al.) *I, Pierre Rivière, having slaughtered my mother, my sister and my brother. . . . A Case of Parricide in the 19th Century.* Translated by F. Jellinek from the French of 1973. New York: Pantheon.

———. 1977a. *Discipline and Punish: The Birth of the Prison.* Translated by Alan Sheridan from the French of 1975. New York: Vintage.

———. 1977b. *Language, Counter Memory, Practice: Selected Essays and Reviews.* Edited with an introduction by R. F. Bouchard; translated by Bouchard and Sherry Simon. Ithaca, N.Y.: Cornell U.P.

———. 1978. *The History of Sexuality.* Vol. I: An Introduction. Translated by Robert Hurley from the French of 1976. New York: Pantheon.

———. 1980. *Power/Knowledge: Selected Interviews and Other Writings 1972–1977.* Edited by Colin Gordon; translated by Gordon et al. New York: Pantheon.

———. 1983. On the genealogy of ethics: An overview of work in progress. In Dreyfus and Rabinow (1983), 229–253. Reprinted in Foucault (1997), 253–280.

———. 1984a. *The Foucault Reader.* Edited by Paul Rabinow. New York: Pantheon.

———. 1984b. What is enlightenment? In Foucault (1984a) and Foucault (1997), 303–320.

———. 1986. *Death and the Labyrinth: The World of Raymond Roussel.* Translated by Charles Ruas from the French of 1963. Garden City, N.Y.: Double-day.

———. 1997. *Ethics: Subjectivity and Truth.* (Vol. I of *Essential Works of Foucault 1954–84*). Edited by Paul Rabinow. New York: The New Press.

Fowler, H. W. 1926. *A Dictionary of Modern English Usage.* Oxford: Clarendon Press.

Frankfurt, H. G. 1966. Descartes' discussion of his existence in the second meditation. *Philosophical Review* 75: 329–358.

Freeman, Joseph John. 1835. *A Dictionary of the Malagasy Language.* Part I, English-Malagasy. Antananarivo, Madagascar: Press of the London Missionary Society.

Frege, Gottlob. 1952. On sense and reference. In *Translations from the Philosophical Writings of Gottlob Frege,* edited and translated from the German by Peter Geach and Max Black. Oxford: Blackwell.

Freud, Sigmund. 1954. *The Interpretation of Dreams.* Translated by James Strachey from the German ed. of 1900 and subsequent edition. London: Allen and Unwin.

———. 1985. *The Complete Letters of Sigmund Freud to Wilhelm Fliess, 1887–1904.* Translated and edited by Jeffrey Moussaieff Masson. Cambridge, Mass.: Belknap Press of Harvard U.P.

Galison, Peter. 1998. *Image and Logic.* Cambridge, Mass.: Harvard U.P.

Galison, Peter, and David Stump. 1996. *The Disunity of Science: Boundaries, Contexts, and Power.* Stanford: Stanford U.P.

Gallop, David. 1990. *Aristotle on Sleep and Dreams.* Peterborough, Ont.: Broadview.

Garber, D. and S. L. Zabell. 1979. On the emergence of probability. *Archive for History of Exact Sciences* 21: 33–53.

Gavroglu, Kostas. 1990. Differences in style as a way of probing the context of discovery. *Philosophia* 45: 53–75.

Glanvill, Joseph. 1661. *The Vanity of Dogmatizing, or Confidence in Opinions, manifested in a discourse on the shortness and uncertainty of our Knowledge and its Causes, with Reflexions on Peripateticism, and an Apology for Philosophy.* London.

Godwin, Malcolm. 1994. *The Lucid Dreamer: A Waking Guide for the Traveler Between Two Worlds.* Shaftsbury, U.K.: Element.

Gombay, André. 1972. *Cogito ergo sum,* inference or argument? In *Cartesian Studies,* edited by R. J. Butler. Oxford: Blackwell, 71–78.

———. 1988. Some paradoxes of counterprivacy. *Philosophy* 63: 191–288. Derived from the paper "Counter privacy and the evil genius" read to the Moral Sciences Club, Cambridge, 30 May 1973.

Goodman, Nelson. 1954. *Fact, Fiction and Forecast.* London: Athlone.

———. 1978. *Ways of Worldmaking*. Indianapolis: Hackett.

Green, Celia. 1990. *Lucid Dreaming: The Paradox of Consciousness during Sleep*. London: Routledge.

Greenblatt, Stephen. 1986. Fiction and friction. In Heller et al. 1986: 30–52.

Gusfield, Joseph. R. 1980. *The Culture of Public Problems: Drinking-Driving and the Social Order*. Chicago: University of Chicago Press.

Hacking, Ian. 1965. *Logic of Statistical Inference*. Cambridge: Cambridge U.P.

———. 1971. The Leibniz-Carnap program for inductive logic. *The Journal of Philosophy* 68: 597–610.

———. 1972. Review of Michel Foucault, *The Archaeology of Knowledge*. *The Cambridge Review* 95: 166–170.

———. 1974. Infinite analysis. *Studia Leibniziana* 6: 126–130.

———. 1975a. *The Emergence of Probability*. Cambridge: Cambridge U.P.

———. 1975b. *Why Does Language Matter to Philosophy?* Cambridge: Cambridge U.P.

———. 1980a. Neyman, Peirce and Braithwaite. In *Science, Belief and Behaviour*, edited by D. H. Mellor. Cambridge: Cambridge U.P.: 141–160.

———. 1980b. Is the end in sight for epistemology? *The Journal of Philosophy* 76: 579–588.

———. 1980c. What is logic? *Journal of Philosophy* 86: 285–319.

———. 1982a. Biopower and the avalanche of printed numbers. *Humanities in Society* 5: 279–295.

———. 1982b. Suicide au XIXe siècle. In *Medicine et probabilités*, edited by A. Fagot. Paris: Didier-Erudition, 165–186.

———. 1983a. *Representing and Intervening: Introductory Topics in the Philosophy of Natural Science*. Cambridge: Cambridge U.P.

———. 1983b. Nineteenth-century cracks in the concept of determinism. *Journal of the History of Ideas* 44 (1983): 455–475.

———. 1984a. Review of Donald Davidson, *Essays on Truth and Interpretation*. *New York Review of Books* (20 December).

———. 1984b. Wittgenstein rules. *Social Studies of Science* 14: 469–476.

———. 1986. The invention of split personalities. In *Human Nature and Natural Knowledge*, edited by Alan Donegan, A. P. Perovich, Jr., and M. V. Wedin. Dordrecht: Reidel, 63–85.

———. 1988a. Locke, Leibniz, language and Hans Aarsleff. *Synthese*: 135–153.

———. 1988b. On the stability of the laboratory sciences. *The Journal of Philosophy* 85: 507–514.

———. 1988c. The sociology of knowledge about child abuse. *Nous* 22: 53–63.

———. 1988d. The participant irrealist at large in the laboratory. *British Journal for the Philosophy of Science* 39 (1988), 277–294.

———. 1990. *The Taming of Chance*. Cambridge: Cambridge U.P.

———. 1991a. The self-vindication of the laboratory sciences. In *Science as Practice and Culture,* edited by Andrew Pickering. Chicago: University of Chicago Press, 29–64.

———. 1991b. Artificial phenomena. *British Journal for the History of Science* 24: 235–241.

———. 1991c. The making and molding of child abuse. *Critical Inquiry* 17: 253–278.

———. 1992a. Statistical language, statistical truth and statistical reason: The self-authentication of a style of reasoning. In *Social Dimensions of Science,* edited by Ernan McMullin. Notre Dame, Ind.: Notre Dame U.P., 130–157.

———. 1992b. World-making by kind-making: Child abuse for example. In *How Classification Works,* edited by Mary Douglas and David Hull. Edinburgh: Edinburgh U.P., 180–238.

———. 1992c. Review of Iris Murdoch, *Metaphysics as a Guide to Morals. London Review of Books* (17 December): 8–9.

———. 1993a. Working in a new world: The taxonomic solution. In *World Changes: Thomas Kuhn and the Nature of Science,* edited by Paul Horwich. Cambridge, Mass.: MIT Press, 275–310.

———. 1993b. On Kripke's and Goodman's uses of 'Grue.' *Philosophy* 68: 269–295.

———. 1993c. Goodman's new riddle is pre-Humian. *Revue internationale de philosophie* 46: 229–243.

———. 1994. Entrenchment. In Stalker (1994): 183–224.

———. 1995a. The looping effects of human kinds. In *Causal Cognition: An Interdisciplinary Approach,* edited by D. Sperber, D. Premack, and A. Premack. Oxford: Oxford U.P., 351–383.

———. 1995b. Imagine radicalmente costruzionaliste del progresso matematico. In *Realismo/Antirealismo,* edited by A. Pagnini. Florence: La Nuova Italia Editrice, 59–92.

———. 1995c. *Rewriting The Soul: Multiple Personality and the Sciences of Memory.* Princeton: Princeton U.P.

———. 1996. The disunities of the sciences. In Galison and Stump (1996): 37–74.

———. 1998. *Mad Travelers: Reflections on the reality of transient mental illnesses.* Charlottesville: University Press of Virginia.

———. 1999a. *The Social Construction of What?* Cambridge, Mass: Harvard U.P.

———. 1999b. Historical meta-epistemology. In *Wahrheit und Geschichte,* edited by W. Carl and L. Daston. Göttingen: Valdenhoeck und Ruprecht, 54–77.

———. 1999c. Review of *I See a Voice,* by Jonathan Rée. *The London Review of Books* (1 July): 15–16.

———. 1999d. Review of Bruno Latour, *Pandora's Box. The Times Literary Supplement* (19 September): 13.

———. 2000. What mathematics has done to some and only some philosophers. In *Mathematics and Necessity*, edited by T. J. Smiley. Oxford: Oxford U.P/The British Academy, 83–138.

———. 2001a. Aristotelian categories and cognitive domains. *Synthese* 126: 473–515

———. 2001b. La qualité. In *Quelle philosophie pour le XXIᵉ siècle*. Paris: Gallimard/Le Centre Pompidou, 105–151.

———. 2001c. An *Introduction to Probability and Inductive Logic*. New York: Cambridge U.P.

Hallyn, Fernand (ed.). 1995. *Les Olympiques de Descartes*. Romanica Gandensia 25. Geneva: Librairie Droz.

Hamann, Johann Georg. 1955–1965. *Briefwechsel*. Edited by W. Ziesemer and A. Henkel. 5 vols. Wiesbaden: Insel-Verlag.

———. 1949–1957. *Sämtliche Werke, Historische-kritische Ausgabe*. Edited by J. Nadler. 6 vols. Vienna: Thomas Morus.

Hardy, G. H. 1929. Mathematical proof. *Mind* 38: 1–25.

Hearne, Keith. 1990. *The Dream Machine: Lucid Dreams and How to Control Them*. Wellingborough, U.K.: Aquarian.

Hegel, Georg W. F. 1956. Ueber Hamann's schriften. Reprinted in *Hegels Berliner Schriften*, edited by J. Hoffmeister. Hamburg: F. Meiner, 221–294.

———. 1971. *Hegel's Philosophy of Mind, being part three of the Encyclopaedia of the philosophical sciences (1830)*. Translated by William Wallace, together with the "Zusätze" in Boumann's text (1845) by A. V. Miller. Oxford: Clarendon Press.

———. 1977. *Phenomenology of Spirit*. Translated by A. V. Miller from the German of 1807. Oxford: Clarendon Press.

Heller, Thomas C., Morton Sosna, and David Wellbery (eds.). 1986. *Reconstructing Individualism: Autonomy, Individuality and the Self in Western Thought*. Stanford: Stanford U.P.

Hervey de Saint-Dénis, Marie-Jean Lyon, Marquis. 1982. *Dreams and How to Guide Them*. Translated from the French of 1857 by N. Fry. London: Duckworth, 1982.

Hintikka, Jaako. 1962. *Cogito ergo sum*, inference or performance? *Philosophical Review* 71: 3–32.

Hobbes, Thomas. 1985. Physical dialogue. Translated by Simon Schaffer from the Latin ed. of 1661 in Shapin and Schaffer (1985), 346–391.

Hoffman, Volker. 1972. *Johann Georg Hamanns Philologie: Hammans Philologie zwischen enzyklopädischer Mikrologie und Hermeneutik*. Stuttgart: W. Kohlhammer.

Homer. 1997. *Iliad*. Translated by Stanley Lombardo. Indianapolis: Hackett.

Horne Tooke, John. *See* Tooke, John Horne.

Humboldt, Wilhelm von. 1988. *On Language: The Diversity of Human Language-Structure and Its Influence on the Mental Development of Mankind*. Translated by Peter Heath from the German of 1836. Cambridge: Cambridge U.P.

———. 1903–1936. *Gesammelte Schriften*. 17 vols. Berlin: B. Behr.

Husserl, Edmund. 1970. *The Crisis of European Sciences and Transcendental Phenomenology: An Introduction to Phenomenological Philosophy*. Translated by D. Carr from the German of 1936. Evanston, Ill.: Northwestern U.P.

James, Susan. 1997. *Passion and Action: The Emotions in Seventeenth Century Philosophy*. Oxford: Clarendon Press.

James, William. 1911. *Some Problems of Philosophy*. London: Longmans.

Janet, Pierre. 1886. Les actes inconscients et le dédoublement de la personnalité pendant le somnambulisme provoqué. *Revue Philosophique* 22: 577–592.

———. 1907. *The Major Symptoms of Hysteria*. New York: Macmillan.

Jardine, Nicholas. 1991. *The Scenes of Inquiry*. Oxford: Oxford U.P.

Johns, D. 1835. *A Dictionary of the Malagasy Language*. Part II, Malagasy-English. Antananarivo, Madagascar: London Missionary Society.

Jung, Carl Gustav. 1970. The meaning of psychology for modern man. In *Civilization in Transition*, translated from the German by R. F. C. Hull. Second edition. Princeton: Princeton U.P., 134–156.

Kant, Immanuel. 1964. *Anthropologie du point de vue pragmatique*. Translated by Michel Foucault from the German of 1798. Paris: Vrin.

———. 1974. *Logic*. Translated from the German by R. S. Hartmann and W. Schwartz. Indianapolis: Bobbs-Merrill.

———. 1978. *Anthropology from a Pragmatic Point of View*. Translated by V. L. Dowdell from the German of 1798. Carbondale, Ill.: University of Southern Illinois Press.

Kenny, A. 1970. *Descartes*. Oxford: Clarendon Press.

Kierkegaard, S. 1989. *The Concept of Irony, with Continual References to Socrates*. Edited and translated from the Danish by H. V. Hong and E. H. Hong. Princeton: Princeton U.P.

Kind, John L. 1906. Edward Young in Germany. *Columbia University Germanic Studies* II, 3, 28–40.

Kituse, John I. and Aaron V. Cewrel. 1963. A note on the uses of official statistics. *Social Problems* 2: 131–139.

Knorr, Wilbur. 1975. *The Evolution of the Euclidean Elements: A Study of the Theory of Incommensurable Magnitudes*. Dordrecht: Reidel.

Kristeva, Julia. 1999. *Le Génie féminin. La vie, la folie, les mots. Hannah Arendt, Melanie Klein. Colette*. Vol. 1. Paris: Fayard.

Kröker, Kenton. 2000. *From Reflex to Rhythm: Sleep, Dreaming, and the Discovery of Rapid Eye Movement 1870–1963*. Ph.D. Dissertation, University of Toronto.

Krüger, Lorenz and Lorraine Daston (eds.). 1987. *The Probabilistic Revolution.* 2 vols. Cambridge, Mass.: MIT Press.

Kuhn, Thomas S. 1962. *The Structure of Scientific Revolutions.* Chicago: University of Chicago Press.

———. 1977a. *The Essential Tension: Selected Studies in Scientific Tradition and Change.* Chicago: University of Chicago Press.

———. 1977b. Objectivity, value judgment, and theory choice. In Kuhn (1977a): 320–339.

———. 1978. *Black-Body Theory and the Quantum Discontinuity: 1894–1912.* Oxford: Clarendon Press.

———. 1987. What is a scientific revolution? In Krüger and Daston (1987), vol. I, 7–22.

———. 1992. The trouble with the historical philosophy of science. Rothschild Lecture, 1991. In *The Road since Structure: Philosophical Essays 1970–1993, with an Autobiographical Interview.* Edited by James Conant and John Haugeland. Chicago: University of Chicago Press, 2000, 105–120.

Kuper, Adam. 1979. A structural approach to dreams. *Man* (N.S.) 14: 645–662.

———. 1989. Symbols in myths and dreams. Freud v. Lévi-Strauss. *Encounter* 73, 26–61.

Kuper, Adam and Alan Stone. 1982. The dream of Irma's injection: A structural analysis. *American Journal of Psychiatry* 139: 1225–1234.

Lakatos, Imre. 1978. *The Methodology of Scientific Research Programmes.* Edited by John Worrall and Gregory Currie. Cambridge: Cambridge U.P.

Latour, Bruno. 1990. Post modern? No, simply amodern! Steps towards an anthropology of science. *Studies in History and Philosophy of Science* 21: 145–171.

———. 1993. *We Have Never Been Modern.* Cambridge, Mass: Harvard U.P.

———. 1999. *Pandora's Hope.* Cambridge, Mass: Harvard U.P.

———. 2000. On the partial existence of existing and non-existing objects. In Daston (2000), 247–269.

Latour, Bruno and Steve Woolgar. 1979. *Laboratory Life: The Social Construction of Scientific Facts.* Beverly Hills: Sage. Second edition retitled *Laboratory Life: The Construction of Scientific Facts.* Princeton: Princeton U.P., 1986.

Leibniz, G. W. 1849–1863. *Mathematische Schriften.* Edited by G. Gerhardt. Vols. 1–2, Berlin: A. Ascher. Vols. 3–7, Halle: Schmidt.

———. 1875–1890. *Die Philosophische Schriften von G. Leibniz.* Edited by G. Gerhardt. 7 vols. Berlin: Wiedmann.

———. 1903. *Opuscules et fragments inédits de Leibniz.* Edited by Louis Couturat. Paris: Alcan.

———. 1975. *Philosophische Schriften.* Reihe 6 of *Sämtliche Schriften und Briefe.* Berlin: Deutsche Akademie der Wissenschaft.

———. 1981. *New Essays on Human Understanding.* Edited and translated by Peter Remnant and Jonathan Bennett. Cambridge U.P.

Levanthal, Robert S. 1986. Semiotic interpretation and rhetoric in the German enlightenment 1740–1760. *Deutsche Viertel-jahrsschrift für Literaturwissenschaft und Geistesgeschichte.* 60: 223–248.

Leys, Ruth. 2000. *A Genealogy of Trauma.* Baltimore: Johns Hopkins U.P.

Locke, John. 1975. *An Essay Concerning Human Understanding.* Edited by Peter Nidditch. Oxford: Oxford U.P.

MacIntosh, Mary. 1968. The homosexual role. *Social Problems* 16: 182–192.

Malcolm, Norman. 1959. *Dreaming.* London: Routledge and Kegan Paul.

Maritain, Jacques. 1946. *The Dream of Descartes.* Translated by Mabelle L. Andison from *Le Songe de Descartes,* 1932. London: Editions Poetry.

Marshall, John. 1981. Pansies, perverts and macho men: Changing conceptions of the modern homosexual. *Social Problems* 16 (1968): 182–192, reprinted with a postscript in Plummer (1981), 133–154.

Maurice, David. The Von Sallman Lecture, 1996: An ophthalmological explanation of REM sleep. *Experimental Eye Research* 66 (1998): 139–145.

Megill, Allan (ed.). 1994. *Rethinking Objectivity.* Durham, N.C.: Duke U.P.

Midelfort, H. C. Erik. 1980. Madness and civilization in early modern Europe: A reappraisal of Michel Foucault. In *After the Reformation, Essays in Honor of J. H. Hexter,* edited by Barbara C. Malament. Philadelphia: University of Pennsylvania Press.

Minsky, Marvin. 1987. *The Society of Mind.* New York: Simon & Schuster.

Monbeig Goguel, Catherine. 1998. *Francesco Salviati (1510–1563) ou La Bella Maniera.* Paris: Musée du Louvre.

Moore, G. E. 1953. *Some Main Problems of Philosophy.* London: Allen and Unwin.

Murdoch, Iris. 1970. *The Sovereignty of Good.* London: Routledge and Kegan Paul.

———. 1992. *Metaphysics as a Guide to Morals.* London: Chatto & Windus.

O'Flaherty, James C. 1967. *Hamann's Socratic Memorabilia: A Translation and Commentary.* Baltimore: Johns Hopkins U.P.

Paracelsus. 1922. *Sämtliche Werke.* Vol. 12. Munich: O. W. Barth.

Parsons, Talcott. 1971. *The System of Modern Societies.* Englewood Cliffs, N.J.: Prentice Hall.

Pears, David. 1987–1988. *The False Prison: A Study in Wittgenstein's Philosophy.* 2 vols. Oxford: Clarendon Press.

Peirce, C. S. 1984. Some consequences of four incapacities (1868). In vol. 2 of *Writings of Charles S. Peirce: A Chronological Edition,* edited by E. C. Moore et al. Bloomington: Indiana U.P., 211–214.

Pickering, Andrew. 1984. *Constructing Quarks.* Edinburgh: Edinburgh U.P.

———. 1989. Living in the material world. In *The Uses of Experiment: Studies in the Natural Sciences,* edited by D. Gooding et al. Cambridge: Cambridge U.P., 275–298.

———. 1996. *The Mangle of Practice.* Chicago: University of Chicago Press.

Plummer, K. (ed.). 1981. *The Making of the Modern Homosexual.* London: Hutchinson.

Poisson, S. D. 1837. *Recherches sur la probabilité des jugements en matière criminelle et en matière civile, précédées des règles générales du calcul des probabilités.* Paris: Bachelier.

Pollen, F. P. L. 1868. Notices sur quelques autres mammifères habitent Madagascar et les îles voisines. *Recherches sur la Faune de Madagascar et de ses dépendances d'après les découvertes de François P. L. Pollen et D. C. van Dam.* 4 vols. 2ème partie. *Mammifères et oiseaux par H. Schlegel et François P. L. Pollen.* Leiden: Steenhoff.

Poovey, Mary. 1998. *A History of the Modern Fact: Problems of Knowledge in the Sciences of Wealth and Society.* Chicago: University of Chicago Press.

Popper, Karl. 1994. *The Myth of the Framework: In Defence of Science and Rationality.* Edited by M. A. Notturno. London: Routledge.

Porter, Theodore M. 1995. *Trust in Numbers: The Pursuit of Objectivity in Science and Public Life.* Princeton: Princeton U.P.

Priestley, J. B. 1937a. *I Have Been Here Before: A Play in Three Acts.* London: French.

———— 1937b. *Time and the Conways: A Play in Three Acts.* London: Heineman.

———— 1939. *Johnson and Jordan: The Play and All About It (an Essay).* London: Heineman.

———— 1946. *The Inspector Calls: A Play in Three Acts.* London: Heineman.

———— 1964. *Man and Time.* London: Aldus.

Proschwitz, Gunnar von. 1964. En marge du Bloch-Warburg. *Studia Neophilologica* 36: 319–341.

Putnam, Hilary. 1962. Dreaming and depth grammar. In *Analytical Philosophy,* First series, edited by R. Butler. Oxford: Blackwell, 211–235. Reprinted in Putnam 1975b, 304–324.

————. 1975a. The meaning of "meaning." In *Language, Mind, and Knowledge,* edited by K. Gunderson. Minnesota Studies in the Philosophy of Science VII. Minneapolis: U. of Minnesota Press, 164–211. Reprinted in Putnam 1975b, 215–271.

————. 1975b. *Mind, Language and Reality.* Philosophical Papers, Volume 2. Cambridge: Cambridge U.P.

————. 1978. *Meaning and the Moral Sciences.* London: Routledge and Kegan Paul.

Quine, W. V. 1960. *Word and Object.* Wiley: New York.

Quine, W. V., Hilary Putnam, Wilfrid Sellars, and Saul Kripke. 1974. General discussion of Sellars's paper. *Synthese* 47: 467–521.

Rée, Jonathan. 1999. *I See a Voice: Language, Deafness and the Senses—A Philosophical History.* New York: HarperCollins.

Reichenbach, Hans. 1947. *Elements of Symbolic Logic.* New York: Macmillan.

Richardson, J. 1885. *A New Malagasy-English Dictionary.* Antananarivo: Press of the London Missionary Society.

Rodis-Lewis, Geneviève. 1992. *Descartes: Biographie.* Paris: Calman-Lévy.

Rorty, Richard (ed.). 1967. *The Linguistic Turn: Recent Essays in Philosophical Method.* Chicago: University of Chicago Press.

———. 1979. *Philosophy and the Mirror of Nature.* Princeton: Princeton U.P.

———. 1982. *Consequences of Pragmatism (Essays: 1972–1980).* Minneapolis: University of Minnesota Press.

———. 1988. Is science a natural kind? In *Construction and Constraint: The Shaping of Scientific Rationality,* edited by Ernan McMullin. Notre Dame, Ind.: Notre Dame U.P., 49–74.

Roussel, Raymond. 1969. *Impressions of Africa.* Translated by L. Foord and R. Heppenstall from the French of 1910. London: Calder and Boyars.

———. 1977. *How I Wrote Certain of My Books.* Translated by Trevor Winkfield from the French of 1935. New York: SUNY.

Rubin, Elizabeth. 1998. Our children are killing us. *The New Yorker* (March 23).

Russell, Bertrand. 1912. *The Problems of Philosophy.* London: Oxford U.P.

———. 1956. The philosophy of logical atomism (eight lectures given in London in 1918). In *Logic and Knowledge: Essays 1901–1950,* edited by R. Marsh. London: Allen & Unwin, 175–282.

Sartre, Jean Paul. 1956. *Being and Nothingness: An Essay in Phenomenological Ontology.* Translated by Hazel E. Barnes from the French of 1943. New York: Philosophical Library.

———. 1980. *Le Nouvel Observateur,* Interview by Benny Levy, No. 800, March 10, "L'Espoir," pp. 26 et. seq.; No. 801, March 17, "Violence et fraternité," pp. 106 et seq.; No. 802, March 24, "L'Histoire juive et l'antisémitisme," pp. 103 et seq.

Sass, Louis. 1994. *The Paradoxes of Delusion: Wittgenstein, Schreber and the Schizophrenic Mind.* Ithaca: Cornell U.P.

Schlick, Moritz. 1936. Meaning and verification. *The Philosophical Review* 45: 339–369.

Schreber, Daniel Paul. 1955. *Memoirs of my Nervous Illness.* Edited and translated from the German of 1903 by Ida Macalpine and R. A. Hunter. London: Dawson.

Shapin, Steven and Simon Schaffer. 1985. *Leviathan and the Air Pump: Hobbes, Boyle and the Experimental Life.* Princeton: Princeton U.P.

Sibree, J. 1893. *Antananarivo Annual and Madagascar Magazine* 5.

Sidgwick, Henry. 1874. *The Methods of Ethics.* London: Macmillan.

Smith, Ronald Gregor. 1960. *J. G. Hamann 1730–1788, A Study in Christian Existence, With Selections From His Writings.* London: Collins.

Sonnerat, Pierre. 1782. *Voyage aux Indes Orientales et à la Chine, fait par ordre du Roi depuis 1774 jusqu'en 1781.* 2 vols. Paris: Chez l'auteur.

———. 1806a. *Voyage aux Indes Orientales et à la Chine, fait par ordre du Roi depuis 1774 jusqu'en 1781.* Second edition. 4 vols. Paris: Dentu.

———. 1806b. *Collection de planches pour servir au voyage aux Indes Orientales et à la Chine.* Paris: Dentu.

Spengler, Oswald. 1918, 1922. *Der Untergang des Abendlandes: Umriss einer Morphologie der Weltgeschichte.* 2 vols. Munich: Beck.

———. 1926, 1928. *Decline of the West: Form and Actuality.* 2 vols. Translated by C. F. Atkinson from the German of 1918, 1922. London: Allen & Unwin.

Stalker, Douglas (ed.). 1994. *GRUE.* La Salle, Ill.: Open Court.

Tooke, John Horne. 1798 (Part I); 1805 (Part II). *EIΠΑ ΠTEPOENTA or, the Diversions of Purley.* London: J. Johnson's.

Unger, Rudolf. 1911. *Hamman und die Aufklärung.* Vol. 1. Jena: Eugen Diederichs.

Van Eeden, Frederick. 1913a. *The Bride of Dreams.* Translated by Mellie van Aun from the Dutch of 1909. London: Mitchell Kennerley.

———. 1913b. A study of dreams. *Proceedings of the Society for Psychical Research,* 67: 413–461.

Weber, Max. 1958. *The Protestant Ethic and the Spirit of Capitalism.* Translated by Talcott Parsons from the German of 1905. New York: Scribners.

Weinberg, Stephen. 1976. The forces of nature. *The Bulletin of the American Academy of Arts and Sciences* 29.

Williams, Bernard. 1990. Auto-da-fé: Consequences of pragmatism. *New York Review of Books* (1983). In *Reading Rorty,* edited by Alan Malachowski. Oxford: Blackwell, 26–37.

———. 1984. The scientific and the ethical. In *Objectivity and Cultural Difference,* edited by S. C. Brown. Cambridge: Cambridge U.P., 209–228.

———. 1985. *Ethics and the Limits of Philosophy.* London: Fontana.

———. 1993. *Shame and Necessity.* Berkeley: University of California Press.

Wisan, Winfred L. 1981. Galileo and the emergence of a new scientific style. *Theory Change, Ancient Axiomatics and Galileo's Methodology: Proceedings of the 1978 Pisa Conference in the History and Philosophy of Science.* Edited by J. Hintikka et al. Dordrecht: Reidel.

Wittgenstein, Ludwig. 1953. *Philosophical Investigations.* Translated from the German by G. E. M. Anscombe. Oxford: Blackwell.

———. 1977. *Remarks on Colour.* Edited by G. E. M. Anscombe, and translated from the German by L. A. McAlister and M. Schättle. Oxford: Blackwell.

———. 1978. *Remarks on the Foundations of Mathematics.* Edited by G. H. von Wright, R. Rhees, and G. E. M. Anscombe, and translated from the German by G. E. M. Anscombe. Third edition (much augmented). Oxford: Blackwell.

———. 1980. *Remarks on the Philosophy of Psychology.* Vol. I edited by G. E. M. Anscombe and G. H. von Wright, and translated from the German by G. E. M. Anscombe. Vol. II edited by G. H. von Wright and Heikki Nyman, and translated from the German by C. G. Luckhardt and M. A. E. Aue. Oxford: Blackwell.

Wolff, Christian. 1730. *Philosophia Prima Sive Ontologia.* Frankfurt and Leipzig: Officina libraria Rengeriana.

Wong, James. 1995. *The Very Idea of Child Development.* Ph.D. Dissertation, University of Toronto.

Young, Allan. 1995. *The Harmony of Illusions.* Princeton, N.J.: Princeton U.P.

———. 1996. Bodily memory and traumatic memory. In *Tense Past: Cultural Essays in Trauma and Memory.* Edited by P. Antze and M. Lambek. New York: Routledge, 89–102.

Young, Edward. 1759. *Conjectures on Original Composition, in a Letter to the Author of Charles Grandison.* London: A. Millar, and D. and J. Dodsley.

———. 1975. *Night Thoughts, or, The Complaint and the Consolation.* Illustrated by William Blake. Reduced version of the edition of 1797, edited by Robert N. Essick and Jeni La Belle. New York: Dover.

Ziff, Paul. 1960. *Semantic Analysis.* Ithaca, N.Y.: Cornell U.P.

Sources

I am grateful to the publishers for permission to reprint, with revisions, the following essays:

2 "Five parables." In *Philosophy in Its Context,* edited by Richard Rorty, Jerry Schneewind and Quentin Skinner (Cambridge: Cambridge University Press, 1984), 103–124.

3 "Two kinds of new historicism for philosophers." *New Literary History,* 21 (1989–90), 343–364. For critical comments by David Hollinger, see pp. 365–372; he wanted to know why I am not simply doing history. A historian himself, he says, "Welcome to the club." For my reply, see pp. 373–378. This issue of the journal was subsequently augmented and published in *History and . . . : Histories within the Human Sciences,* edited by R. Cohen and M. S. Roth. (Charlottesville, Va.: University of Virginia Press, 1995).

4 "The archaeology of Foucault." *The New York Review of Books,* 14 May, 1981.

5 "Michel Foucault's immature science." *Noûs,* 13, 1979, 39–51.

6 "Making up people." In *Reconstructing Individualism,* edited by Thomas Heller, Morton Sosna, and David Wellbery (Stanford: Stanford University Press), 1986, 222–236.

7 "Self-improvement." *University Publishing* no. 13 (Berkeley: University of California Press, 1984), 5–6.

8 "How, why, when, and where did language go public?" *Common Knowledge,* 1 (2) (1992), 74–91.

9 "Night thoughts on philology." *History of the Present,* 4 (Spring 1988), 3–11.

10 "Was there ever a radical mistranslation?" *Analysis,* 41 (1981), 171–176.

11 "Language, truth and reason." In *Rationality and Relativism,* edited by Martin Hollis and Steven Lukes (Oxford: Blackwell, 1982), 48–66.

12 "'Style' for historians and philosophers." *Studies in History and Philosophy,* 23 (1992), 1–20.

13 "Leibniz and Descartes: Proof and eternal truths." 19th Annual Dawes Hicks

271

Lecture for the British Academy. *Proceedings of the British Academy,* 59 (1973), pp. 175–188.

14 "Wittgenstein as philosophical psychologist" appeared as "Wittgenstein the psychologist" in *The New York Review of Books,* 1 April, 1982.

15 "Dreams in place." *Journal of Aesthetics and Art Criticism,* 59 (2001), 245–260.

Index

Aarsleff, Hans, 7, 124, 127–131
Adam, 7, 138f, 150
Adanson, Michel, 90
Addison, Joseph, 45, 50
Adrienne/Lucie, *see* Multiple personality
Agamemnon, 236
agenda-setting, 68
algebra, 186, 203
"Al-gorismi," 186
Allen, Barry, 195
Althusser, Louis, 76, 162, 185
analysis and synthesis (mathematical proof), 206
analysis, philosophical, 51, 68, 70f, 88, 122, 135f, 223
analytification, 194
anarcho-rationalism, 162f
anatomo-politics, 99, 112
Annales d'hygiène publique et de médecine, 80
Annales school, 83
Anscombe, G. E. M., 48, 108, 139
a priori, historical, 5, 79, 81, 91; synthetic, 5, 91, 137, 203
archaeology, Foucault's, 5, 26, 93, 213
Archimedes, 174
architectonic reasoning, 208
arch-rationalism, 162f
Arendt, Hannah, 149
Aristotle, 2, 25f, 51, 57, 89, 181, 183, 208–10, 227, 236–39
Arnauld, Antoine, 205
Artaud, Antonin, 149

asceticism, 118
Asclepius, 236
Atran, Scott, 197
August der Stark, 28–30
Augustine, 117
Ausonius, 230
Austin, J. L. 26, 33f, 51, 67f, 191, 223

Bachelard, Gaston, 9, 44, 76, 93
Bacon, Francis, 57, 89, 208, 212
Baillet, Adrien, 229, 245–47
Baltas, Aristide, 178
Balzac, Honoré de, 179
Barnes, Barry, 16, 159
Bayes, Thomas, 13
Becquerel, A. H., 44
Beeckman, Isaac, 246
Belaval, Yvon, 201
Belshazzar's feast, 235
Benjamin, Walter, 133
Bennett, Jonathan, 55
Berens, Johann Christoph, 133–35
Bergman, Gustav, 34
Berkeley, George, 32, 57, 63, 98, 137, 139
Berlin, Isaiah, 121, 125, 128–30
Bernhardt, Thomas, 240
bio-politics, 49, 99, 112
bivalence, 165, 190
Bloomfield, Leonard, 127
Bloor, David, 16, 159
Boccaccio, Giovanni, 238
Boethius, 229, 238
Bopp, Franz, 126f, 141–44, 185

Boswell, John, 104
bourgeois, 81; individualism, 124
Brecht, Bertolt, 27, 32–34, 43
Bréhier, Emile, 205, 210
Britten, Benjamin, 250
Broad, C. D., 51
Buchdahl, Gerd, 206
Buchwald, Jed, 11, 15
Buffon, G.-L. L., 179
Burnyeat, Myles, 241

caloric, 166
camera, 10
Canguilhem, Georges, 5, 76, 79, 91, 93
Carnap, Rudolf, 203
cause and effect, 208
Cervantes, Miguel de, 231
Charles/Eric/Mark, *see* Multiple personality
Chaucer, Geoffrey, 238, 240
child abuse, 4, 69
child development, 20–23
Chladenius, J. M., 146
Chomsky, Noam, 7, 53, 85, 90, 125–7, 130f,
    162, 167, 176, 179, 184f
Church, Alonzo, 201
Cicero, 113
Clausewitz, Karl, 84
Clifford, James, 113
codes, moral, 116
cogito ergo sum, 204f
Cohen, I. B. 179
Cole, John, 229, 246
Coleridge, Samuel Taylor, 243
Collingwood, R. G., 162
color, 225
Columbine school murders, 2
Comte, August, 4, 58, 63, 89, 164–67, 190
concepts, 35–38
conceptual scheme, 159, 168, 172–75
Condillac, E. B. de, 63, 129f
Condorcet, M. J. A. N. de Caritat, 63
Conrad, Joseph, 115
Conring, Hermann, 201
construction: social, 16, 64–67, 191f, 197;
    ethical, 119
Cook, James, 152f
Cosimo I, 239
cosmopolitics, 17
couch (psychoanalytic), 248f
Cousin, Victor, 101

Crombie, Alistair, 5, 159, 167–73, 178–80,
    190–92, 196–99
culture-concept, 129
Cuvier, Georges, 76, 126, 141, 155, 185

Daniel (biblical), 234f
Daston, Lorraine, 7f, 17, 24, 199
Davidson, Arnold, 8, 99, 107f, 179, 195, 225
Davidson, Donald, 60, 159, 167, 169f, 172–
    75.
Deleuze, Gilles, 6, 60
Democritus, 237
Derain, André, 189
Descartes, René, 89, 77, 94, 116, 121;
    dreams of, 229f, 239–42, 245–48, 253;
    eternal truths, 200–13; *Olympica*, 164;
    popularity of, 27, 30–33, 56; *Regulae*, 84;
    skepticism, 63; and Wittgenstein, 214–16,
    221f
Dewar, James, 180
Dewey, John, 31, 59
Diaz, Diogo, 158
discipline, 81
discourse, 78–82, 90
dispatch (speed of communication) 144–46
disunity, 4
divination, 237
Drake, Stillman, 185
Dreams, 7, 227–54; Agamemnon's, 236;
    Chantecleer's, 238; Descartes's, 229f, 239–
    42, 245–48, 253; divination, 237; at
    Epidaurus, 236, 248, 251; Freud's of
    Irma, 230f; internet, 250; genres of, 229,
    232, 236; Joseph's fat and lean cattle, 239;
    Leibniz's, 242; lucid, 244, 252; Dunne's,
    249f.; Nebuchadnezzar's, 234f; and
    objectivity, 227, 254; significant, 227; in
    Sumer, 235; Wordsworth's, 231
Dreamwork, 37
Dresden, 28
Dreyfus, Hubert L., 3, 115, 118
dualism, 216
Duhem, Pierre, 93, 193
Dummett, Michael, 164–67, 190f, 225
Duncan, A. R. C., 34
Dunne, J. M., 249
Dyson, Freeman, 180

ego, 84
Einstein, Albert, 44

Enlightenment, the, 145, 147, 231, 253; dreams and enlightenment, 252; "What Is Enlightenment," 3

"endrina," 156f

énoncé, 91

Epidaurus, 236, 248, 251

epistemology, 25, 88, 178, 200, 203, 210; historical, 7f; meta-epistemology, 9f

Esquirol, J. E. D., 112

ethics, 2, 10, 19, 66–69, 115–20

etymology, 144f

Euclid, 207, 231

evidence, 189

existence, 192

existentialism, 22, 112

explanation, 227

expressionism, 128

Fancher, Mollie, 103

Faraday, Michael, 43

fauvisme, 189

Félida X, 101

Fermi, Enrico, 45

Feyerabend, Paul, 96, 163, 167, 169–170, 176

Flacourt, Etienne de, 158

Fleck, Ludwik, 38, 180

Fliess, Wilhelm, 249

Forrester, John, 195

Fort-Dauphin, 158

Foucault, Michel, v, 18,, 28, 31, 48, 52, 151; archaeology 5, 24, 50, 213; bio-politics, 49; *Birth of the Clinic*, 70, 75, 77; and Chomsky, 85; criticisms of, 76, 140–51, 195; *Discipline and Punish*, 70, 79; episteme, 121, 180; ethics, knowledge, and power axes, 3–5; genealogy, 3, 24, 84, 114, 119; on grammar, 125f, 140–42; gulag, 83–85; on Hegel, 45f; historical ontology, 2, 20; *History of Sexuality*, 80; history of the present, 24, 51, 182; Hume, 90; *Introduction à l'anthropologie de Kant*, 78; *I, Pierre Rivière*, 80; and Kant, 3, 78, 86, 119f; *Language, Countermemory, Practice*, 79; *Madness and Civilization*, 70f, 75f; "On the genealogy of ethics," 115; on Man, 78, 84, 86; Maoists, 85; *The Order of Things*, 23, 77–79, 84, 125, 131, 142; positivity, 190; power, 70, 73, 75, 81; *Power/Knowledge*, 3, 73–86; Roussel, 47;

on the sovereign, 81f; truth, 46; "What Is Enlightenment," 3

Fowler, H. W., 35

Frederick the Great, 128, 148

freedom, 119

Frege, Gottlob, 71, 121, 123, 165

Freud, Sigmund, 71, 254; couch of, 248; on Descartes's dreams, 245; explanation, not cure, 36f, 71; Irma dream, 233; tablet commemorating his discovery, 249; trauma, 18; Wittgenstein on, 221

Galileo, 162, 176, 179, 209; Galilean style, 184f

Galison, Peter, 8, 184, 189

Garber, Daniel, 12

garçon de café, 109

Gavroglu, Kostas, 178, 180, 190

genealogy, 3, 84, 113, 115, 119

general grammar, 89, 125, 140, 144

genetic fallacy, 63

Gentzen, Gerhardt, 200

Gessell, Arnold, 21

Gingras, Yves, 9

God, 107, 139, 204–10

Gombay, André, 204, 206, 227

Goodman, Nelson, 60, 66, 105f

Graham, Malcolm, 102

Graubard, Alan, 140

green family, 27

Grice, H. Paul, 51

Grimm, Jacob, 141f

gulag, 83–85

Gusfield, Joseph, 68

h, silent, 150

Hall effect, 14–16

Hamann, Georg, 57, 121f, 128f, 132–39, 147f

Hardy, G. H., 204

Havilland, John, 153

Hearne, Keith, 252

Hegel, Georg Friedrich, 29, 31, 71; Foucault on, 45f; on Hamann, 133; historicism, 24, 54, 58; language private and public, 123f; *Phenomenology of Spirit*, 123; unhappy consciousness, 36

hegemony, 83–86

Heidegger, Martin, 1, 6, 59f

Herder, Johann Gottfried von, 57, 125, 128, 130

hermeneutics, 93, 146–48
Hermes, 144
Herschel, William, 173f
Hertz, Heinrich, 15
Hervey de Saint Denis, 244
Hintikka, Jaakko, 33
historicism, 24, 54, 58; new, 51
Hobbes, Thomas, 135; laboratory, opposed
    to, 15; *Leviathan*, 3, 82; nominalism, 105;
    private language, 121f
Hoffman, Volker, 148
homeopathy, 176
homosexual, 82, 99, 103, 110f; Freud on
    Descartes as, 245
Horne Tooke, John, 143–46
Humboldt, Alexander von, 126
Humboldt, Wilhelm von, 57, 126f, 141, 148
Hume, David, 121, death of, 118; Foucault
    on, 90; and Goodman, 105f; Hamann on,
    132, 137, 148; *History of England*, 54;
    idéologue, 63; induction, 12–14, 24, 61;
    and Kant, 13; on suicide, 113; vivacity of
    ideas, 223
Huron, 124
Husserl, Edmund, 6, 179, 185
Hypolyte, Jean, 31
hypothetico-deductive reasoning, 207, 212

idéologues, 124, 129
immortality, 250
incommensurability, 96f, 159f, 167, 169–72
indeterminacy of translation, 160, 167,
    169–71
indri, 154–57
induction, problem of, 11–13, 24, 61, 167,
    190, 211f; evasion of problem, 13; new
    riddle, 165
internet dreams, 250
introspection, 220
intuitionism, 165f
Invest in Kids, 21
Irma dream, 230

Jacobi, Friedrich Heinrich, 136
James, Susan, 235
James, William, 12, 23, 35, 60f, 65, 71, 220,
    240
Janet, Pierre, 101
Jardine, Nicholas, 180

Jews, 132f
John the evangelist, 138
Joseph (biblical), 239
Joyce, James, 149
Jung, C. G., 7, 228, 254

"kangaroo," 152f
Kant, Immanuel, 29, 34, 61, 89, 116, 121,
    168, 181; *Anthropologie*, 78, 118, 132;
    critique, 57; on existence, 192; and
    Foucault, 3, 83, 118f; and Hamann, 132–
    36, 148; hope, 86; and Hume, 13;
    promenades of, 253; synthetic *a priori*, 5,
    91; What Is Man", 78
Kierkegaard, Søren, 132f
Kleist, Hermann von, 113
Klemm, Gustav, 29
Knorr, Wilbur, 183
knowledge, depth and surface, 77f, 90, 95
Koyré, Alexandre, 93, 181
Krafft-Ebing, Richard, 108
Kripke, Saul, 106
Kristeva, Julia, 149
Kröker, Kenton, 249, 251
Kuhn, Thomas S., 65f, 71, 87–89, 93f, 106,
    159, 167–70
Kuper, Adam, 228

labeling theory, 67, 103, 110
laboratory 184f, 189; stability of, 192
language game, 217, 224
Laplace, P. S. de, 96, 166
laser, 15
Latour, Bruno, 11, 16f, 185, 197
Leibniz, G. W., 29f, 34, 54, 57, 121; and
    Descartes's notebook, 229, 245; on
    dreams, 242f; on language, 124f, 128;
    Nouveaux Essais, 125; on proof, 200–13
lemur, 155–58
Lenard, Philip, 44
Leventhal, Robert, 147f
Lévi-Strauss, Claude, 78, 91, 228
Lewis, David, 154
Leys, Ruth, 18
linguistic idealism, 138, 150
Linnaeus, Carl von, 90
Locke, John, 57, 63, 113, 121; Lockean
    imperative, 70; language, 125
logic, 167, 190

logos, 138
Lukes, Steven, 159

MacIntosh, Mary, 103
MacNish, lady of, 101
Madagascar, 155–58
Maine de Biran, 63
Malagasy language, 155–58
Malcolm, Norman, 232f
malin génie, mauvais génie, 246–48
Malinowski, Bronislaw, 113, 115
malostension, 154
Man, 78f, 88, 119, 151
Maoists, 85, 131
Maritain, Jacques, 247
Marx, Karl, 36, 85f, 188
mathematics, 137, 182–85, 189f, 194, 201–26
Matisse, Henri, 189
Maupertuis, P. L. M. de, 128
Maxwell, James Clerk, 14, 166f
McGeer, Victoria, 135
McTaggart, J. M. E., 249
memory, 18
Merleau-Ponty, Maurice, 6
Michelangelo, 239
Michelson, A. A., 167
Microbes, 108
microsociology, 16, 64, 188
Midelfort, H. C. Eric, 76
Mill, John Stuart, 123
Minkowski, Hermann, 250
Minsky, Marvin, 122
Moore, G. E., 12, 31f, 51, 61, 71
morals, 10, 66–70, 115–20, 187; extrinsically meta-moral, 70; intrinsically moral, 70
Morand, J. F. C., 154
multiple personality, 99, 101–103, 106f
Murdoch, Iris, 67

Nebuchadnezzar, 239f
necessity, 206
Nestor, 236
neurosis, 18
Neyman, Jerzy, 168
Nicaragua, 19
nihilism, 70, 86
nominalism, 39, 98, 104, 106; dynamic, 26, 48f, 100, 106, 113f; Foucault, 83, 115,

168; historicist, 65; Quine, 168; revolutionary, 42–45, 48f
numbers, avalanche of printed, 100

objectivity, 6–8, 161, 181, 188, 191, 198, 227, 238, 254
objects, 10f, 188–90
observation sentences, 161, 171f, 191
Ockham, William of, 106
Olympica, 224
ontology, 1f, 26, 189, historical, 1–26, 61, 98, 211f
originality, 149

pain, 219
Paracelsus, 96, 171, 195
paradigm, 5, 40, 170
Parks, Kathleen, 8
Paz, Octavio, 57
Pears, David, 240
Peirce, C. S., 13, 31, 38, 123, 168, 217
perversion, 99, 107f
Pharaoh, 239
phenomena, creation of, 14, 43, 45
phenomenology, 6, 78, 90
philology, 89, 126–28, 140, 146; philological seminar, 138
Pickering, Andrew, 16, 64–69, 193
picture theory of meaning, 218
Planck, Max, 39
Plato, 2, 8, 57, 61f, 138, 230, 233; Platonism, 189
poetry and philosophy, 230f
Pollen, François, 156
Poovey, Mary, 8, 12
Popper, Karl, 5, 163, 176, 212
Porter, Theodore, 8, 199
Port Royal grammar, 126
porcelain, 28–30
possibility, 97, 189
positivism, 4, 58f, 63f, 71, 90, 164; logical, 59, 64; positivist psychology, 101; and dreams, 232–236; positivity, 175, 190
post-traumatic stress disorder, 18
power, 2f, 19, 47, 50, 70, 73, 116
pragmatism, 38
prison, 70, 79, 85
private language argument, 122, 135f, 215, 219

probability, 4, 142, 185, 203, 211
problems, philosophical, 12, 35, 37f, 52, 59–
    61, 71f, 201
progress, 58
proof, 200–11, 254; computer-generated,
    180
psychology, philosophical (Wittgenstein),
    214; positivist, 101
Putnam, Hilary, 87, 139, 154, 187, 233

Quine, Willard van Orman, 92f, 152f, 167–
    170, 173f, 193

Rabinow, Paul, 3, 113, 115, 118
rapid eye movement, 233, 251f
rationality, 41
Rée, Jonathan, 6–8
reference, inscrutability of, 152
relativism, 23, 30, 66, 118, 159f, 167
Rembrandt, 235
Reynolds, Mary, 141, 185
Ricardo, David, 126, 141, 185
Richardson, Samuel, 149
Rodis-Lewis, Geneviève, 247
Rorty, Richard, 9, 30f, 34, 45, 52–54, 59–61,
    71, 195
Rothstein, William, 102
Rousseau, Jean-Jacques, 85f
Roussel, Raymond, 47
Rowland, Henry, 14
Russell, Bertrand, 35, 51, 61, 68, 71f, 122

Sade, Marquis de, 108
Salviati, Francesco, 239
Sartre, Jean-Paul, 23, 31, 109f, 177
Sauvages, P. A. B. de, 112
Schaffer, Simon, 12, 16, 65, 185
Schlegel, Friedrich, 140–143
Schlick, Moritz, 4, 52, 72, 164f
Schopenhauer, Arthur, 80
Schreber, Daniel Paul, 240
Schweber, Sam, 235
seeing as, 220
self-authenticating, 191–93
self-improvement, 191–93
Sellars, Wilfred, 60
Sextus Empiricus, 12
sexuality, 80, 117
Shapin, Steven, 12, 15, 65, 185

Sibree, J., 155
Sidgwick, Henry, 34
similitudes, 97, 170, 176, 195
Skepticism, 13, 33, 63, 203, 240, 248
Smart, J. J. C., 153
social contract, 7
Society for Psychical Research, 244
Socrates, 183
solipsism, 135, 240f
Sonnerat, Pierre, 154–57
Sophocles, 233
soul, 136, 216, 219, 222, 231
sovereign, 81f
speech act, 226
Spengler, Oswald, 179
Spinoza, Baruch, 31, 85, 242, 202
Spock, Benjamin, 21
stability of results, 192–94; self-
    stabilization, 194
Stanford sleep laboratory, 228, 251
statistics, 103, 111, 160, 182, 184, 193f
Staurophorus, Rudophilus, 229
Strindberg, August, 206
structuralism, 91, 221
styles of reasoning (thinking), 6, 38, 89,
    160f, 178–99; Crombie's, 161, 181f
Suárez, Francisco, 205
suicide, 112

taxonomic style, 161, 182, 194
technology, philosophical, 198
telepathy, 237
Thales, 185
Tooke, John Horne, see Horne Tooke
topology, 186, 202
trading zone, 184
trauma, 17–21
truth, 46, 81, 173, 188; correspondence
    theory, 59, 191; eternal, 107, 205;
    evaporation of, 210; Leibniz on, 203;
    true-or-false, 79, 84, 95, 97, 160, 164, 175,
    188, 190, 195; truth-keeping, 10
Tschirnhaus, Ehrenfried Walter, 201
tuberculosis, 105

Uganda, 19, 224
undoing, 57f
universal characteristic, 203, 211

Van Eeden, Frederick, 244
"vasistas," 154
verbalism, 138f, 150
verification principle, 4, 165, 191
victimology, 18
Vienna Circle, 60, 62, 138, 164
vivacity of ideas, 223
Vivieros de Castro, Eduardo, 233
voltaic cell, 42

W (weak elementary particle), 46
Washington, George, 107f
Weinberg, Steven, 162, 179, 184f
Whewell, William, 196
Williams, Bernard, 45f, 62, 67, 196
Wisan, Winifred, 162, 185
Wisdom, John, 37
Wittgenstein, Ludwig, 22, 26, 51; de-
    politicizing effect of, 136; and Descartes,
214–16, 221f; dreaming, 232f; language
games, 191; philosophical anthropology,
196; philosophical psychology, 214–26;
private language argument, 122f, 135f;
psychology, 50; *Remarks on the
Foundations of Mathematics,* 194, 212;
solipsism, 240f; therapy, 37, 71f; undoing,
59
Wolff, Christian, 1, 29
Wong, James, 20
Wordsworth, William, 231
writing in dreams, 229, 250

Young, Allan, 18
Young, Edward, 137, 148–50

Zabell, S. L., 12
Zeus, 226
Ziff, Paul, 236